STUDIES IN EVANGELICALISM
edited by
Kenneth E. Rowe &
Donald W. Dayton

1. Melvin E. Dieter. *The Holiness Revival of the Nineteenth Century.* 1980.

2. Lawrence T. Lesick. *The Lane Rebels: Evangelicalism and Antislavery in Antebellum America.* 1980.

3. Edward H. Madden and James E. Hamilton. *Freedom and Grace: The Life of Asa Mahan.* 1982.

4. Roger H. Martin. *Evangelicals United: Ecumenical Stirrings in Pre-Victorian Britain, 1795-1830.* 1983.

5. Donald W. Dayton. *Theological Roots of Pentecostalism.* 1985.

6. David L. Weddle. *The Law as Gospel: Revival and Reform in the Theology of Charles G. Finney.* 1985.

7. Darius L. Salter. *Spirit and Intellect: Thomas Upham's Holiness Theology.* 1986.

8. Wayne E. Warner. *The Woman Evangelist: The Life and Times of Charismatic Evangelist Maria B. Woodworth-Etter.* 1986.

SPIRIT AND INTELLECT: Thomas Upham's Holiness Theology

by

DARIUS L. SALTER

Studies in Evangelicalism, No. 7

The Scarecrow Press, Inc.
Metuchen, N.J., & London
1986

Library of Congress Cataloging-in-Publication Data

Salter, Darius, 1947-
Spirit and intellect.

(Studies in evangelicalism ; no. 7)
Bibliography: p.
Includes index.
1. Upham, Thomas Cogswell, 1799-1872. I. Title.
II. Series.
BX7260.U64S24 1986 230'.58'0924 [B] 86-10048
ISBN 0-8108-1899-X

Manufactured in the United States of America

To my wife, Brenda,

for her long-suffering patience and labor

CONTENTS

EDITORS' NOTE

The current resurgence of Evangelical religion has highlighted the important role of this force in the formation of American and British culture. This series will explore the movement's roots in the Evangelical Revival and Awakenings of the eighteenth century, its nineteenth-century blossoming in revivalism and social reform, and its twentieth-century developments in both sectarian and mainline churches. We will be particularly concerned to emphasize the diversity within Evangelicalism--the search for holiness, the Millennial traditions, Fundamentalism, Pentecostalism, and so forth. We are pleased to publish Darius Salter's ground-breaking study of a popular nineteenth-century proponent of holiness, Thomas C. Upham, as number seven in the series.

Darius Salter received his theological training at Asbury Theological Seminary and at Drew University from which he received the Ph.D. degree in 1984. He is currently professor of religion at Western Evangelical Theological Seminary (Portland, Oregon) and Executive Director of the Christian Holiness Association.

Donald W. Dayton
Northern Baptist
Theological Seminary
Lombard, Illinois

Kenneth E. Rowe
Drew University
Madison, New Jersey

PREFACE

Never in the history of America have religion and education been more at odds with each other. The courts are presently ruling on "equal access" for student worship and tax exemptions for religious schools; the White House is attempting to overturn the Supreme Court school-prayer ruling; angry Christian parents are fighting to remove obscene books from the school library; creationists are battling evolutionists; fundamentalists are in revolt against the public school system; Christian colleges are at odds with the federal government over whom they may fire and hire. Incompatibility is the key word for the relationship that exists between confessional religion and academic pursuit, their peaceful cohabitation suffering increasing conflict because of the ongoing tension occurring between those who advocate minority rights and those who stand for religious freedom. Looking back over a century, Ernst Christian Helmreich, in his _Religion at Bowdoin College: A History_, states: "It took pages to deal with religious matters in the first printed by-laws of the college; today one sentence forbids the imposition of any religious tests that might influence either the selection of officers and faculty or the admission of students."

In antebellum America, religion and education were not only compatible, they were almost synonymous. From the years 1830 to 1860, the romance between the two was at its apex. Religion was not a private matter but readily accepted as the substance belonging both to public domain and classroom discussion. Indoctrination--far from being considered taboo--was expected. Merle Curti reminds us that the 1848 _Webster's Elementary Speller_, which sold one million copies annually, taught that "God governs the world with infinite wisdom, and is to be worshipped with prayer on beginning the day and before retiring at night." In 1846, the trustees of Bowdoin College issued a declaration that they regarded religion "as a permanent principle in the administration of the College that science and literature are not to be separated from morals and religion."

Between 1840 and 1860, Thomas Cogswell Upham's (January 30, 1799-April 2, 1872) textbook on mental philosophy was one of the most widely used in America. The 700-page tome was laced with references to morals and religion. The Bowdoin professor was a prototype of the integration between Spirit and intellect. He was the perfect matchmaker between academics and religion. Suspicion and jealousy between the two were nonexistent. Perhaps we can best decipher their congeniality by examining the heart and mind of one individual.

Upham's story is the account of a man's contribution to the religious thought of antebellum American society. It was an attempt to construct a theology that was both academically challenging and spiritually stimulating. Upham gathered from historical roots and simultaneously grappled with many of the intellectual winds that blew through the corridors of America's institutions of learning. He not only mirrored intellectual and spiritual currents but attempted to apply his convictions to issues as well as to individuals.

Thomas Upham was widely respected academically. He wrote approximately twenty major works; his best known within the academic community was <u>A Philosophical and Practical Treatise on the Will</u> (1834), called by Frank Hugh Foster "one of the first original and comprehensive contributions of American scholarship to modern psychology." His work <u>Outlines of Imperfect and Disordered Mental Action</u> (1840) is said by Herbert W. Schneider to be the first full treatise on abnormal psychology written in the United States. Upham's work entitled <u>Elements of Mental Philosophy</u> (1841) stirred Schneider to call him "the first great American textbook writer in mental philosophy."

Three Congregationlists made heavy contributions to holiness theology in the nineteenth century: Charles G. Finney, Asa Mahan, and Thomas C. Upham. Much attention has been given to Finney, increasing attention has been given to Mahan in recent years, but virtually none has been given to Upham. No definitive work has been written on Upham. Most historical mention of Upham identifies him within a philosophical or psychological context. Indeed, he was both a philosopher and a psychologist, but he also published a dozen books that explored a relationship with God. His *Principles of the Interior or Hidden Life* went through eighteen editions, and though it is difficult to determine the number of books issued in each reprint, a case could be made that Upham was the most prolific American, nineteenth-century, "holiness" author.

Upham's writings are the first attempt to weigh the tenets of holiness theology within the rubrics of psychological investigation. His findings are integral to the history of the psychology of religion. Upham's *Principles of the Interior Life* (1843) may be the best attempt to stress experiential holiness theology within a psychological context. Within all of the antebellum holiness movement and quite possibly the entire American religious scene before the Civil War, his writings provide the most extensive and most gratifying contribution to spiritual nurture. It was observed by Frank Hugh Foster that Upham's *Treatise of the Will* was "more largely influenced than many later productions by the conception of psychology which is now controlling, viz., it is a chapter in the natural history of the soul." This is a chapter that I hope to at least partially rediscover in this study.

Acknowledgments

A word of thanks is due the many persons who have helped me gather pieces of information. Not wishing to allow my faulty memory to jeopardize friendships, however, I will not list all of them.

Special appreciation is due Dianne Gutscher, who forwarded me significant materials from the library of Bowdoin College. I thank Thomas Oden, Kenneth Rowe, and Melvin Dieter for having participated with me in this project, and for having made many helpful suggestions.

Throughout this endeavor, the faithfulness and work of my wife, Brenda, have been invaluable.

Chapter I

A BIOGRAPHICAL SKETCH OF THOMAS UPHAM WITH ASSESSMENTS OF HIS PHILOSOPHY AND PSYCHOLOGY

Genealogy

In 1635, at the age of thirty-five, John Upham, with his wife Elizabeth and three children, sailed from England to Weymouth, Massachusetts.[1] They were part of a group consisting of fifty-two members sponsored by the Hull Company of England. John was certainly one of the leaders of the newly arrived group. It is recorded that he was one of a few who, along with two others elected as a "selectman" (one who is appointed to settle small claims within a colony), initiated negotiations with the Indians.[2]

In 1648, John moved his family to Malden, Massachusetts; he was appointed as a "selectman" there, too. Later he was to serve as commissioner of the Supreme Court and as a grand juror. John Upham died on February 25, 1681 and was buried at Malden.

Of particular interest in the genealogy is the grandfather of Thomas Cogswell Upham, Timothy Upham. A graduate of Harvard, Timothy served for thirty-nine years as the first pastor of the Congregational Church in Deerfield, New Hampshire.[3] His wife, Hannah, was a descendant of General Daniel Gookin, who distinguished himself during the Revolutionary War. The church record called Rev. Upham "a prudent, active, and faithful labourer in Christ's vineyard."[4] His temperament (as described by his grandson Albert) somewhat foreshadows the character of Thomas Cogswell.

> His mind was perfectly balanced, his judgment excellent, and his temper, though naturally quick, was

> under perfect control. Distinguished for the rectitude of his character, for quiet dignity, and constant self-possession, he won the admiration of his people, while his hospitality and benevolence, extending to the very verge of his means, awakened their love and esteem.[5]

Within all the Upham genealogy, probably the most distinguished personage preceding our subject was the oldest son of Rev. Timothy and the father of Thomas Cogswell, Nathaniel Upham, born in 1774. When he was a young man, Nathaniel moved his family to Rochester, New Hampshire, where he became the town's chief merchant and leading citizen. In 1814, he was nominated for Congress but defeated by the opposing party, which included the famed Daniel Webster.[6] Though defeated in the 1814 election, Nathaniel was elected, in 1817, to the Fifteenth Congress of the United States.

Some of his more strategic actions included a vote against a bill that would have made more ample provisions for the recovery of fugitive slaves in the United States; Nathaniel also supported a bill that would allow Congress to appropriate money for the building of military roads.[7] The Congressional Record shows that Nathaniel Upham voted consistently against the slave trade.

Upham was fond of debate and theological investigation; he was a strong promoter of local education and distinguished by his power to memorize lengthy prose. Nathaniel was described physically as a man six feet four inches high, well formed and perfectly erect with high forehead and black hair, blue eyes, clear complexion, and a Roman nose. The Rochester Courier characterized him as courteous and affable, a gentleman of the old school who "always wore ruffled-bosomed shirts like the aristocratic Portsmouth merchant, and enjoyed smoking his cigar every morning before his place of business."[8]

All of Nathaniel's eleven children distinguished themselves through either personal accomplishment or marriage (one child died in infancy). Four were medical doctors or married medical doctors; three were lawyers or married lawyers; one son became a merchant, and another daughter married James Bell, who eventually became a United States senator from New Hampshire. Nathaniel Gookin Upham, the second oldest son, became an associate justice of the superior court of New Hampshire. He has left on record a valuable discourse, delivered in 1864, which represents his recommendations concerning policies necessary to conclude the Civil War and also concerning powers of the government to abolish slavery and negotiate peace.[9]

The following anecdote concerning Nathaniel Upham, Sr., appeared in the "Rochester Courier" of December 14, 1888:

> Squire Upham was very proud of his boys and much pleased with their success in the world, and well he might have been. It is related that one day a customer or villager, was at his store when the old merchant, as if to enlighten him a little, with an air of satisfaction, said: "I have brought up my boys to look after my several interests. I have educated Tim to look after my health, I have educated Nat to look after my worldly affairs, and Tom I have educated to look after my spiritual affairs." "Well, I pity poor Tom," rejoined the customer.[10]

Thomas Cogswell Upham

"Poor Tom" was not so poor, at least in regard to his heritage. Thomas Cogswell Upham was born January 30, 1799, in Deerfield, New Hampshire.[11] In March 1802, the Upham family moved to Rochester, New Hampshire, where Thomas spent his boyhood days. We know very little of his life, before his taking his first pastorate at the church across from his boyhood home in Rochester. One of the few anecdotes on record was related by a younger brother:

> So well-mannered and studious a child was he that for a long while he, alone, of the pupils of Henry Orne, escaped the flogging administered for cause to every other one. When at last his time came, to the amazement of all the school, of its stern master, too, the gentlest of the village boys so stoutly resisted, that for once, Henry Orne, gave in, feeling that there must be some mistake, as there proved to be.[12]

There can be no doubt that Thomas was precocious as a child. Later, at both Dartmouth College and Andover

Theological Seminary, he demonstrated excellent academic abilities. One of the most intimate glimpses that Upham gives of himself is revealed in a letter he wrote to William Hale for the purpose of requesting financial aid for a study trip to Europe. In the letter, Upham requests, specifically, that Mr. Hale become his patron, "father," and have "the kindness to take my chote for a small sum, perhaps, an hundred dollars or three fourths of that amount.... As true as the soul of a real scholar is found of generous temperament, that man would not be a loser! There would be gratitude to him while living, and tears when he was departed." Before getting to the request, Upham reminds Hale

> For many years I have pursued with unwearied application the acquisition of knowledge, and it is not self-deception and flattery to say, that I have never resided in any institution without gathering a respectable share of its laurels.[13]

Anyone familiar with the temperament of Upham (of which, more later), would know that the request must have been difficult to write. The appeal must not have been met since no account exists that Upham took the hoped-for trip.

Except for the anecdote above and the revival mentioned in Chapter III, we know very little concerning Upham's years at Dartmouth, other than that he graduated from college at the age of nineteen. The years 1818 to 1821 were spent at Andover, where Upham fell under the influence of Leonard Woods and Moses Stuart. Woods, Andover's first professor of Christian theology, was a Calvinist, but not as extreme a Hopkinsian as Nathanael Emmons.[14] Upham inherited the evangelical doctrines that were the earmarks of Andover. These included belief in the following: the plenary inspiration of scripture, the depravity of man, "the eternal, uncaused existence of God, the scripture doctrine of the Trinity, the atonement, and the endless punishment of the impenitent."[15] The following description of Woods by Williston Walker bears similarity to our later discussion of Upham's characteristics:

> His cast of mind was naturally cautious; on the sharper distinctions between the shades of Calvinism of his day he sometimes seemed indefinite; he

> lacked in a measure, that power which comes in the classroom from having a full, definite promptly expressed, and dogmatically asserted opinion on every question that student inquiries may present.[16]

In 1810, Moses Stuart was appointed professor of sacred literature at Andover. It was Stuart's proficiency at languages that helped equip Upham to publish a translation of Jahn's Biblical Archaeology in 1823. Woods observed, in his History of Andover, that Stuart's "frequent repetition of scraps of Latin and Greek gave a peculiar zest to his instructions, and made the time spent in his lecture room appear very short."[17] Stuart chose Upham to assist him in the Greek and Hebrew instruction of the Seminary. When H. M. Pierce, president of Rutgers Female College, granted an honorary doctorate to Upham in 1870, he noted the influence of Stuart on Upham and called the former, "a man who did as much for biblical learning in this country as any man ever did."[18]

Upham's Only Pastorate

A History of the Churches in New Hampshire gives only a brief account of Upham's tenure at the Congregational Church in Rochester (July 1823-July 1825), but there is sufficient evidence that his two years there were profitable ones.

> In July, 1823, Rev. Thomas C. Upham, feeling a deep interest in the spiritual welfare of his native town and of the church to which he belonged, became the associate pastor of this flock. "The half-way covenant" was exchanged for one better adapted to the advancement of piety in the church. The sanctuary was once more filled with attentive listeners and devout worshippers. The people of God began to rejoice in the evident tokens of the divine favor, and the restoration of light, and salvation to this people. A large number were added to the church, and an foundation laid for what we may hope will yet be the glorious spiritual temple of the Lord.[19]

A History of the Town of Rochester, New Hampshire gives us a more intimate account. Upham was of the opinion that both the preaching and the church were so run down that the life expectancy of the church had been shortened.[20] He decided that the only way to renew interest was to spend four days of the week visiting his parishioners. The pastoral concern paid off; during Upham's twenty-two months of service, fifty-three persons were admitted to the church and forty-four baptisms were administered.[21] But as the following anecdote demonstrates, not everyone was so easily won over to the gentle young man.

> Soon after Mr. Upham was settled as pastor, he called on his father's old friend, and said, "I don't see you at church, as I should like to." "No," said Siah, "the fact is I have no suitable clothes to appear in there, but I make use of my Bible all the same." "Yes," spoke up his wife, "he uses it to hone his razor Sunday mornings." "Parson," said Josiah, "do you know why a woman doesn't grow a beard?" "No," said Mr. Upham. "Because," was the reply, "She can't hold her tongue long enough to get it shaved."[22]

Bowdoin and Mental Philosophy

Whether other teaching positions had been offered Upham before he accepted the one as professor of mental and moral philosophy at Bowdoin College in the fall of 1825, we do not know. According to Louis Hatch, Moses Stuart recommended him for the Bowdoin position, and Upham was to spend the rest of his working life in that particular academic chair.[23] An article in the September 1838 issue of the Christian Review, defined mental philosophy as "that branch of science which pertains to the mind, its faculties, its operations, and its laws."[24] In an 1847 article for the British Quarterly Review, Robert Vaugh referred to the mental philosophy of S. S. Schmucker and Thomas Upham and defined philosophy in terms of physical science--"an inductive method which utilized consciousness as the field of its observation."[25] Vernon Howard describes mental philosophers as those who marked the transition between the speculative philosophy of Jonathan Edwards and the empirical psychology of William James. He states that "mental philosophy was essentially an outgrowth of a theological and psychological critique of Jonathan Edwards' Inquiry into the Freedom of the Will."[26]

But why a chair of mental and moral philosophy? Because if man could understand the ways of the mind, he could understand the ways of the universe, and furthermore, he could understand the ways of God. The fixed ways of God were the absolute laws for man. Mental philosophy was an anthropological source for doing theological ethics. As to its importance to the Christian minister, mental philosophy will lead the minister to "perceive the foundations of religious duty, which are laid in the mind itself--the means of strengthening our social and religious feelings, and of bringing to their highest perfections all our intellectual and moral faculties."[27] Mental laws could be intuitively discovered, and the mental fact most evident was that man had a moral law within. Wilson Smith writes:

> Although moral philosophy as academic ethics was a treatment of worldly affairs, much of it was set to operate within a fixed firmament. It described a universe of moral laws in which the uncertainties of life could be met with theologically satisfying preconceptions and fixed plans of actions.[28]

German Philosophy and Scottish Commonsense Realism

H. M. Pierce, Louis Hatch, and Alpheus Packard all recalled that Upham, on the recommendation of Moses Stuart, was called to Bowdoin College to refute Kant and German philosophy.[29] That was the understanding also of George Peck in an 1846 article "Doctor Upham's Works."[30] Vernon Howard takes the opposite view: "That Upham defended the 'cause of orthodoxy' in his religious works and frequently in moral asides in the Elements is true. But that he did so via a refutation of Kant or even that the Elements were designed to refute 'German metaphysics' is patently false."[31] The contemporaries of Upham are right in saying that he was ostensibly called to combat the German idealism that was incomprehensible to the American mind. But Vernon Howard is equally right in stating that Thomas did not pursue this as his overt agenda. In his writings, Upham mentions Kant only a couple of times.[32]

Still, a clear distinction between the Scottish commonsense realism of Upham and the idealism of German philosophy did exist. One minor Kantian that Upham does mention is Johann Fichte.[33] Citing an imaginative conversation that took place between the two helps demonstrate the difference between German idealism and Scottish commonsense realism. Upham might have said: "I perceive that there are apples on the tree because I can see, feel, smell, and taste them." Fichte would probably have responded, "To make that statement, you have actively posited something, an act which is more than just passively experiencing sensation; therefore, you have made a statement which expresses more than you really know. What one should really say is that 'the thought appears that there are apples on the tree,' or 'I know that I think there are apples on the tree.'"

For Fichte, the connection between nature and man destroys man's independence. Because the individual is conscious of consciousness, he knows that he exists. Upham would have agreed with this, but he would have added that this consciousness is immediately dependent upon the real existence of external objects. Upham's realism was, for Fichte, synonymous with a deterministic nature, that destroys freedom and moral consciousness. The latter would have answered that what is perceived is really ourselves; "our consciousness of external things is absolutely nothing more than the product of our own presentative faculty, and that, with respect to such things, we know only what is produced through our consciousness itself; through a deterministic consciousness subject to definite laws."[34]

The Three Mental Departments

Though Pierce, Packard, and Hatch may have been partially right in saying that Upham, at least indirectly, refuted the German idealists, they are doubly wrong in implying that Upham had discovered something original in his separation of the mind into three separate faculties--the intellect, the sensibilities, and the will--thus making the will independent and destroying determinism. First of all, this had little to do with the difference between his philosophy and the philosophy of the German metaphysicists. In fact, the Germans had gone to the extreme in making the will paramount in their understanding of the mind. Upham's contemporary, Fichte, had reverted to a philosophical reductionism in making the will supreme and totally free:

"My will is mine, and it is the only thing that is wholly mine and entirely dependent on myself."[35]

For Upham, the will actually was highly dependent on the laws of nature as determined by God. Over and over again, he reiterates in his Philosophical and Practical Treatise on the Will, that both freedom and the necessity of laws are compatible--in fact synonymous--while the absence of laws is automatically determined by the strongest motive. For Edwards, the strongest desire (motive) and the will are synonymous. For Upham, Edwards made the will, at best, superfluous, and at worst, meaningless. The Bowdoin professor reiterated throughout the treatise:

> But if the result, (that is to say, the volition) is the measure of the intensity, when motives differing in kind are compared together, then in all cases of this description, to say that the will is governed by the strongest motive, is an identical proposition and imparts the same as to say, that the will is governed by the motive by which it is governed.[36]

Pierce, Packard, and Hatch are also wrong that the separation of the will and the sensibilities was some kind of original discovery for Upham. As early as 1793, Samuel West suggested a threefold division of the mental faculties: perception, propension, and will.[37] A. A. Roback states concerning Asa Burton's 1824, Essays on Some of the First Principles of Metaphysicks, Ethicks, and Theology that

> Burton opposed Edwards' bipartite division of the mind, himself adopting three faculties, viz, understanding, taste, and will, taste of course, presiding over the feelings, which to him are reduced to pleasure and disgust, and since the feelings are the main springs of action and determine the qualities of right and wrong, Burton regards the faculty of taste as paramount.[38]

The organization of mental processes above was to influence Upham's work. The second division was also called "taste" and gave a clear philosophical and psychological basis for the evolving evangelical theology, i.e., religion was primarily of the affections of the heart. Henry Boynton Smith, in his review of "Upham's Mental Philosophy," suggests at least three others who had constructed a tripartite division of the mind before Upham; Burton, Jeremy Bentham, and Thomas Brown.[39]

At any rate, Upham was a true eclectic; he borrowed whatever help he could for his psychological system. It is in his systematization that his originality lies, not in novel or ingenious ideas. Henry Smith gave a clear overall view of Upham's modus operandi in constructing his mental philosophy:

> His originality is natural, not studied. The method is strictly inductive. From literature and biography, history and narrative, from medical and physiological works, from poetry and art, he has collected a vast number of facts, and evolved the mental laws and principles contained in them. A large and various general reading, a thorough study of his own mind, and of philosophy in all its phases, are exhibited in these volumes. He is the exclusive partisan of no sect in philosophy, neither an idealist, nor a sceptic, nor a dogmatic, nor a mystic; but from all has borrowed aids and illustrations to the perfecting of his system.[40]

Despite the commonsense reliance on "sensation,"[41] Upham also used John Locke to support internal sources of knowledge, such as perception, thinking, doubting, believing, and reasoning.[42] Upham did not perceive Locke and Kant as antithetical as did Pierce and Packard.[43]

Assessments of Upham's Psychology

The assessments of Upham's philosophical psychology are quite varied, but most are favorable. In 1848, Robert Blakey evaluated Upham's debt to Locke and Dugald Stewart. Blakey characterized Upham as comprehensive, systematic, and judicious, and "there is a healthy spirit of philosophical discussion pervading the whole."[44] After criticizing beginning elementary mental science textbooks the British philosopher Robert Vaughn--comparing Upham's Elements of Mental Philosophy with the works of Henry P. Tappan and S. S. Schumucker--wrote the following:

> The lucid arrangement of the subjects in Upham's work, the candor everywhere displayed the true spirit of inductive investigation which characterizes all his inquiries, and the simple, easy, and natural yet vigorous and precise style in which his work is written, render it eminently suitable for the purpose of instruction. It is, in other respects, admirably adapted for an elementary work; and we think its circulation in this country would contribute to revive and invigorate a taste for the cultivation of sound philosophy. We earnestly recommend it to the attention of the student of mental science.[45]

Upham's popularity had somewhat cooled off a half century after his death. George S. Brett wrote in his magnum opus, A History of Psychology (1921, Volume III) that Upham's Elements "still lingers on the bookshelves of literary antiquarians." He then admits that Upham was more original and less stereotyped than his contemporaries.[46] But theologian Frank Hugh Foster more charitably calls Upham's Treatise on the Will, "one of the first original and comprehensive contributions of American scholarship to modern psychology."[47] Recent interpretations have also been favorable. Herbert Schneider describes Upham as "the first great American textbook writer in mental philosophy," and reminds us that Upham's Outlines of Imperfect and Disordered Mental Action (1840) is the first full treatise on abnormal psychology written in the United States.[48] Most unequivocally charitable is Jay Wharton Fay in his American Psychology Before William James (1939). Fay states that Upham "anticipates many ideas commonly supposed to be modern,"[49] had a gift for clear and ordered exposition,[50] and exemplifies "a spirit of seriousness, piety, and fair-mindedness."[51]

A. A. Roback keeps more critical distance from Upham than Fay does.[52] While admitting that Upham is an unusually astute observer, Roback sees "no need of turning him into a genius a century ahead of his time."[53] Roback concedes that Upham did foreshadow such twentieth-century psychological expressions as introversion and extroversion, rationalization, and the emergence of suppressed desires in perverted forms. He suggests that the most original contribution of Upham's is a treatment of the psychology of character included in his Mental Philosophy.[54]

In a recent Ph.D. dissertation, Vernon Howard correctly summarized Upham's forte as Upham's ability to utilize both psychological evidence as well as philosophical argument.[55] Howard believes that Upham's investigation of the mind is a "half-way house between the speculative philosophy of Jonathan Edwards and the empirical investigation of William James."[56]

Edwards and Upham were each using different approaches. Edwards was trying to solve the dialectical struggle that existed between determinism and indeterminism, and Upham was appealing to the intuitive evidence of the mind or consciousness. Edwards philosophized; Upham simply looked within.

In that Upham's argument for the freedom of the will was unique, inductive and empirical, he made a genuine contribution to American psychology and philosophy. Howard, especially, is helpful in demonstrating how Upham was more Lockian than Kantian in his understanding of intellect and sensation, even though Kant's "thinking," "sensibility," and "will" somewhat foreshadow Upham's tripartite division of the mind.[57]

Scholarship and Works

Since we do not know the number of copies sold of the various editions of Upham's works, it is difficult to estimate his books' distribution and from that gain some understanding of his total influence. The National Union Catalog Pre-1956 Imprints lists twenty major works. Upham's Mental Philosophy went through an astounding fifty-seven editions (1826-1899). For approximately the first fifteen years of the editions, Upham continued to revise the work so that each new edition would demonstrate the development of his thought. It could be argued that Upham, because of the primacy of his textbook, was the prototype mental philosopher of the nineteenth century. Of his religious writings, his biography of Madame Guyon (thirty-seven editions) enjoyed the greatest popularity. The Interior Life went through eighteen editions. This book, along with Madame Guyon's biography, had a wide reading in England, especially within the Keswick holiness movement.[58]

Upham was a scholar--almost to the point of stereotype.[59] Even though his philosophical writings are heavily indebted to Locke and the Scottish philosophers and his religious writings are grounded in the French mystics, Upham read everything he could possibly obtain. His Letters: Aesthetic, Social and Moral demonstrates his tremendous grasp of world history and literature. On February 27, 1915, a writer for the Lewiston Journal characterized Upham as an "omnivorous" reader who was willing to make a trip from Bowdoin to Baltimore to obtain a single book.[60] George Little, librarian at Bowdoin during the latter part of Upham's tenure, reported that when a book was missing in the library, as a last resort for finding it, he would always check Professor Upham's "loan list" or Upham's personal library.[61]

Characteristics and Idiosyncrasies

In respect to his physical characteristics, Upham was tall, bent, and slightly built.[62] Regarding his character, he was pious and industrious. In psychological temperament, he was sentimental, sensitive, introverted, soft-spoken, self-effacing and "nervous." For almost the whole of his professorship, it seems, he was unable to speak in public or lead in formal worship because of the anxiety he experienced when he attended large gatherings. "He was a most lovely character," one newspaper article stated, and though he lived his faith fearlessly in the eye of the world day by day, he was so definite and bashful as to be unable to conduct the public chapel services of the chapel."[63] A former pupil recalled:

> His excessive nervous timidity to my mind accounted for traits of character that awakened unfavorable comment. He trembled at, and shrank from public speech. He hesitated at a bold assertion, however true. He loved the most retired, not to say secret, ways of investigation for either practical or philosophical purposes, more because his nerves were weak, than because his convictions were feeble or his moral courage faint.[64]

But the above in no way diminished Upham's spiritual effectiveness, which was particularly demonstrated in his one-on-one encounters with individual students. Henry Boynton Smith stated that Professor Upham conversed with him calmly and reasonably. The former student had confidence in his teacher as a counselor, and it seems that Upham was a pivotal person in regard to Smith's conversion.[65] Still another student described how Upham approached him and requested him to come to the privacy of his room:

> "I have long desired to have some conversation with you on the subject of your religious faith and duty." He proceeded to admonish me in the most tender manner and with a depth of feelings, unmistakable by the moistened eye and trembling voice, exhorted me in impressive language, and pleaded with me to give my life to the Lord's service. Before concluding the interview, he surprised me by apologizing for the liberty he had presumed to take in thus reminding me of my religious obligations; hoped I would take no offense, and on my expressing much pleasure and grateful appreciation of his thoughtful interest, he retired with a bright soul gleam of happiness on his face.[66]

His natural humility and self-effacement are uniquely illustrated in his correspondence. In a letter dated March 8, 1854, Upham is requesting a daguerreotype, which had been recently made of him to be sent to the "Guide to Holiness," since the latter wanted to use it in a future publication. Upham asked,

> Do you mean to put the name at the bottom of the engraving? If so, omit the honorary title to mine. Delicacy forbade me refusing it when it was conferred; but I have always had some doubts about allowing it to be appended to my name.[67]

In a letter just before his death, March 26, 1872, his wife wrote, "It was his request to have a plain coffin and everything in great simplicity."[68] Alpheus Packard further wrote:

> The most lowly found one more lowly than themselves. However much he had accomplished by personal effort, he did not claim credit for what he had done. In a public meeting, even in a church meeting,

> his chosen seat was in a retired corner. He seldom spoke of his own agency in affairs of moment, never appeared as a leader, everywhere in truth he was the heart and soul of the movement.[69]

His three volumes of poetry, as well as his ability to pen a poem on the spur of the moment, were products of his romantic imagination, keen powers of observation, knowledge of literature, and sensitive emotional inclination.[70] Learning of the senseless killing of an eagle in Egypt, Upham wrote, "I am not ashamed to say that I wept."[71] His poetry was probably influenced by Robert Burns, as much as by any other.[72] He used the American farm and village setting as his most frequent motif. The American farmer, wedded to nature and in harmony with the world around him, was the prototype of inner strength and tranquility. Upham wrote in his preface to American Cottage Life (1852), which contains 135 poems:

> And as it is religious feeling which, more than anything else, has made the American farmer and cottager what they are; I have introduced the religious sonnets and hymns in the hopes of encouraging and strengthening this feeling. It is the Bible accompanied with prayer, which gives the American farmer his consistency of life, his strength of purpose, his strong and serene alliance with truth, freedom, and humanity. Like the furrow which he turns, he may be said to be nourished in the rains and sunshine of an overruling providence and amid the wonderful works of nature, to be trained up for the acknowledgement and the worship of the God of nature.[73]

Interests and Commitments

Thomas Upham was highly committed to Bowdoin College and sought to insure both its financial and theological stability. He foresaw that if funds were going to be committed to the institution, the benefactors would need to be assured of the college's future doctrinal commitment. Thus, in 1846, Upham was instrumental in finding support among the trustees and leadership of the school for a "declaration" of theological and denominational commitment within its constitution.[74] Using the "declaration," Upham obtained more than $70,000, money which was crucial in keeping the doors of Bowdoin open; over a period of years, he gave as much as $6,000 of his own money. After forty-three years of service to the institution, a portion of the resolution passed by the Board of Trustees read:

> That the College Board most highly appreciates the uniform and earnest endeavors of Prof. Upham by his self denying labors, his constant solicitude, and care, and his personal sacrifices and toils, to promote the welfare of the College throughout the entire period of his official connection with it; and would particularly record the obligations of the College to him for his devotion to its interest at that period of its history when in its financial affairs the College was in serious want.[75]

Upham devoted himself to pacifism, temperance, foreign mission,[76] the abolition of capital punishment and the emancipation of slaves, though concerning the latter he was not an immediate abolitionist. We will have the opportunity to discuss his views on each of these subjects in Chapter VI. Just a couple of remarks at this point will suffice. The Uphams were friends of Calvin and Harriet Stowe, and it is evident they entertained Harriet during the writing of Uncle Tom's Cabin (1850-1852).[77] But what influence Upham had on Harriet Stowe is difficult to determine. No letters of substance are extant that might indicate any kind of theological contribution to the understanding of Stowe by Upham.[78] Catherine Gilbertson claims Upham's Interior Life had comforted Mrs. Stowe and that Mrs. Upham's serenity was a special witness to her in contrast to her own irritability and restlessness.[79] On May 29, 1850, Harriet wrote:

> Mrs. Upham has done everything for me, giving up time and strength and taking charge of my affairs in a way without which one could not have got along at all in a strange place and in my present helpless condition. This family is delightful, there is such a perfect sweetness and quietude in all its movements. Not a harsh word or hasty expression is ever heard. It is a beautiful pattern of a Christian family, a beautiful exemplification of religion.[80]

A 1915 article for the Lewiston Journal claims that the

Upham house was "an underground railroad during the last days of slavery."[81] Though difficult to document, the claim makes sense, taking into consideration the sentiment of the Upham's, the location of Bowdoin, and the large size of the Upham house.[82]

Alpheus Packard recalls that Upham took so much interest in a local option for the sale of alcohol that he made it a personal campaign to recommend privately to as many individuals as possible that the sale should be disallowed. The vote went for the cause of temperance, and the influence of Upham was recognized so markedly that the referendum was called "Upham's victory." Packard wrote: "All questions of public moment, whether regarding religion or morals and manners, found him a vigilant observer and active participant in all good measures."[83]

Family

In 1825, Thomas married Phebe Lord, who, dying at the age of seventy-eight in March of 1882, survived him by ten years. From all accounts, Phebe was a beautiful woman --physically, socially, and spiritually.[84] Phebe was an author and poet in her own right, and was a constant contributor to the Guide to Holiness. Her best known work, the Crystal Fountain (1887), was a spiritual diary. Her portrait was painted by Gilbert Stuart when he was seventy; it hangs in the Walker Art Building at Bowdoin College.

The Uphams did not have any biological children. Of the six children they adopted, we know something of only three.[85] Upham's Genealogy gives an account of two of these children. One son, George Barnard Upham, for many years practiced medicine in the city of New York. He also served as an "examining surgeon" for drafted men during the Civil War.[86] Another child took the name of Susan Elizabeth Upham and married a Mr. DeLong of Nunda, New York.[87] The other son, Thomas Lord Upham, at the approximate age of fifteen, was lost at sea with the rest of his ship's crew.

In his Letters, Upham gives a moving account of the adoption and death of the son. He tells that he saw the boy in the streets one day and, having pity on him as the son of a deceased mother and a sea captain lost at sea, he "took him home, gave him [his] own name, and adopted him as a son."[88] Concerning his death:

> So painful was the event that I seldom alluded to it in conversation. Perhaps I may say that I never told my sorrow, because language has no expression for it. And yet I nourished it in my memory. Often, very often, has my heart alone gone down into the depths of the ocean, and held communion with the solitary tomb.[89]

The Uphams moved to Kennebunkport, Maine, during the years of retirement, but evidently they spent the winters with their physician son in New York City.[90] Thomas became extremely feeble. He was a semi-invalid and nearly blind during the last years of his life. For the last several weeks, he was only periodically conscious. According to his wife, his last words were: "My soul is with God."[91] Thomas Upham died on April 2, 1872. He and his wife are both buried in the Bowdoin College cemetery in Brunswick, Maine.[92]

Conclusion

Three significant characteristics stand out concerning Upham, all of which were to have bearing on his later involvement in the holiness movement. First of all, his affluent, cultural background led him to Dartmouth College. Subsequently, he was trained at Andover, this the vital link to his being appointed professor at Bowdoin College. Also, Upham's upper-class New England background was not unlike the social class that gravitated around Dr. Walter and Mrs. Phoebe Palmer.

Secondly, Upham was not an evangelist such as Finney, a college president such as Francis Wayland, nor an outspoken preacher such as Lyman Beecher. Though he was a pivotal figure in American academic development (his textbook Mental Philosophy was possibly as popular as any from approximately 1830 to 1860), he has not attracted the attention he deserves. As a mental philosopher, he was the most intellectual of all the contributors to antebellum holiness literature and the best equipped to understand the psychological implications of "entire sanctification."

Thirdly, the psychological quirks of Upham's temperament were what motivated him--partially, at least--to seek spiritual answers within mysticism and Wesleyan perfectionism. Thus, some of the answers to his psychological crisis and quest for wholeness were worked through in his voluminous commentary on experiential piety. Also, Upham's pensive, sentimental romanticism lent itself to his search for spiritual perfection.

Notes

1. Frank Kidder Upham, Genealogy and Family History of the Uphams of Castine, Maine, and Dixon, Illinois (Newark, N.J.: Advertiser Printing House, 1887), p. 7.
2. Frank Kidder Upham, Descendants of John Upham of Massachusetts (Albany, N.Y.: Joel Munsell's Sons, 1892), p. 42.
3. Robert F. Lawrence, The New Hampshire Churches Comprising Histories of Congregational and Presbyterian Churches in the State (Claremont, N.H.: The Claremont Manufacturing Co., 1856), p. 36.
4. Frank Kidder Upham, Descendants, p. 114.
5. Ibid., p. 175.
6. Ibid., p. 176.
7. Ibid., p. 186.
8. "Early Rochester Sketches," Rochester Courier, 14 December 1888, number 6, second series, number 1. The Upham house, which Nathaniel had built, was the most expensive within the community and stood on an adjacent corner to the Congregational Church, which his son would pastor.
9. Nathaniel G. Upham, "Rebellion, Slavery, Peace," address delivered at Concord, New Hampshire, March 2, 1864. (Concord, N.H.: E. C. Eastman, 1864).
10. "Early Rochester Sketches," Rochester Courier, 14 December 1888.
11. Ibid. Cogswell is the maternal surname. The Rochester Courier stated that "Nathaniel Upham married Judith Cogswell of Gilmanton. She was the daughter of Hon. Thomas Cogswell, and the family is one of honorable mention in our state like the Wentworth family. Mrs. Upham was a true woman, and a lady beloved by all who knew her. She is said to have been above the medium height and quite portly in person, with a kind motherly face and pleasing

manner. As mistress of the beautiful Upham mansion her social success was great. I am not certain that she accompanied her husband to Washington during his congregational career, but she was fitted to adorn any position in life."

12. Franklin McDuffee, History of the Town of Rochester, New Hampshire: From 1722 to 1890. Edited and revised by Silvanus Hayward, Vol. I. (Manchester, N.H.: The John B. Clarke Company, 1892).

13. Hale Family Papers (New Hampshire Historical Society). Written by Thomas C. Upham to William Hale from Andover Theological Seminary, September 8, 1821.

14. See a thorough discussion of Woods' relationship to the Hopkinsians in E. A. Lawrence's article: "Leonard Woods," The Congregational Quarterly (April 1859), pp. 105-124. Lawrence wrote: "He was never a partisan. He had no love for controversy. In his disagreements with those holding the ground principles of the Christian faith; he always sought for conciliation as well as correction." p. 117.

15. "Dedicatory Address" prefixed to Leonard Woods' Works, quoted in Williston Walker, Ten New England Leaders (New York: Silver, Burdett, and Company, 1901), pp. 392-393.

16. Ibid., p. 390.

17. Leonard Woods, A History of the Andover Theological Seminary (Boston: James R. Osgood and Company, 1885), p. 152.

18. H. M. Pierce. Addresses at the Commencement of Rutgers Female College (New York: Cushing, Barbua, and Company, 1870), p. 4.

19. Robert F. Lawrence, p. 342.

20. Franklin McDuffee, p. 243.

21. Ibid., p. 243.

22. Ibid., p. 568.

23. Louis C. Hatch, The History of Bowdoin College (Portland, Me.: Loring, Short, and Harmon, 1927), p. 58.

24. "Importance of a Knowledge of Mental Philosophy to the Christian Minister," Christian Review, Vol. III (September 1838), p. 430.

25. Robert Vaughn, "American Philosophy," British Quarterly Review (February-March 1847), pp. 88-119.

26. Vernon Howard, "The Academic Compromise on Free Will in the Nineteenth Century American Philosophy." Unpublished Ph.D. dissertation, University of Wisconsin, 1965, p. xx.

27. Importance of a Knowledge of Mental Philosophy, p. 431.

28. Wilson Smith, Professors and Public Ethics: Studies of Northern Moral Philosophers Before the Civil War (Ithaca, N.Y.: Cornell University Press, 1956), p. 28.

29. Pierce, pp. 5-6; Hatch, p. 58; Alpheus S. Packard, Address on the Life and Character of Thomas C. Upham, D.D. (Brunswick, Me.: Joseph Criffin, 1873), p. 8.

30. George Peck, "Dr. Upham's Works," Methodist Quarterly Review, Vol. XXVIII (April 1846), p. 260. Peck sides Upham with English philosophy and draws a sharp dichotomy between it and German philosophy. "We would admonish them (readers) against the decorated illusions of this exotic philosophy; we would teach them to despise its emasculated spirit, which would dilute our vigorous literature, unnerve the old energy of our tongue, and evaporate our wholesome religion. We comment to them the above psychological works at the head of this article, as specimens of the true English Philosophical spirits."

31. Howard, p. xv. Apparently, as Howard suggests, this idea was first made public by H. M. Pierce at the 1870 Commencement of Rutgers Female College, when Upham was given an honorary doctorate. Speaking of Upham and his early academic work, Pierce stated: "In these researches he had the cordial sympathy and encouragement of his former master, Stuart, who foresaw the pernicious consequences of the transcendental German metaphysics rolling in upon the country, and who looked to him to stem the flood. Thus encouraged he went on with unwearying labor, fourteen hours a day, for ten years, and, as yet, no firm land." Pierce, p. 6.

32. Thomas C. Upham, Elements of Mental Philosophy, Vol. I (New York: Harper and Brothers, 1850), p. 226. Also see Jay Wharton Fay, American Psychology Before William James (New York: Octagon Books, 1966), p. 95.

33. Thomas C. Upham, Divine Union (Boston: George C. Rand and Avery, 1856), p. 39.

34. Johann G. Fichte, The Vocation of Man (Indianapolis: The Bobbs-Merrill Company, 1956), p. 75.

35. Ibid., p. 119.

36. Thomas C. Upham, A Philosophical and Practical Treatise on the Will (Portland, Me.: William Hyde, 1834), p. 217.

37. Jay Wharton Fay, p. 75.

38. A. A. Roback, History of American Psychology (New York: Library Publishers, 1952), p. 49.

39. Henry B. Smith, "Review of Upham's Mental Philosophy," Literary and Theological Review, Vol. XIV (December 1837), pp. 630-631.

40. Ibid., p. 628.

41. Thomas C. Upham, Elements of Mental Philosophy, Vol. I., p. 61. Upham quotes from Stewart: "Let us suppose, then a particular sensation to be excited in the mind of such a being. The moment this happens, he must necessarily acquire the knowledge of two facts at once: that of the existence of the sensation and that of his own existence as a sentient being." Upham then remarks: "This language clearly implies, that the notions of existence and of person or self are attendant upon, and subsequent to, an affection of the mind, caused by an impression on the senses."

42. Ibid., p. 222.

43. See Merrill R. Davis, "Emerson's Reason and the Scottish Philosophy," New England Quarterly, Vol. XVIII (June 1944), pp. 209-228; and Merle Curti, "The Great Mr. Locke--America's Philosopher, 1783-1861," The Huntington Library Bulletin, No. 11 (April 1937), p. 132. The articles of both Davis and Curti suggest a revision of such nineteenth-century views which pitted Locke and the Scottish sense triumvirate of Stewart, Reid, and Brown against transcendentalism and German metaphysics.

44. Robert Blakey, History of the Philosophy of Mind, Vol. IV (London: Trelawney William Saunders, 1848), p. 530.

45. Robert Vaughn, p. 118.

46. George Brett, A History of Psychology, Vol. III (London: George Allen, 1921), p. 256.

47. Frank Hugh Foster, A Genetic History of the New England Theology (Chicago: The University of Chicago Press, 1907), p. 249.

48. Herbert W. Schneider, A History of American Philosophy, second edition (New York: Columbia University Press, 1963), p. 210.

49. Fay, p. 106. See G. Stanley Hall on "The History of American College Textbooks and Teaching in Logic, Ethics, Psychology, and Allied Subjects," American Antiquarian Society (April 1894), pp. 137-161. He states, "As Berkeley's problem widened into Hume's scepticism and that went on to Kant and the heroic age of German philosophy, American professors drew back. The Scotch philosophy represented by Reid, Stewart, Brown, and Hamilton, opened a far safer way.... In this form psychology was very widely

introduced in American colleges" p. 158. Found in the Firestone Library, Princeton University, Princeton, New Jersey.

50. Fay, p. 108.

51. Ibid., p. 106. I thank Jay Wharton Fay for the following excellent summary paragraph, which lists the sources for Upham's psychology. "The 1827 book is decidedly Lockean in spirit and terminology. He cites or refers to Bacon, Locke, Cudworth, Berkeley, Hume, Hartley; Hutcheson, Reid, Beattie, Oswald, Stewart, Brown, Priestley; More, Wollaston, Butler, Price, Clarke, King, Chubb; Duncan, Watts, Gambier, A. Smith, Mackintosh; Campbell, Harris, Tooke; Hogarth, Reynolds, Alison, Burke, J. G. Cooper, Cogan; Edwards; Feinagle; Barrow, Jenun, Good; Montaigne, Descartes, Malebranche, Buffier, Condillar, de Tracy, Diderot, Helvetius, Cabanis, Buffon, de Stael, Pinel, Esquirol, Hibbert, Rush, (abnormal psychology); Brucker, de Gerando, Bayle, New Edinburgh Encyclopedia, Dictionaire des Sciences Medicales; Kant; Aristotle, Cicero, Longinus.

"In the 1840 edition in two volumes his heaviest direct borrowings are from Reid (375 lines), Stewart (175), Brown (84), Locke (165), Cudworth (98), and Buffon (one citation of 145 lines). However, large amounts are taken indirectly from Reid and Stewart, perhaps by unconscious plagiarism, perhaps because the sources were so familiar to the reader as not to need reference. E.g., Vol. I, pp. 175-179, are almost verbally taken from Stewart's _Elements_ without a word of acknowledgment" p. 196.

52. Roback, pp. 51-54.

53. Ibid., p. 54.

54. Ibid.

55. Vernon Howard, p. xxv.

56. Ibid., p. xxviii.

57. Ibid., p. 68. See recent assessments of Upham's works by J. A. Cardno in "Idiocy, Imbecility: An Early American Contrast," _The Psychological Record_, Vol. 18, No. 2 (1968), p. 244; "The Aetiology of Insanity: Some Early American Views," _Journal of the History of the Behavioral Sciences_, Vol. 4, No. 2 (1968), p. 100; and "The Birds Are Rather Big for Ducks: Criterion and Material in History," _Journal of the History of the Behavioral Sciences_, Vol. V, No. 1 (1969), p. 69.

58. Charles F. Harford (ed.), _The Keswick Convention_ (London: Marshall Brother, 1907), p. 224; J. B. Figgis (ed.), _Keswick from Within_ (London: Marshal Brother, 1914), p. 9.

59. Dictionary of American Biography, article by Kenneth C. M. Sills (New York: Charles Scribner's Sons, 1936), Vol. 19, pp. 123-124.

60. "Bowdoin College's Gentle Apostle of Peace," Lewiston Journal, 27 February 1915, from the archives of Bowdoin College.

61. Ibid.

62. Ibid.

63. "Professor Upham," no newspaper title, date or page given; from Bowdoin Archives.

64. Louis C. Hatch, p. 60.

65. Elizabeth L. Smith, Henry Boynton Smith: His Life and Work (New York: A. C. Armstrong and Sons, 1881), p. 14. "I have had several conversations with Hamlin, and last evening Professor Upham came in, and we conversed a long while. I stated to him fully and explicably, my doubts, fears, hopes, and, in fine, my situation in every respect, and he talked to me, calmly, reasonably. I aim to see him again this afternoon."

66. "Professor Upham," no newspaper title, date or page given, from Bowdoin Archives.

67. Bowdoin Archives.

68. Ibid.

69. Alpheus S. Packard, p. 20.

70. Thomas C. Upham, American Cottage Life (Portland, Maine: Sanborn and Cater, 1852), pp. v and vi; Thomas C. Upham, Christ in the Soul (New York: Warren, Broughton, and Wyman, 1872); Thomas C. Upham, Religious Offerings (New York: Published by Leavitt, Lord & Company; Boston: Crocker & Brewster, 1835).

71. Thomas C. Upham, Letters, p. 277.

72. "Eminent Author," newspaper article, no newspaper title, date or page given, from Bowdoin Archives. "Professor Upham was evidently a great admirer of Robert Burns, and he followed his Cotter's Saturday Night very closely in his long poem, The Farmer's Fireside, but it is a series of pictures of the New England of his early years in their way as perfect as those of Burns' of the Scottish peasants of his time."

In regard to poetry, there is an interesting letter written to Dr. George Bush of New York University, which is in the Simon Gratz Autograph Collection in the Philadelphia Historical Society. In it (the July 7, 1834, letter), Upham recommends a fellow teacher, Henry Wadsworth Longfellow, for a Spanish professorship at New York University: "It is hardly necessary for me to say, that Mr. L. is a young gentleman of distinguished talents and acquirements, since I doubt not you are already familiar with his reputation. He is not only very highly valued here as possessing the requisite qualifications and tact in the discharge of the duties of the recitation room; but also as a judicious and efficient officer in the government of the college...."

73. Thomas Upham, American Cottage Life, p. vi.

74. Louis Hatch, pp. 112-113. Also see History of Bowdoin College.... From 1806 to 1870, Inclusive, by Nehemiah Cleaveland (Boston: James Ripley Osgood and Company, 1882), pp. 131-133. The most recent word has been written by Ernst Christian Helmreich. Upham initiated the declaration, which for the first time officially stated that the school "has been and still is of the Orthodox Congregational denomination." Ernst Christian Helmreich, Religion at Bowdoin College: A History (Brunswick, Me.: J. S. McCarthy Company, Inc., 1981), p. 76.

75. Bowdoin College Archives.

76. Missionary letter, Bowdoin College Archives (Brunswick, Me.: April 15, 1829). Phebe Upham reports in a letter to a missionary that even as she writes, her husband is reading a copy of Mrs. Judson's Memoirs. Phebe states: "My own family and a few other friends are preparing some ready made garments, which we hope will reach you safe and remind you of our affectionate remembrance of you and also of our prayers."

77. Calvin Stowe took a teaching position at Bowdoin College in 1850. His meager salary of $300 a year may have been at least part of the motivation for Harriet to continue her writing.

78. Gayle Kimball, in an unpublished Ph.D. dissertation, The Religious Ideas of Harriet Beecher Stowe: Her Gospel of Womanhood, makes no mention at all of Thomas C. Upham, much less any theological influence he might have had on Mrs. Stowe. (University of California, 1976).

79. Catherine Gilbertson, Harriet Beecher Stowe (Port Washington, N.Y.: Kennekat Press, Inc., 1937), pp. 124-131.

In an article for the New York Evangelist, Harriet B. Stowe commends Upham's Interior Life because it "furnished a tangible and definite point to the efforts of those who are longing for higher spiritual attainments." Harriet Beecher Stowe, "The Interior Life or Primitive Christian Experience," Guide to Christian Perfection, Vol. VIII, 1845, pp. 13-18.

80. Charles Edward Stowe, Life of Harriet Beecher Stowe (Boston and New York: Houghton, Mifflin and Company, The Riverside Press, 1889), p. 133.

81. Lewiston Journal (1915), Bowdoin College Archives.

82. The house that Thomas and Phebe Upham lived in, a large two-story structure, was known as the Dunlap-Upham House. When it was constructed in 1818, it was the most expensive dwelling built in Brunswick up to that time. William D. Shipman, The Early Architecture of Bowdoin College (Brunswick, Me.: Brunswick Publishing Company, 1973), p. 45.

83. Alpheus Packard, p. 18. There is some family irony in Upham's stance for tee-totalism, since his father sold liquor in his store. A December 21, 1888, article in the Rochester Courier states concerning Nathaniel Upham and Jonas March: "Each trader kept in a conspicuous part of his store hogsheads of rum, a brand they called 'Tobago rum,' and gin also, a cheap kind distilled from potatoes, being known as 'potato gin.' Then there was rye gin and corn gin flavored with the ale of juniper which gave it the proper 'gin taste.'" Obtained from the Rochester, New Hampshire Public Library.

84. Joseph Williamson, A Bibliography of the State of Maine, from the Earliest Period to 1891, Vol. II (Portland, Me.: The Thurston Print, 1896). Phebe was a sister of the co-owner of the publishing firm, Leavitt, Lord, and Company. See a letter to George Bush from Thomas Upham, July 7, 1824, the Simon Gratz Autograph Collection of the Pennsylvania Historical Society in Philadelphia. Her obituary stated: "Equally conspicuous was Mrs. Upham's religious character, her earnest and effective work in many ways, at all times, and under all circumstances, to promote the cause of the religion which she professed. Mrs. Upham wrote with great facility, in earlier years writing considerably for the public eye, her writings attracting favorable criticism, and she also often addressed public assemblies, speaking with ease, precision, with so evident a sincerity as to win attention, if all her view were not accepted by her hearers." Telegraph, March 24, 1882. Bowdoin College Archives.

85. Phebe Lord Upham, The Crystal Fountain (Philadelphia: J. B. Lippincott and Company, 1877), p. 8. She wrote concerning her spiritual autobiography: "This is not a history, in any sense, of my external life and labors. There are long intervals of years, of which no records are

here given, and during which time, as at all other times, I was occupied, 'first,' in the care of my family, which was considerable, having adopted six orphan children without father or mother, who were made a great blessing to me. I was led also to engage in special efforts to benefit the poor, neglected children of our vicinity--a labor attended with the blessing of God at every step, and perserveringly followed."

86. Frank Kidder Upham, Upham Genealogy, p. 307.

87. Ibid., p. 309.

88. Thomas C. Upham, Letters, p. 76.

89. Ibid., p. 79.

90. Ibid., a letter addressed to "Friend Oliver" (Kennebunkport, Me.: May 17, 1868), "I have just returned from New York, where I have spent the winter."

91. Handwritten account by Phebe Lord Upham in Bowdoin College Archives.

92. Obituary of "Dr. T. C. Upham," The Guide to Holiness, Vol. 16 (1872), p. 152.

Chapter II

CONGREGATIONALISM AND THE AMERICAN CONTEXT: THE PHILOSOPHICAL AND THEOLOGICAL BACKGROUND OF UPHAM'S THEOLOGY

Jonathan Edwards, Sr., Nathanael Emmons, Samuel Hopkins, Joseph Bellamy, Timothy Dwight, Nathaniel Taylor, Leonard Woods, Asa Mahan, Charles Finney, Edward Beecher, and Thomas Upham shared three readily apparent characteristics. They were all native Americans; they were all Congregationalists; and they were all theologians attempting to arrive at a biblically based and philosophically cogent theology that would speak to the rapidly changing religious climate. (Comparisons would reveal that a Timothy Dwight was more existentially oriented than a Nathanael Emmons, the latter whose historical Calvinistic dogma was not flavored to appeal to the populus. But, deciding whose theology best complemented the American matrix, will not be the subject of this chapter.)

A significant theological shift was occurring in America, a shift that helped prepare Upham for his transition from New England theology to Phoebe Palmer's Wesleyan holiness. Upham was not some Congregationalist anomaly who had lost his Calvinistic bearings.[1] The previous 100 years had paved the way for the perfectionism of Finney, Mahan, and Upham, and many of the theological components of Palmer's perfectionism were simply handed to her for assemblage. The materials for constructing a holiness theology were already there; Palmer simply signed the purchase order that the package had been received.

The Puritans began preparing it for her when they arrived on the shores of the new land. Their newly formed covenant began to weaken the arbitrary power of the sovereign God of Geneva and Westminster. They would not have gone as far as the Methodist bishop, Matthew Simpson, who two hundred years later would say, "God cannot do without America."[2] Nonetheless, John Winthrop and the Massachusetts Bay Colony, fired by a millenarian vision, had made a pragmatic, utilitarian agreement with God.[3] A lot of changes would have to take place to arrive at the manifest destiny and perfectionism of Matthew Simpson. These changes would evolve within the framework of New England theology, and no one would be more blatant and critical of the changes than Richard Niebuhr:

> A single line of development leads from Jonathan Edwards and his great system of God-centered faith through the Arminianism of the Evangelical revival, the Unitarianism of Channing and Parker, and the humanism of transcendental philosophy, to the man-centered, this worldly, lift yourself-by-your-boot-straps doctrine of New Thought, and Christian Science.... Here the gospel of self-help has excluded all remnants of that belief in fatality, which formed the foundation of Puritan heroism.[4]

At the heart of the changing climate was revivalism, the method for taking the new land for God; unequally were the method and the theology yoked together. Sidney Mead called it a "forced marriage."[5] It was difficult to call men to repentance--to instantaneous "decisions" for Christ--and at the same time, work from the philosophical basis that man's will is bound and predetermined. America would no longer tolerate Parson Simpson's dilemma, which Harriet Beecher Stowe depicted in Old Town Folks. Sam Lawson quoted the Old Town pastor as saying: "We was clear down in a well fifty feet deep, and the sides all round nothin' but glare ice; but we was under immediate obligations to get out, 'cause we was free, voluntary agents."[6] Jonathan Edwards was among the first who attempted to solve the dilemma. Maintaining his Calvinism, and, at the same time, preaching "Pressing into the Kingdom of God," his attempt is admirable:

> Here is this to induce you to a compliance with what you have been directed to; if you sit still, you die, if you go backward, behold you shall surely die; if you go forward, you may live. And though God has not bound himself to any thing that a person does while destitute of faith, and out of Christ, yet

> there is great probability, that in a way of hearkening to this counsel you will live; and that by pressing onward, and persevering, you will at last, as it were by violence, take the kingdom of heaven.[7]

Whether one believes that the church shapes society or society shapes the church,[8] it is difficult to argue with Frank Hugh Foster's statement that "the evolution of New England theology was more the work of the age than of the leaders in whose works it was gradually formulated."[9] Foster's summary statement makes it easier to understand the direction our thinking needs to take.

> For the arbitrary will of God they had substituted his character, love; for a sinful nature, a nature occasioning sin; for imputation, a strict personal responsibility; for a limited, a general atonement; for a bound, a free will; for a satisfaction to justice in the atonement, a governmental example; for irresistible grace, unresisted.[10]

A Benevolent God

What kind of God did America need psychologically and socially in the New World? There was creature against unruly nature, creature unprotected by monarch and by the state church. The American "jeremiad" was able to coerce man to obey God through fear of divine wrath, a fear which was accepted by the existential anxiety that existed among the harsh elements. But only a benevolent God could reach man's heart. Both Edwards and Upham, as many others between them, did away with the "half-way" covenant because their evangelicalism was opposed to a simple, outward conformity. Thus, benevolence became the chief attribute of God within New England theology. Joseph Haroutunian states that "our compassionate heavenly father" was the deity who was coming to dethrone the "Creator and Ruler of the universe." He calls this "the heavenly coup d'etat."[11] Upham repeatedly reiterated that love is the central characteristic of God. He wrote, "It cannot be too often repeated in relation to God, that love stands as the centre of his being. For more than anything else, it is the essential element of his life as God."[12]

The hallmark of Americans has been pursuit of a better life; this being the case, only a benevolent God could help them pursue earthly happiness. Holiness, happiness, and harmony all went together. Edwards believed that the happiness of God's creature is what would best bring glory to the creator. "God communicates himself to the understanding of the creature, in giving him the knowledge of his glory; and to the will of the creature, in giving him holiness consisting primarily in the love of God; and in giving the creature happiness chiefly constituting in joy in God."[13]

Samuel Hopkins went a step further. He argued that the glory, holiness, and perfection of God were actually dependent upon man's happiness.[14] By the time we get to Oberlin theology, God is so totally defined by benevolence that "the universe is conceived ideally as a vast harmony in which divine resources are perfectly adapted to creaturely needs."[15] The attributes of God were defined teleologically in that God created, controlled, and ruled the universe primarily for the happiness of humanity.[16] Haroutunian writes, "A providence which had blessed the people of the land with all manner of good could be none other than good. What could be more evident that God was on their side, and made their happiness His chief concern."[17] In commenting on Mark Hopkins' Romantic and Pragmatic Lectures on Moral Science (1862), Timothy Smith states that he "arranged the wedding of Puritan virtue and the pursuit of happiness; man's end was neither holiness nor happiness alone, but a holy happiness, a happy holiness."[18]

With the foregoing, Upham was not out of step at all. One could take for granted that God had allied himself with the endeavors of man. God's activities are for the purpose of promoting and improving the welfare of men.[19] Upham's God is a happy God, and whoever does the will of God partakes in God's happiness.[20] Neither suffering nor sorrow nor any adversary could separate man from happiness; only selfishness could do that.[21] The assurance of happiness was as certain as the presence of an immanent God who personally concerned himself with the affairs of man.[22] It was a mutual arrangement, man for God's happiness and vice versa.[23] Upham believed that making God happy is the highest destiny of man[24] and that man could be assured of accomplishing this feat through direct consciousness.[25] He wrote: "We come, then, to the conclusion, that another and very great source of God's happiness is the contemplation of the holiness and happiness of his creatures. If they are holy, they cannot be otherwise than happy; and if they are happy, God must be happy in them."[26] Again Upham wrote: "God himself is happy, both in accomplishing whatever is accomplished and also in permitting whatever is permitted; and those who live in God by an unreserved union of their wills with his will, necessarily partake in his happiness."[27]

But Upham was to save himself from the easy-going pragmatic utilitarianism of the nineteenth century. (Chapter V on mysticism will demonstrate that more fully.) He agreed with both Hopkins and Fenelon "that Christian submission implies the willingness to endure the just penalty of the law, and sacrifice our own external happiness or to be cast off forever, if the glory of God requires it."[28] Upham stated: "Holiness is something which must stand, independently of its pleasant results, first in the mind's eye, first in the heart's affections."[29] But in spite of the nonutilitarianism, there was an essential link between holiness and happiness. This association had been inherent to Wesley's rationale, which proclaimed a message of experiential righteousness. Heart-changing religion made people happy. Intrinsic to Wesley's definition of good was doing that which promoted "the happiness of our fellow creatures."[30]

God as a Moral Governor

There needed to be a coherent system to promote harmony, holiness, and happiness, and the answer was found in a moral governor. God would carry out his justice in a fashion that made sense to man. Arbitrary election and reprobation made less and less sense, but a moral governor could hand out rewards and punishments, and, at the same time, make justice and benevolence compatible. God was no longer an angry dictator, whose wrath had to be satisfied; he was the great ethical judge whose principles were to be kept intact. Americans could not have a social contract of fairness and equity if their God was something less than the ethical system.

Joseph Bellamy was probably as instrumental as anyone in utilizing Hugh Grotius' "governmental theory of the atonement." Virtue and vice, rewards and punishment, could be upheld in a manner consistent with God's law, holiness, justice, and authority. Bellamy wrote: "God does not appear to be a being influenced, actuated, and governed by a groundless, arbitrary self-will, having no regard to right reason to the moral fitness and unfitness of things; nor does he appear to be a thing governed and actuated by a groundless fondness to his creatures...."[31] By the time of Lyman Beecher, the case for God as a moral governor had fully developed. Beecher spoke of God's "determination to create a universe of free agents, to exist forever under the public laws of his moral government, perfectly administered; for the gratification and manifestation of his benevolence, for the perfect enjoyment of all his obedient subjects...."[32] Haroutunian summarizes the trend:

> Public good, public order, and legal justice, the keynotes of the political philosophy of the eighteenth century, supplied the keynotes of later New England Calvinism, the "good of the moral creation," "the moral government of God, and the glory of the vindicative justice of God."[33]

The moral government theory fitted into the teleology of the Oberlin system quite well. It was compatible with Finney's passion for law and justice. For Finney, the universe was one great courtroom where God was judge, carrying out His immutable law with infinite precision. This immutable law was not beyond man's comprehension. But it was to be understood that God's justice was an outflow of God's central characteristic, benevolence, and the purpose of justice was to protect the rights and happiness of man. Finney defined benevolence for both God and man as "willing the highest well-being of God and the universe for its own sake, in devoting the soul and all to this end."[34]

Universal Moral Law

Upham's concern was somewhat different from Finney's. Upham was not as concerned about vindicating God's action as he was about trusting God's providences and maintaining confidence in the rhyme, rhythm, and harmony of the universe. As was hinted in the last chapter, a moral philosopher could trust the laws of the mind, the laws of nature, and the laws of God. Wilson Smith writes:

> Although moral philosophy as academic ethics was a treatment of worldly affairs, much of it was set to operate within a fixed firmament. It described a universe of moral laws in which the uncertainties of life could be met with theologically, satisfying preconceptions of fixed plans of action.[35]

But a subtle shift took place; the law of the governor became more important than the governor himself. Law was written in the universe, and God became subservient to the indelible law written in the nature of things. Upham wrote: "God's choice never varies and never can vary from the facts and incidents of that state of things which now exists."[36] Foster observes "the shift away from God's arbitrary sovereign will";[37]

> But if right is right in the nature of things, and God himself is obligated to exercise love and to act for the welfare of beings; thus, not even the interests of sovereignty can justify the use of phrases which put the divine action above reason.[38]

Stanley French reminds us that "if anyone had seriously proposed to the moral philosophers that there might not be objective universal moral laws, that values might in fact be 'relative', they would have been incredulous."[39] Upham wrote that, "Rectitude stands in its own nature, immutably and eternally based, not in the fickle foundations of personal interest and of mere positive enactments, but in the unalterableness of the constitution of things."[40] James Hamilton comments on the conclusion of Mahan on the same issue:

> There was no teleological suspension of the moral in his religious commitment nor was there the slightest identification of morality with God's will. The right is independent even of God's will and God always chooses to do right for its own sake.[41]

A contemporary of Mahan and Upham attempted to correct the premise that the law was antecedent to God, but at the same time, he maintained that the law was independent of God's arbitrary command.

> The true solution seems to be, that an eternal

> standard of rectitude exists to which the will of God conforms, and requires all moral agents to conform; but that this is not extraneous to his own being. It is the eternal, immutable, immaculate sanctity and goodness of his own nature, to which his will infallibly conforms, for he cannot deny himself.[42]

The Employment of Reason

If the laws and character of God are written in mind and matter, and the nature of things can be understood, then the reason can be employed in knowing God. Newtonian physics had taken some of the transcendence out of God, or at least, put the upstairs office within commuting distance. Natural theology, only perceived through spiritual eyes, had been raised almost to the same level as revelation. One author wrote:

> The truths of science differ from the truths of revelation, not in the certainty of their evidence, but in the source from which they are derived. The truths of revelation rest upon the testimony of God, the truths of science are derived from the testimony of our senses, our inward consciousness, and the development of reason.[43]

The Christian Spectator asserted that "all that we know with regard to the divine nature or proceedings, must be ascertained by referring a series of facts in heaven, to principles which, from our own nature, we know to produce similar, though infinitely less momentous effects on earth."[44] Upham's Andover teacher, Leonard Woods, went so far as to groan,

> Oh! when will the time come in which God, the object of divine science, shall be recognized by reason, in the manifestations he makes of himself in the world, as well as in those contained in Revelation, and in which the world (as its material, its law, its history), the object of the human sciences, shall be referred to God as its first cause, its grand centre and last end.[45]

No one expressed the relationship of mental laws to God's laws more succinctly than Asa Mahan did: "Thus as a person becomes more conscious of the correspondence between the great truth of Christianity and the basic requirements of human nature, he becomes increasingly convinced of the truth of Christianity."[46]

As a mental philosopher, Upham was fully in agreement with all of the above. The more he studied the order of the mind, the more he was convinced that God's ethical order in the universe could be perceived by humanity. Faith and perception were inseparably linked together. It was a law of mental science that man cannot believe in that of which he has no intellectual knowledge. Upham wrote: "Faith is necessarily based upon antecedent acts of intelligence. By the use of those powers of perception and reasoning, which God has given us, we have the knowledge of the existence of God."[47] And again, "The manifestation of God therefore, in some important respect, so that we can speak of him intelligently and give him both thought and affection, may be regarded as a necessity."[48] For Upham, reason was a gift from God in knowing and understanding the divine sovereignty.

Upham also claimed that a qualitative leap was essential in actually knowing and having a relationship with God. Mental philosophy and theology had been irrevocably wedded together. Intellect and natural theology could demonstrate to the human mind that God exists, but evangelical faith could come only from God. Upham wrote: "Religious faith, that faith which recognizes and realizes the existence and perfection of God, relating as it does to things which must always be beyond direct human cognizance, is and must be, a gift of God."[49]

Commonsense Realism

In spite of the qualitative leap, there was a certitude about nature and God, held by Upham and his contemporaries, that eclipsed French deism and German idealism. Add the realism of Thomas Reid, Dugald Stewart, and Thomas Brown to common-sense intuition, and the American scholastics and theologians had themselves a neatly packaged, well-defined philosophical method. Upham said it succinctly:

"There can be no knowledge without an object of knowledge, without something known, without a thing or existence to which the knowledge corresponds."[50] Sydney Ahlstrom writes concerning Scottish commonsense realism, "During the first two-thirds of the nineteenth century, at least, it was to become among American Protestants the chief philosophical support to theological and apologetical enterprises."[51] Commonsense realism would be used to safeguard theology against Hume's skepticism, Berkeley's idealism, Voltaire's atheism, and Hobbes' atomism. It could prevent an undermining of the faith by guaranteeing a unified approach among orthodox seminaries and colleges. It was so easily understood and taught that it could guarantee "well-constructed machines," which turned out "uniform sets of opinions."[52] As George Marsden argues, neither American churchmen nor laymen were ready to admit that a subjective interpretation could stand between their perception and the objective truth.[53] Truth was as available to the theologian or philosopher as the surrounding land and wealth were available to the American entrepreneurs. In the same way, for Upham and many others, so was righteousness available --also the consciousness that it would be attained.

Consciousness

Because of its utilization of immediate consciousness, the Scottish commonsense philosophy was particularly attractive to the mental philosopher. Vernon Howard reminds us that Upham, as a mental philosopher and psychologist, "avoided speculation, and rested mainly upon faith and the obvious deductions from them."[54] For his theory of knowledge from external sensations, Upham quoted from Locke. But Upham's concept of internal ideas and original states perceived by consciousness was drawn from Reid and Stewart. His dependence on the latter two largely surpassed his dependence on Locke. Stewart and Reid accented many of the beliefs of Upham and his contemporaries: proof of God from the design and laws of the universe,[55] benevolence of God providing man's happiness,[56] and resignation to God's providence.[57] The following from Stanley French, Jr. concerning Reid, Stewart, and Brown, explains well the philosophical basis from which Upham worked:

> That which enables them to be collectively referred

to as "the Scottish Common Sense Philosophers"--was their presuppositions about the nature of the universe, their general attitude toward philosophy, and their method. The three philosophers conceived of the totality of creation essentially in terms of Newton's mechanistic explanation of the physical universe. Because the physical world was conceived of in terms of the immutable laws which governed it, these philosophers assumed that there are immutable laws which govern the universe, which are the laws which determine the universal character of man. Taken together the laws of the physical and mental universe from God's design; the laws are the structural reification of God's will. According to the Scottish philosophers, the purpose of philosophy was to analyze the nature of the human mind in order to discover the laws of human nature so that man would be able to know them and follow them to comply with God's design. It was "common sense" philosophy in that the laws of human nature were universally manifest and could be "commonly sensed" through the process of introspection.[58]

Theological Implications

What did all this mean theologically? Foster reminds us that Calvinism was essentially a system of abstract logic. The whole framework of the system derived from the sole causality of God by logical deduction, without much--if any --appeal to consciousness.[59] Less and less were American theologians to agree with doctrines simply because they were in agreement with a single *a priori* premise, but yet not in keeping with just "good plain common sense." Mahan wrote that "Calvinistic determinism not only flatly contradicted the teachings of the leading thinkers of the primitive church, but also the reports of ordinary consciousness."[60] The new moral and theological certitude could not stand the mysteries inherent to Calvin's fervent theocentricity. Ahlstrom concluded that "There resulted a new-rationalism which rendered the central Christian paradoxes into stark, logical contradictions, that had either to be disguised or explained away."[61] Haroutunian wrote, "It was no longer possible to accept events as divine decrees unless they measured up to the ethical principles which had come to constitute the standards of righteousness, human intercourse, and to which even the creator of the universe had to conform."[62] To be sure, Upham and the holiness movement needed standards of righteousness that were immediately perceivable and that were salvaged from the dilemmas of Calvinism, and the doubts of German philosophy.

Depravity

Over all others, one doctrine inherent to Calvinism needed clarification. No sensible moral philosopher would accept a God who would reckon man totally depraved, without his first having committed sin. Edwards began to weaken the Westminster catechism before Scottish philosophy ever arrived. God did not will the fall; He was the author of the system to which the fall was inherent.[63]

Edwards believed that man's depraved innate condition resulted more from a deprivation of the Spirit than from a positive existence of disease or corruption.[64] Sin is not actually imputed to man until he voluntarily sins; hence, there is no guilt inherited from Adam. From this, all kinds of philosophical approaches were to come forth.

Joseph Bellamy vindicated God's permission of sin by saying that it was God's plan to bring the greatest happiness to man. Without the fall, God could not have made angels and men as holy and happy as they are now. Bellamy asked: "And now, who can doubt but that the humility, holiness, and happiness of the saved, will be much greater, perhaps a thousand times, perhaps ten thousand times greater than if these things had never happened?"[65] Hopkins said essentially the same thing, i.e., that the world is a better place to live because of the sin of man. But Bellamy's word "permission" did not suit Hopkins' hyper-Calvinistic concept of God's sovereignty, so God "willingly suffered it to take place."[66]

It was left to Taylorism to give Calvinism a completely new thrust and to divert New England from its reformation bearings. To Nathaniel Taylor, sin was consistent with the nature of man; it was man's moral agency but not as certain as the laws of nature; for instance, sin was not as sure a law as gravity.[67]

Sin was inherent to the moral agency of humanity; God, merely by withholding His grace, permitted individuals to sin. For Taylor, this withholding of grace was better than a system of innate depravity that made sin automatic and God the author of it. "Naturally depraved," for Taylor, did not mean some physical, substantive attribute that would disallow man's "power to the contrary."[68] Unlike the way he was depicted by the Councils of Dort, man could theoretically go without ever having sinned (but it was "certain" that he would).

Upham's understanding of depravity is very similar to Taylor's, i.e., it is a philosophical approach. God had given humans power to turn from their creator and seek support and fulfillment elsewhere.[69] Depravity is essentially selfishness:[70] to the free agency of individuals, it may even be a moral necessity.[71] Men and women are born innocent,[72] and "the ability to sin is a necessary result of the great faculties and capabilities, which are man's inheritance."[73] At some point, there exists what is almost a dualism, though Upham said virtue demands the possibility of wrong; he did not say it demands evil. But then he asked: "Without evil, what idea would we have of the holiness of God?"[74] As usual, Upham was being nondogmatic.

> Whether there be in men principles, which are naturally and originally evil, or whether the evil exists, not so much in the nature, as it does in the unrepressed and inordinate tendencies of those principles, are questions upon which we do not feel required by the present to offer any opinions.[75]

But the Bowdoin professor consistently opted for the latter.

Freedom of the Will

On no doctrine did the two "great awakenings" have a greater effect, than on freedom of the will and on the free moral agency of man. Revival fires had gradually diminished Edwards' "moral inability." It was left for the New School men--Nettleton, Beecher, and Taylor--to completely sever the knot and proclaim unequivocally that man is morally free. No one took moral freedom further than Finney did when he taught that man, by taking the right measures, could actually obligate God to bring revival. Man was now the sovereign cause--not God; God was the effect, all this as simply demonstrated as the physical laws of nature.[76]

The pragmatic revivalistic measures affected the doctrine of free moral agency, and the doctrine of predestination no longer fit the emerging image of the self-made man and the philosophy of individualism, both of which had become so uniquely American. Egalitarianism and individual rights were the leftovers of the enlightenment and integral to the new Jacksonian democracy. Success was not measured by aristocracy, or even by education, but by the self-initiative a person demonstrated in pursuing wealth. "In democratic countries," de Toqueville observed, "however opulent a man is supposed to be, he is almost always discontented with his fortune, because he finds that he is less rich than his father was, and he fears that his sons will be less rich than himself."[77] Edwin C. Rozwenc painted a picture of Upham's era as not only the age of the common man but as an era marked by an obsessive pursuit of wealth, status, and power. This kind of individualistic initiative and pursuit of fulfillment was not entirely unrelated to the spiritual conquest of Phoebe Palmer and those whom she influenced.

Freedom of the will was an a priori assumption of John Wesley, Upham, and the holiness exponents. Still, it is safe to say that Upham's theory concerning the will was not so much affected by economic and political exigencies as it was by scientific investigation. In order to discover the truth of the matter, Upham probed the issue as a true scientist would have. He wrote, "The inquiries before us, so far at least as the mode of conducting them is concerned, ought to be presented in essentially the same manner as our inquiries into the physical world."[78] An appeal to consciousness testified to the separation between obligation and desires within the sensibilities, and pointed out that the will is always free to choose between the two.[79] Though he is not bound to it, man can always choose the greatest good over mere impulses of the immediate good.

Upham did not arrive at this conclusion by saying that the will is absolutely free and self-determining. Rather, the will is subject to the laws of causality, and the laws of causality are uniform in the mind and throughout nature.[80] The will is only free within a circumscribed set of laws, instituted and controlled by the supreme intelligence of God.[81] The conscience is the mental act that allows man most awareness of his freedom, of his ability to obey or disobey God's moral law.[82]

The appeal to consciousness was not unique to Upham; even his teacher, Leonard Woods, had used introspection in support of the premise that man was free within himself, while at the same time he was controlled by the sovereignty of God.[83] But Upham, by means of extensive original thinking, was the first person to systematize the argument. "Where there is perfect liberty," he said, "as we have already had occasion to notice, there is perfect harmony, but there cannot be perfect harmony, nor harmony in any degree without law."[84]

Law and freedom are compatible while freedom and absence of law or anarchy are antithetical. "If the acts of the will were guided by no principles whatever, if they were beyond the reach of all superintendence and regulative control, they would necessarily be thrown into the arms of a blind and inflexible destiny."[85] Upham argued for the harmony of power and dependence. At the same time, however, he admitted to the mystery of God working in us while we work out our own salvation.[86] At any rate, blind and inflexible destiny were not suited for perfectionistic theology, and neither were they suited for the American nineteenth-century context.

Upham's treatise on the will was almost universally well received. Congregationalist Enoch Pond wrote that Upham's "deep and varied research, but profound and laborous thought ... will add much to the reputation of its author, and entitle him to rank among the ablest metaphysicists of our country."[87]

Praise was not the only response, however. Methodist William McKendree Bangs, pointed to the semantical problems within the work, to the confusion of physical and moral laws, to the lack of differentiation between laws and the results of laws. Bangs also claimed that man may be essentially free according to intelligence but not essentially free according to morality; freedom according to morality can come only through the Holy Spirit and the

death of Christ.[88] Criticizing Upham's meticulous argument was far less difficult than substituting a more lucid explanation. Vernon Howard offered insightful historical retrospect as, in his thesis, he concluded that Upham's argument made a bridge between Jonathan Edwards and William James.

> Upham's scientific determinism is, then, like his concept of free will, based on inductive evidence; and while freedom of the will must be conformable to the laws of the will, the two are not incompatible. In this respect Upham drove an opening wedge into the then prevailing view that the most important evidence for determinism is *a priori* and necessary, which requires an "explanation" of any contrary empirical evidence so as to bring it into harmony with necessary truth. He could well agree with James that the conflict between deterministic and indeterministic systems of philosophy is "altogether metaphysical", and that the aims and achievements of scientific determinism do not conflict with freedom of the will. Upham's mistake was in trying to serve both masters at once. It is enough, perhaps, that he saw the alternative and introduced it into the American dialogue on free will.[89]

Imparted Righteousness

At this point, we are ready to look at an essential element of holiness theology. The belief that depravity was a positive taint and an essential part of man's nature had been dealt a serious blow by American theologians. Sin, for many, was a matter of the will and no longer synonymous with Augustine's concupiscence. Regenerate the will and sin is gone. Transform the sentiments that control the will by the grace of God, and you have a person who is not only imputed or accounted righteous, but who actually is righteous. The acknowledgement of imparted righteousness was a major conciliatory step that Congregationalists, Presbyterians, Episcopalians, and Unitarians--or anyone else heading toward Wesleyan perfectionism--had to take. The American Wesleyans had inherited the doctrine of imparted righteousness from their founder, and the very first systematic theology published in America by Richard Watson expressed the idea succinctly:

> Believing in his Redeemer and Saviour with the heart unto righteousness, he knows for himself the power of his merit, and the strength of his grace, to regenerate. Thus, he becomes a holy man ... and his holiness will increase.[90]

The Methodist doctrine was gradually to lose its stigma among the neighboring denominations, but the change seen in the leading theologians was antecedent to the influence of the Methodists. The following statement by Hopkins--made in reference to the obedience of Christ--evidences far more than imputation:

> By this he has purchased and obtained the Holy Spirit, by whom sinners are so far recovered from total depravity, and revived, as to be prepared and disposed to believe on Christ and receive him being offered to them; and he carries on a work of sanctification in their hearts, until they are perfectly holy.[91]

Theology was becoming more practical and less speculative, more influenced by a psychological understanding of man and less by theological reasonings. Timothy Dwight used Asa Burton's taste metaphor in his argument that regeneration took place in the disposition and that man was given a new relish for spiritual things. Hyper-Calvinist Nathanael Emmons opposed this position. Emmons believed that righteousness consisted in "holy exercises" or "activity."[92] Nathaniel Taylor argued in his "Regeneration: The Beginnings of Holiness in the Human Heart," that actual good was imparted to the human heart and that the grace of God as taught by the Methodists could restore lost powers. He wrote that:

> Although all that is merely natural in men is sinful, in other words, although there is no moral goodness in men, except it be produced by the Divine Spirit, yet, that in consequence of the first promise of a saviour, light and grace are given to all men; and that thus something good is produced in the heart of all men by the Spirit of God.[93]

No antebellum document stated more clearly the need for imparted righteousness and inward piety than Edward Beecher's series of sermons: "The Nature, Importance, and Means of Eminent Holiness Throughout the Church." Beecher spoke of the present indispensable necessity of holiness that would be unfulfilled if no belief existed that adequate efforts would secure it.[94] He made a clarion call for "perfect purity ... under the renovating influence of the pure and holy mind of God."[95] God is able to impart his own emotions, character, and moral sensibilities into the mind of the Christian as the two commune together,[96] conditioned on the believer's fully consecrating his powers and faculties to God.[97] Beecher spoke of "eradication" of sin and the possibility of "a habit of mind, deep, fixed, and permanent, a trait of character wrought into the very texture of the soul, even as it will be in heaven."[98] Any of the Wesleyan perfectionists would have been pleased with the following from this Congregationalist:

> But arduous and difficult as it is, it may be carried to an extent far beyond our highest conceptions, if we constantly aim at the standard of entire perfection; and no one should aim at anything lower. No one should aim at any thing less than an entire and radical crucifixion of the old man, in all his members and parts, and to put on entire and in full proportion, the Lord Jesus Christ, and to make no provision for the flesh to serve the lusts thereof.[99]

Transcendentalism

Transcendentalism, an intellectual expression of nineteenth-century optimism striving for the perfectability of man, was closely akin to the holiness movement. Melvin Dieter points to the parallel between transcendentalism's emphasis on a man fulfilling his natural powers and purposes in body and spirit, and Wesleyan perfectionism's teaching of entire sanctification, which "would free a man to be all that a loving God originally had intended him to be."[100] Timothy Smith states that the "quest for Christian holiness seems to have been a popular expression of strivings which on a more sophisticated level produced the transcendentalist revolt of Emerson and Thoreau."[101] In an unpublished monograph, "Transcendental Grace: Biblical Themes in the New England Renaissance," Timothy Smith documented a search which contained a "doctrine of the Holy Spirit, ... the ethics of Christian perfection, and the idea of salvation by grace, that is, of transcending evil through the initiative and faithfulness of God."[102] For instance, the sentiment in Emerson's sermon, "Holiness," delivered in Boston in 1838, is very similar to Channing's sermon, "Likeness to God," published in 1829. Emerson wrote:

> It is the perception of this living in God that makes the propriety of the commandment to the Jews; Be ye holy because I am Holy (Lev. 11:44, I Peter 1:16), and that by Jesus Christ, Be ye merciful, and Be ye perfect as your Father in heaven is perfect (Matt. 5:48), commandments which would be wholly incomprehensible but for the great truth that men, in the words of Saint Peter, are partakers of the divine nature.[103]

W. E. Channing interpreted transcendentalism as a journey away from creeds and rituals toward the triumph of God in the soul and that the instruction of the single-eyed and pure-hearted had put to silence tradition and formulas.[104] Grace was not only in the human heart but in nature (which Smith denies was an actual pantheism). Nature and man are inseparably bound together, and the beauty of the earth depends upon man's response to the commandments of God. Holiness, truth, justice, love, and the construction of man are made for each other.[105] Channing lamented the fact that the Old Calvinists had so demeaned human potential that men had plunged into despair.[106] Timothy Smith wrote:

> This reconciliation of divine sovereignty and human freedom, though sounding paradoxical, mirrored precisely the one that Charles G. Finney, Nathaniel Taylor, Lyman Beecher, and his children, and a generation of Arminianized Calvinist revivalists made during the 1830's. And all these appealed to the same biblical texts John Wesley had used in making a similar reconciliation a century earlier.[107]

If there was any single person within the entire nineteenth century, that merged holiness theology and transcendental romanticism, it was Thomas Upham. The grace of

God extended not only to man but flowed throughout all creation. There are key similarities between Thoreau's On Walden Pond and Upham's extolling of the virtues of the New England farmer and the Maine countryside. Upham wrote: "there is a sense in which God is the life of everything,"[108] and God is within "the incarnations of himself which exist in the things that are made in the great robe of created forms and life which hangs as a garment around the brightness of his essential being."[109] The following would have not seemed at all out of place in the transcendentalist Dial, though Margaret Fuller might not have emphasized the biblical focus:

> Our doctrine is supported abundantly by the scripture, as we believe that there is something beyond the brotherhood of humanity, namely the brotherhood of life; something beyond the love of humanity, the wider and deeper love of everything that exists.[110]

Romanticism

Both Timothy Smith[111] and Ralph Gabriel[112] point to the common denominator of sentimentality that existed between nineteenth-century protestantism and romanticism. As Upham traveled in Europe, he admiringly reflected on American transcendentalism. The romantic flavor is evident: "Love of living in general ... wide and universal attachments ... a sublime doctrine ... the restoration of universal harmony..., that great and sacred tie which binds together all existences."[113]

The Bowdoin professor had a romantic and optimistic mind; he enjoyed life and reveled in its surroundings. On his trip abroad, he consistently demonstrated his reverence for nature by lamenting that a lamb had been killed or a flower crushed.[114] The story of a girl communicating with fish was related on at least two occasions in his writing.[115] Feeling and emotion went out to all the world, to particular parts of nature, and to special places for retreat and reflection.[116] Nowhere was a utopian harmony of nature, beast, and man more apparent than in Upham's poetry.

> Nor man alone is blest. The lowing herd,

> That crowd around his door, express their joy:
> The wild beast of the wood, the mounting bird,
> That high at heaven's gate finds sweet employ,
> Imbibe the chartered mercies of the day.
> No longer by the faithless hook betrayed,
> The spotted trout darts in his wonted play.
> The hare, that nestled in the thickest shade,
> Now leaps across the path, and o'er the sunny
> glade.[117]

Unitarianism

The tracing of theological change within Congregationalism certainly has to include mention of Unitarianism, which has been considered more the antecedent of transcendentalism than of Christian perfection.[118] Again, Thomas Upham provided a common ground.

The Unitarian magazine, the Christian Examiner, did not fail to take notice of his writings. In an 1846 article discussing Upham's Life of Faith, the periodical's reviewer spoke favorably of "perfectionism," emphasis on "perfect love," "consecration of the heart," "turning from sin," and "study of the Bible."[119] The author of the article agreed with Upham's philosophical premise that no moral obligation or volition exists concerning a task one believes is impossible to do.[120]

The two contributions of Upham most appreciated in the Christian Examiner were his nonsectarian emphasis and his lack of reliance on "religious emotions, of striking and vivid religious experiences."[121] Mention was made in the Unitarian periodical of Upham's work, the Interior Life:

> While it has not diminished zeal in outward efforts for the promotion of the moral improvement of man and the spread of the Redeemer's kingdom on the earth, it has awakened a deeper sense of the importance of ever keeping the inner state of the soul pure before God and ever cherishing a spirit of acquiescence in the will of God in regard to the result of our exertions.[122]

The next year, a review of Upham's biography of

Madame Guyon was equally favorable.[123] The book "compels the mind to turn in upon itself ... brings out our own secret or slighted errors and sins ... kindles pure and high aspirations."[124] The writer is in agreement that the "pure love" taught by Fenelon and Madame Guyon is not enthusiasm but the doctrine of Christ and the Gospel.[125] There are no qualms with Upham's assessment that the essential difference between Madame Guyon and the Roman Catholic Church was that Madame Guyon believed Christ "can save not only from the penalty of past sins; that he has power not only to make us holy, but to keep us holy."[126]

Upham as a Spiritual Prototype

Changes in theology--free will, impartation, accent on God's benevolence, the antebellum era's increasing romantic naiveté--had set the tone for Upham's perfectionism. The effect was not isolated, but it lodged in unsuspecting places and hearts.

In 1843 after the death of his son, Horace Bushnell began reading Upham's Life of Madame Guyon and the Interior Life.[127] While studying these works, Bushnell realized there was a higher Christian life to be experienced. As late as 1871, he referred to the new concept of Christ, the life of the soul, and the power of righteousness for humanity all as passing a boundary. In 1848, Bushnell's wife refers to the experience; during this year, Bushnell was submerging himself in the writings of Upham and in the Gospels:

> In these studies, and in the devout application by which he sought to realize, in his own experience, the great possibilities unfolding to his conception, the New Year came in. On an early morning of February, his wife awoke, to hear that the light they had waited for, more than they that watch for the morning, had risen indeed. She asked, "What have you seen?" He replied, "The gospel." It came to him at last, after all his thought and study, not as something reasoned out, but as an inspiration --a revelation from the mind of God himself.[128]

Upham was conditioned by his times, but his simple

religion, unfettered by high ecclesiasticism and sectarianism, would provide an evangelical element for the more liberal streams which flowed around him; it was a two-way street. Both Horace Bushnell and James Walker, editor of the Unitarian Examiner, were refreshed by the spiritual nourishment that flowed from Upham's pen. Congregationalists, Methodists, Unitarians, or nonsectarians, whether they were transcendentalists or just plain romantics, hungered for the spirit--not just the letter--of the law. Institutionalism could not provide the freshness of the spirit that was needed. Madame Guyon's tension with the established church was not totally unlike Phoebe Palmer's extraecclesiastical activities in her parlor, though Phoebe Palmer was far more institutional than Madame Guyon. It is not coincidental that both Upham and Emerson were attracted to Fenelon.[129] There was an unbroken line from Fenelon to Wesley to Phoebe Palmer; each person tried to stimulate deeper spiritual life beyond the church walls.

Upham found himself the common denominator, or prototype, among Methodists, Unitarians, Transcendentalists, and many of his own denomination who sought higher spiritual experience, even if that search meant skirting the strictures of theological tradition. The Unitarian editor had found consolation in Madame Guyon's waywardness when he wrote:

> The church of Rome has enough to answer for; but it is not alone, perhaps not the most inconsistent in punishing those who place inward goodness before and above everything, and regard as practical and imperative the injunction, "Be ye perfect."[130]

Conclusion

Many of the historical figures mentioned in this chapter were Congregationalists or persons who had come from a Congregationalist heritage. Congregationalism was somewhat paradigmatic of the changes that had been taking place in American thought, paving the way, as it did, for wide acceptance of the evolving holiness theology. What may be considered the capstone to this development within Congregationalism came in 1855 when the Congregational Board of Publication awarded Henry C. Fish $200 for his 249-page essay: Primitive Piety Revived. The author called for a complete consecration, which is "the grand characteristic of that holiness which the scriptures enjoin upon the followers of Christ,"[131] and also a confidence and faith in the word of God that secures our sanctification.[132] Fish differed from Upham only by the fact that Fish never met with the group that gathered in Phoebe Palmer's parlor.

Mental philosophy, Scottish commonsense philosophy, and Newtonian physics all served to provide assurances regarding existence. These were not unlike the assurances regarding spiritual life that were inherent to holiness theology. Arminian-Wesleyan theology was not only better adapted to the academic climate of antebellum America but existentially oriented to the optimistic-economic-millenarian fervor. Understanding and confidence concerning God and his universe were the intellectual precedents for the certitude existing within perfectionism. Holiness theology and transcendentalism were not unlike Upham's study of inner consciousness; each focused on an immanent God who was interested in man's harmony, happiness, and holiness.

Notes

1. The Guide to Christian Perfection had more articles from Congregationalists than any other denomination other than Methodism. The editors of the Guide believed that the articles by Enoch Pond and Leonard Woods, Sr., on Wesley's theology and the current doctrine of entire sanctification, were written because the latter two feared the rapid acceptance of the doctrine within their denomination. The editors stated in 1840: "We hardly need stronger proof that the subject of entire sanctification is arresting the attention of the church, and gaining an influence, than that our opponents have taken the field, with their mightiest men in the van of the battle. Among their productions is a sermon by Dr. Pond, Professor of Theology, Bangor, Me., the evident design of which is to counteract the influence of those eminent men of the Congregationalist Church, who entertain such views as are maintained by the Guide." Volume II (Boston: T. Merritt, 1840), p. 282.
Also see "Entire Sanctification: Its Nature," Guide to Christian Perfection, Volume IV (1842), pp. 224-225. A reprint from the Congregational Observer.

Also see Rev. S. W. Dutton, "The Relation of the Atonement to Holiness," The Monthly Religious Magazine, Volume XV (January 1856), pp. 19-35. The central argument of the message is that the atonement effects that which the law could not, i.e., the ability to live righteously. "The holiness and blessedness of his creature is the ultimate object God aims at in the atonement, and in all his measures both of law and of grace" pp. 22.

Also see "Man's Dependence on the Grace of God, For Holiness of Heart and Life," The Christian Spectator, Volume VII (1835), pp. 76-89. While the article does not make any mention of sanctification as an instantaneous work of grace, the author emphasizes a day-by-day reliance on the Holy Spirit for holy living.

2. James H. Moorhead, American Apocalypse: Yankee Protestants and the Civil War: 1860-1869 (New Haven: Yale University Press, 1978), p. 145.

3. Alan Simpson in "The Covenanted Community," states that although the New England Israelites did not believe the covenant of God was confined to them, it "had acquired a more concrete and durable form in their experience than elsewhere." John Mulder and John Wilson (eds.), Religion in American History, (Englewood Cliffs, N.J.: Prentice-Hall Inc., 1978), pp. 17-27.

4. Richard Niebuhr, The Social Sources of Denominationalism (New York: Henry Holt and Company, 1929), p. 104.

5. Sidney Earl Mead, Nathaniel William Taylor (Chicago: The University of Chicago Press, 1942), p. 7.

6. Harriet Beecher Stowe, Old Town Folks (Cambridge, Mass.: The Belknap Press of Harvard Univ., 1966), p. 115.

7. the Works of President Edwards, IV Volumes (New York: Jonathan Leavitt and John F. Trow, 1843), 4: p. 392.

8. Richard Niebuhr postulated the premise that the church is shaped by society in his The Social Sources of Denominationalism (New York: Henry Holt and Co., 1929), and his The Kingdom of God in America (New York: Harper and Row Publishers, 1937). Sidney Mead would not be so harsh as Niebuhr, but would interpret such American novelties as denominations and voluntary societies as healthy adaptations to the freedom and unique opportunities that the New World offered. See Sidney E. Mead, "Denominationalism: The Shape of Protestantism in America," Russell E.

Richey, (ed.), Denominationalism (Nashville: Abingdon Press, 1907), pp. 70-105.

9. Frank Hugh Foster, A Genetic History of the New England Theology (Chicago: The Univ. of Chicago Press, 1907), p. 127.

10. Ibid., p. 282.

11. Joseph Haroutunian, Piety Versus Moralism (New York: Henry Holt and Company, 1932), p. 24.

12. Thomas C. Upham, Divine Union (Boston: George C. Rand and Avery, 1856), p. 216.

13. Jonathan Edwards, "Dissertation Concerning the End for Which God Created the World" (1765), in Giles Gunn (ed.), New World Metaphysics (New York: Oxford University Press, 1981), pp. 112-114.

14. Joseph A. Conforti, Samuel Hopkins and the New Divinity Movement (Grand Rapids, Mich.: University Press, 1981), p. 118.

15. James Lee, The Development of Theology at Oberlin (Madison, N.J.: Drew University, 1952), p. 21, unpublished Ph.D. dissertation.

16. Ibid., pp. 39 and 41.

17. Haroutunian, p. 182.

18. Timothy L. Smith, Revivalism and Social Reform (New York and Nashville: Abingdon Press, 1957), p. 93.

19. Thomas C. Upham, Life and Religious Opinions and Experience of Madame De La Mothe Guyon (New York: Harper and Brother, 1847), Volume II, p. 346.

20. Thomas C. Upham, Life of Catherine Adorna (Boston: Charles H. Peirce, 1845), p. 168.

21. Ibid.

22. Ibid.

23. Upham, Divine Union, p. 372.

24. Ibid., p. 371.

25. Ibid., p. 369.

26. Ibid., p. 371.

27. Upham, Life of Catherine Adorna, p. 169.

28. Leonard Woods, D.D., History of the Andover Theological Seminary (Boston: James R. Osgood and Company, 1885), p. 35.

29. Upham, Life of Faith (Boston: Charles H. Peirce, 1847), p. 250.

30. The Works of John Wesley (London, England: Wesleyan Conference Office, 1872; reprinted, Grand Rapids, Mich.: Zondervan Pub. House, no date), Volume VII, p. 7.

31. Frank Hughs Foster, p. 115.

32. H. Richard Niebuhr, The Kingdom of God in America, p. 173.

33. Haroutunian, p. 167.

34. Lee, p. 38.

35. Wilson Smith, Professors and Public Ethics: Studies of Northern Moral Philosophers Before the Civil War (Ithaca, N.Y.: Cornell University Press, 1956), p. 28.

36. Upham, Divine Union, p. 398.

37. Frank Hughes Foster, p. 113.

38. Ibid.

39. Stanley G. French, Jr., Some Theological and Ethical Uses of Mental Philosophy in Early Nineteenth Century America (unpublished Ph.D. dissertation, University of Wisconsin, 1967), p. 208.

40. Henry Boynton Smith, pp. 646-647.

41. Edward Y. Madden and James E. Hamilton, Freedom and Grace: The Life of Asa Mahan (Metuchen, N.J.: Scarecrow Press, Inc., 1982), p. 67.

42. "Archibald Alexander's Outlines of Moral Science," The Princeton Review (New York: January 1852), p. 25.

43. "Importance of the Knowledge of Mental Philosophy to the Christian Minister," p. 429.

44. Leonard Woods, Jr. "Thoughts on the Relation of Mental Philosophy to Theology," Christian Spectator, Volume VII (1825), pp. 28-33.

45. "Christianity and Philosophy," Literary and Theological Review, Volume I (September 1834), p. 499.

46. Quoted in James E. Hamilton, "Nineteenth Century Philosophy and Holiness Theology: A Study in the Thought of Asa Mahan," Wesleyan Theological Journal, Volume 13 (Spring 1978), p. 56.

47. Upham, Madam Guyon, Volume II, p. 105.

48. Thomas Upham, Absolute Religion (New York: G. P. Putnam's Son, 1873), p. 80.

49. Upham, Divine Union, p. 59.

50. Ibid., p. 64.

51. Sydney E. Ahlstrom, A Religious History of the American People, Volume I (Garden City, N.Y.: Image Books, 1975), p. 433.

52. Woodbrige Riley, American Thought (Gloucester, Mass.: Henry Holt and Company, 1915), p. 120.

53. George Marsden, Fundamentalism and American Culture (New York: Oxford University Press, 1980), p. 14. Marsden gives an excellent discussion of how Scottish common-sense realism fortified American conservative theology, which built its main fortress at Princeton.

54. Vernon Howard, p. 146.
55. Stanley G. French, Jr., p. 60.
56. Ibid., p. 63.
57. Ibid., p. 65.
58. Ibid., p. 85.
59. Frank Hughs Foster, p. 80.
60. Madden and Hamilton, p. 10.
61. Sydney E. Ahlstorm, "The Scottish Philosophy and American Theology," Church History Volume XXIV (1955), p. 269.
62. Haroutunian, p. 291.
63. Frank Hughes Foster, p. 80.
64. Representative Selections--Jonathan Edwards, ed. Clarence H. Faust and Thomas H. Johnson (New York: Hill and Wang, 1962), p. xxi.
65. H. Shelton Smith, Robert T. Handy, Lefferts A. Loetscher (eds.), American Christianity, "Bellamy on the Problem of Evil." Volume I (New York: Charles Scribner's Sons, 1963), p. 351.
66. Conforti, p. 66.
67. Sidney Earl Mead, Nathaniel William Taylor, p. 189.
68. Ibid., p. 90.
69. Upham, Divine Union, p. 24.
70. Ibid., p. 414.
71. Upham, Absolute Religion, p. 105.
72. Ibid., p. 102.
73. Ibid., p. 116.
74. Ibid., p. 157.
75. Thomas C. Upham, A Philosophical and Practical Treatise on the Will (Portland, Me.: Wm. Hyde, 1834), p. 219.
76. The classic statement from Finney was that "The connection between the right use of means for a revival and a revival, is as philosophically sure as between the right use of means to raise grain and a crop of wheat. I believe in fact, it is more certain and that there are fewer instances of failure." Mendall Taylor, Exploring Evangelism: History, Methods, Theology (Kansas City, Mo.: Nazarene Publishing House, 1964), p. 448.
77. Edwin C. Rozwenc (ed.), Ideology and Power in the Age of Jackson, "Democracy in America" by Alexis de Toqueville (New York: University Press, 1961), p. 19.
78. Upham, Will, p. 3.
79. Ibid., p. 62.

80. Ibid., p. 138.
81. Ibid., p. 167.
82. Ibid., p. 235.
83. Frank H. Foster, pp. 304-306.
84. Upham, Will, p. 245.
85. Ibid., p. 245.
86. Ibid., p. 283.
87. Enoch Pond, "Review of Upham on the Will," Literary and Theological Review, Volume II (March 1835), p. 168.
88. W. M'K. Bangs, "Strictures on Prof. Upham's Philosophical Works," Methodist Magazine and Quarterly Review, Volume XVII (1836), p. 313.
89. Howard, p. 151.
90. The Works of the Rev. Richard Watson, III, pp. 52-53, as quoted in John Peters, Christian Perfection and American Methodism (Nashville: Abingdon Press, 1956), p. 108.
91. Frank H. Foster, p. 181.
92. Williston Walker, A History of the Congregational Churches in the United States (New York: The Christian Literature Co., 1894), p. 303.
93. Mead, p. 84.
94. Rev. Edward Beecher, "The Nature, Importance, and Means of Eminent Holiness Throughout the Church," American National Preacher, Volume X, No. 110 (June and July 1835), p. 195. No family within Congregationalism was more influenced by the evolving holiness theology than the Beechers. The Morning Chronicle reprinted Lyman Beecher's testimony to "the blessing of sanctification by simple faith in Christ." The requisites which he listed for obtaining the blessing were 1) a firm belief that it is practicable; 2) a strong conviction that it is a duty to possess it, and a sin to be without it; 3) a fixed determination to seek it, and to seek it now; 4) a willingness to sacrifice everything, no matter what, that obstructs its attainment; and 5) a diligent use of all the means of grace, especially the word of God and prayer. Guide to Christian Perfection, Volume VII (1845), p. 23.

Not too long before Lyman Beecher's personal testimony, his daughter, Harriet, had commented on Upham's Interior Life by saying: "Its object is to treat of the higher forms of Christian experience, as they have been recognized and treated in all ages, whether by Catholic or Protestant writers--as they have been recognized, under different terms, by all denominations of Christians. The advantages to the Christian church in setitng before it such distinct points of attainment, are very nearly the same in result, as the advantages of preaching immediate regeneration, in preference to indefinite exhortation to men to lead sober, righteous and godly lives." Originally in the New York Evangelist, reprinted in the above preceding publication, p. 13.

95. Ibid., p. 195.

96. Ibid., pp. 195-196.

97. Ibid., p. 205.

98. Ibid., pp. 199-200.

99. Ibid., p. 98.

100. Melvin Dieter, The Holiness Revival of the Nineteenth Century (Metuchen, N.J.: The Ścarecrow Press, 1980), p. 5.

101. Timothy L. Smith, Revivalism and Social Reform (Nashville: Abingdon Press, 1955), p. 113.

102. "Biblical Themes in the New England Renaissance," unpublished essay sent to this writer by the author, Timothy L. Smith, p. 4.

103. Ibid., p. 11.

104. Ibid., p. 19.

105. Ibid., p. 26.

106. Ibid., p. 33.

107. Ibid., p. 34.

108. Upham, Divine Union, p. 350.

109. Upham, Absolute Religion, p. 47.

110. Ibid., p. 283.

111. Timothy Smith writes: "Indeed the whole stream of nineteenth-century popular romanticism was a fitting context for the optimism which ruled in Phoebe Palmer's parlors as Americans sought 'immediate sanctification by faith.' A similar mood lay back of New Harmony, the Oneida Community, and the Washingtonian movement, as well as Brook Farm. The merging of the romantic spirit with the boundless hopefulness of the postwar years in no wise lessened the receptiveness of multitudes awakened by a generation of revivals to the confident promise, 'if we walk in the light as He is in the light, we have fellowship one with another, and the blood of Jesus Christ God's son cleanseth us from all sin.'" Revivalism and Social Reform, p. 143.

112. Ralph H. Gabriel, "Evangelical Religion and Popular Romanticism in Early Nineteenth Century America," Church History, Volume XIX (1950), pp. 34-47. The following from Gabriel provides excellent reasons for the

receptivity of Upham's thought: "Between New England transcendentalism and the folk religion of the frontier ran the main current of American Protestantism in an age in which cities were growing swiftly but whose outlook was still dominated by that of the countryside and the rural village. As the century rolled forward, New England theology lost some of that granite hardness of Puritan Calvinism and took on the adaptable rationality of Scottish common sense. Jonathan Edwards in the eighteenth century, moreover, had introduced the idea of the importance of emotion into what had been a coldly logical intellectual structure. Emotion had made its way in the churches despite a somewhat stubborn conservatism of theologians." p. 42.

113. Thomas C. Upham, Letters: Aesthetic, Social, and Moral (Brunswick, Me.: J. Griffin Press, 1855), p. 390.

114. Ibid., p. 392.

115. Ibid., pp. 394-396.

116. Ibid., p. 495.

117. Thomas C. Upham, American Cottage Life (Portland, Me.: Sanborn and Carter, 1852), p. 234.

118. See Timothy L. Smith's "Evangelical Unitarianism" in his Revivalism and Social Reform, pp. 95-102.

119. "Perfectionism: Upham's Life of Faith," Christian Examiner, Volume XL (1846), pp. 397-398.

120. Ibid., pp. 400-401.

121. Ibid., p. 403.

122. Ibid., p. 401.

123. "Madame Guyon," Christian Examiner, Volume LXLIII (November 1847), pp. 317-324.

124. Ibid., p. 318.

125. Ibid., p. 319.

126. Ibid., p. 322.

127. Mary Bushnell Cheney, Life and Letters of Horace Bushnell (New York: Charles Scribner's Sons, 1903), p. 191.

128. Ibid., p. 192.

129. For a discussion of the influence of Fenelon on Emerson, see Austin Warren, "Fenelon Among the Anglo-Saxons," New England Saints (Ann Arbor, Mich.: The University of Michigan Press, 1956), p. 67. Warren writes that Upham "is a curiously isolated figure, without doubting Rufus Jones' statements concerning the extent of Upham's influence, one is left with no notion of how this Congregationalist professor came by his remarkable range of

speculative theology and knowledge of the classics of earlier mysticism" p. 68.

130. "Madame Guyon," The Christian Examiner, p. 324.

131. Henry C. Fish, Primitive Piety Revived (Boston: Congregational Board of Publication, 1855), p. 68.

132. Ibid., pp. 138-139.

Chapter III

THE SANCTIFIED LIFE

This chapter will set Thomas Upham's theological thought within the context of nineteenth-century antebellum Wesleyan and Oberlin perfectionism. In order that it be confined within realistic parameters, the discussion will include explication of only the chief issues involved in Upham's and his contemporaries' pursuit for holiness of heart and life. We have already mentioned many of the antecedent and surrounding theological streams that influenced Upham; now the focus narrows to what specifically stimulated Upham's experience of "entire sanctification," i.e., his encounter with the Wesleyan theology of Phoebe Palmer.[1]

Christian Perfection Defined

Chapter IV will focus more sharply on Wesley's theology, but it is necessary, at this juncture, to define his understanding of Christian perfection; this understanding was at the core of Palmer's thought and writings. Through the grace of God, Wesley believed, a person could reach such a state of righteousness that he would not commit a known and willful transgression against the law of God; though not able to reach a state of faultlessness, a person could live blamelessly before God and community. Infirmities, human frailties, limitations, and errors of judgment would remain, but pure love would govern all motives and intentions.[2]

In his message that expounded on the text, Hebrews 6:1, "let us go on unto perfection," Wesley used several terms for Christian perfection: "entire sanctification," "sanctified throughout," "entire dedication," and "to the uttermost."[3] He quoted Archbishop Usher's definition of a perfect man as one who unceasingly offers up "every thought, word, and work as a spiritual sacrifice, acceptable to God, through Christ."[4] Analogous to the death of the physical body, entire sanctification will be both progressive and instantaneous; "if ever sin ceases, there must be a last moment of its existence, and a first moment of our deliverance from it."[5] And even after instantaneous or entire sanctification, the person would continue to grow in grace. The following well represents Wesley's thought on the matter:

> All experience, as well as scripture, shows this salvation to be both instantaneous and gradual. It begins the moment we are justified, in the holy, humble, gentle, patient love of God and man. It gradually increases from that moment, as "a grain of mustard seed," which at first, is the least of all seeds; "but afterwards, puts forth large branches, and becomes a great tree; till, in another instant, the heart is cleansed from all sin, and filled with pure love to God and man." But even that love increases more and more, till "we grow up in all things into Him that is our Head"; till we attain "the measure of the stature of the fullness of Christ."[6]

Phoebe Palmer

Phoebe Palmer no doubt saw herself in direct theological lineage to John Wesley. A careful reading of Palmer reveals that she correctly understood the substance of Wesley's teaching on perfection. She made it the personal crusade of her life to call Methodism back to its original "design," the teachings of the scriptures, and John Wesley. Palmer believed Christian perfection should be preached to "believers constantly, strongly, and explicitly."[7] According to her perception, if the "crowning" and "distinguishing" doctrine of Methodism was not preached, the work of God would not prosper.[8] She constantly exhorted the leadership to use their "glorious privilege" in promoting the cause of holiness in the church.[9] In her own way of thinking, and in the view of many others, she devoted herself to keeping Methodism true to its historical mission, the "spreading of scriptural holiness." Nathan Bangs "pronounced her teachings substantially orthodox, and Wesleyan";[10] he wrote:

> Some object to her phraseology. I do not pledge myself to the correctness of every word she may

> utter any more than I can expect every other person to agree with me in all my words and phrases. But why should I dispute about words so long as the substance is retained? I care not by what name this great blessing be designated, whether holiness, sanctification, perfect love, Christian perfection, so long as is meant by it an entire consecration of soul and body to God accompanied with faith that he accepts the sacrifice through the merits of Christ alone.[11]

The primary instrument for calling Methodism back to its theological roots was the "Tuesday Meetings for the Promotion of Holiness," held in the home of Walter and Phoebe Palmer. In the beginning, the meetings were largely for Methodists and attended only by women, but they later became quite ecumenical and equally attended by men as well as women. As we shall see, Thomas Upham was the key to both the latter changes. Charles Jones sums up Palmer's influence:

> Mrs. Palmer's Tuesday Meeting for the Promotion of Holiness (so popular that it outlived her thirty years), influenced a dedicated core of the Methodist ecclesiastical elite, as well as prominent members of other communions. Her following included not only Methodists such as Stephen Olin, president of the Wesleyan University in Connecticut, Nathan Bangs, editor of the New York _Christian Advocate_; and bishops Edmund Janes, Leonidas Hamline, and Jesse Peck; but Congregationalists, Thomas Upham, professor at Bowdoin, and Asa Mahan, president of Oberlin; Episcopalian Charles Cullis, A. B. Earle, ministers in Philadelphia and Boston respectively; and Friends Hannah Whitall Smith, author of the popular _A Christian's Secret to a Happy Life_, and David B. Updegraff, leader in the Ohio Yearly Meeting.[12]

Sanctification of Phebe Lord Upham

In 1840, Phebe Lord Upham, wife of Thomas Upham, wrote a letter to the _Guide to Christian Perfection_ relating the spiritual experience she had undergone during the past year. She stated that she had been a Christian for sixteen years but had never heard of "heart holiness" until she met and heard Phoebe Palmer in February of 1839.

This encounter was the impetus for Phebe Upham's eight-week study of the Bible. She began praying, fasting, and endeavoring to control and perfect herself,[13] but with no rest or peace.[14] She then testified to the sweet assurance she felt that her prayer had been heard. The consequences were "new emotions," "a oneness with Christ," "rest to [her] soul," and the "sun-light of God's countenance."[15] Phoebe Palmer wrote concerning Mrs. Upham's experience: "According to her faith, it was done unto her. She no sooner found the doctrine in the Bible, than she at once received the blessing in her heart."[16]

Thomas Upham's Testimony to Entire Sanctification

Mrs. Upham influenced her husband to attend the Tuesday meetings. He recalled that he had experienced religion during a spiritual awakening at Dartmouth in 1815.[17] Since that time, he had striven for high religious attainments, but the belief that sanctification was not attainable until death had inhibited him. The July before he attended the Tuesday meeting in December of 1839, Upham stated, he had come to the "undoubting conclusion that God required me to be holy, that he had made provision for it, and that it was both my duty and my privilege to be so."[18] Even though he communicated his purpose to no human being, Upham, by simple volition, had consecrated himself "to God, body and spirit, deliberately, voluntarily, and forever."[19] He testified to two immediate results--a loss of a sense of condemnation and an intense love for the Bible. "Before this time, reading everywhere my own condemnation, I had insensibly but voluntarily closed my eyes to the doctrine of present holiness, which shines forth so brightly and continually from the sacred pages. But now I found holiness everywhere, and I felt that I began to love it."[20]

Upham's remaining testimony states, in essence, that the "Tuesday meeting" he attended in December of that year was a catalyst for him to appropriate faith. On the last Friday of the month, Upham claims he underwent a "great moral revolution," i.e., he was removed from the condition of a servant and adopted to that of a son.[21] At this point, Upham's language resembles Wesley's understanding of his own Aldersgate experience.[22] Upham then said he renewed his consecration: "God had given me great blessings, such as a new sense of forgiveness, increased love, a clear evidence of adoption and sonship, closer and deeper communion with himself, but I felt there was something remaining to be experienced."[23]

He stated that in the middle of January 1840, he journeyed back to Maine. Still not able to give personal witness to an experience of holiness, he revealed that he was deeply troubled by a sense of selfishness.[24] On February 2, he was still "greatly afflicted in mind," but through an unshaken faith stripped of either intellectual excitement or marked joy, he was able to claim "the victory" on the morning of February 3.[25]

> I was distinctly conscious when I reached it. The selfish exercises which had recently and as it were, by a concentrated and spasmodic effort, troubled me so much seemed to be at once removed; and I believed, and had reason to believe, that my heart, presumptuous as it may appear to some to say it, was now purified by the Holy Spirit and made right with God. I was thus, if I was not mistaken in my feelings, no longer an offering to the world, but sanctified unto the Lord; given to him to be his, and no longer my own; redeemed by a mighty power, and filled with the blessing of "perfect love."[26]

Though Satan never ceased his hostility, from that time on, the enemy of Upham's soul remained cast out. A calm sunshine and the praise of God became abiding characteristics. On February 14, Upham recalled experiencing "some remarkable operations" on his mind; these would appear intermittently throughout his Christian life. For Upham, this experience was the evidence that God had sealed him and given him the "earnest of his Spirit." His summary statement affirmed that the experience of sanctification is most commonly characterized in a person's becoming "distinctly conscious of a new but powerful and delightful attraction towards the divine mind."[27]

There were seven distinct steps to Upham's sanctification experience: consecration in the summer of 1839; realization that sanctification comes by faith, December 1839; the adoption as a son, late December 1839; a renewed solemn consecration, late December 1839 or early January 1840; increased condemnation for selfishness, the middle of January 1840; complete victory, February 3, 1840; divine manifestation, February 14, 1840.

The part of Upham's experience that Phoebe Palmer calls Upham's sanctification, refers to the late December experience (1839) of "full assurance of faith as the adoption of a son."[28] Palmer claims to have taken Upham as a special test case of prayer and pleading with God; if God would sanctify Upham, Phoebe believed she would "be more truly instant--in season and out of season--in urging the subject of holiness on persons of this description."[29] Basing her claim on the authority of the word, Phoebe noted the exact time of Upham's sanctification, and, after waiting with a great struggle to hold fast her confidence, Upham confided to her two days later that "At about such an hour yesterday morning, I received such clear view of faith, of its simplicity and power, as I never before had a conception of."[30]

No doubt exists in regard to Upham's spiritual indebtedness to Phoebe Palmer. He was especially grateful that Palmer had made him the expressed subject of a personal vow, and he recognized her intellectual contribution to his practical attainment of the blessing. On March 31, 1841, after receiving a letter from the Uphams, Palmer wrote: "I can never look back upon the solemn covenant engagements entered into at that time, in reference to the specific object, without adding fresh fuel to the fire of devotion."[31]

The historical truth of the matter is that Palmer diminished the complexity of Upham's sanctification experience and regarded it as a single step of faith. Whether Palmer simplified Upham's actual experience intentionally or unintentionally is not a pertinent question. The relevant issue is that simplicity was at the heart of Palmer's sanctification theology, and it would have been quite natural for her to unconsciously impose this simplicity on the testimony of others.[32]

Wide Acceptance of the Holiness Message

Before Upham, not many of the mainline Protestant denominations accepted holiness theology; after him, acceptance increased. Upham was the first prominent outsider to enter the domain of perfectionistic Methodism. George Hughes recorded that from Upham's time forward, the Tuesday meetings were open to all of "God's children, without regard to sex or denomination."[33] Hughes, reflecting on the Upham's opening sessions--in their own home--that were patterned after the Tuesday meetings, triumphantly asserted that the Uphams "by their courageous example, are boldly saying to all around, we are well able to go up and possess the good land. Glory be to God in the highest, for such witnesses."[34] A person who intended to testify to the experience of entire sanctification, if he obtained this experience while attending "a prayer meeting in the Dutch Reformed Church in Harlem," claimed that previous to this occasion his desires for holiness were strengthened by reading Upham's works.[35]

Similar testimony could have been obtained from countless other people. In a sense, Upham was the progenitor of the ecumenicity created by the American search for entire sanctification. This interdenominationalism reached its apex from approximately 1867 to about 1885, during the camp meetings of the National Camp Meeting Association for the Promotion of Holiness.[36]

Pragmatism and Altar Theology

As Finney wedded revivalism to technique, so Palmer combined individual pietism with American pragmaticism. No one before her had ever made sanctification so simple. What Palmer did was utilize the symbolism of the Old Testament sacrificial system. The ceremony of placing the gift upon the altar was analogous to the Christian offering himself in full consecration. Palmer's logic consisted, simply, of placing oneself on the altar of God. Because the scriptures declare that the offering will be accepted, it is believed to be accepted and faith becomes fact.37

According to Palmer, the witness of the Spirit would come, but one had to claim the victory or the fact of sanctification before God would give the witness. Her doctrine of entire sanctification was essentially the same as Wesley's, but the structures (technique and form) were her own special contribution to perfectionistic teaching. Melvin Dieter gives us a valuable historical perspective:

> The newness then, essentially was a change in emphasis resulting from a simple, literal Biblical faith and the prevailing mood of revivalism combined with an impatient, American pragmatism that always seeks to make a reality at the moment whatever is considered at all possible in the future. Edwards' "immediateness" and Finney's "directness" joined with Wesley's claim to full release from sin to create a powerful logic for the new perfectionist movement's challenge to Methodism and the whole Christian Church.[38]

Palmer's reasoning was teleological in that results justified her methods. She penned, accordingly, that "the experience of a glorious number of living witnesses who have attested the excellency of the knowledge of this grace, proves that just so soon as they were willing in reality to count all things loss, just so soon they found it perfectly easy to believe."[39] One testified that though he had repeatedly but vainly sought the blessing for some time, he was sanctified within twenty-four hours of beginning to read _Faith and Its Effects_.[40] Concerning Palmer's book, _Notes by the Way_, he witnessed that "it was the first book which gave me _tangible_ views of the great doctrine of holiness. In that book, I saw this blessing standing out before my hopes in a substantial, _practical_ form."[41]

One of the secrets to supplicants' believing and receiving the blessing was their realization of the magnificence and power associated with God's altar. It was paramount for the seeker to remember that the "altar is greater than the gift." Palmer explained that "this altar was now the Lord's altar in such a peculiar sense that whatsoever touched the altar became holy by virtue of the touch."[42] Her emphasis resulted, historically, in Old Testament typology becoming the central sacrament for holiness sects.

By the turn of the century, the rail at the front of the typical holiness church was not used nearly as much for the eucharist as it was for the seeker to place his wholly-consecrated self before God. The altar was the foremost means of grace for the growth of the Christian. Though John Wesley and Phoebe Palmer were theologically compatible, a practical difference emerged between her and the founder of Methodism. Possibly, if the altar had retained its association with the eucharist, there would have been less losing and reseeking entire sanctification. As it was, the altar became the most prominent instrument of ritual for holiness worship.[43]

Consecration and Consciousness

Upham was clear that consecration and sanctification were not synonymous.[44] But at the same time, he emphasized the combination of consecration and faith in the promises of God, which is equivalent to sanctification.[45] Upham testified to the witness of the Spirit in his own life,[46] but you would never have found him admonishing individuals to persevere in their consecration until they had the witness of the Spirit. If there is perfect self-abandonment and no failure within the consecration, the answer will be sure to come.[47] Upham drew from Jonathan Edwards and Wesley's encounter with the Moravians for his understanding of justification as it differs from a full assurance of faith.[48] God will be sure to answer promptly if there is really and absolutely no failure in the individual's consecration and faith. For Upham, consecration and faith were a matter of inward consciousness:

> And, he, who breaks off from every known sin, and at the same time is in full reliance upon the word of God, and with childlike simplicity leaves himself entirely and in all things in the hands of God, unresistingly to receive the suggestion and to fulfill the guidance of the Holy Spirit necessarily in the scripture sense of the term, is a holy or sanctified person.[49]

Although Upham periodically mentioned the witness of the Spirit, he was adamantly opposed to any seeking of God that would specifically rely upon a sign.[50] His mysticism taught him that God is to be sought for God himself and that God will manifest himself to the creature according to divine wisdom.[51] For the believer who simply stands on the word and character of God, there will be greater continuity and stability of experience.[52] It is selfishness for the creature to seek from the creator a particular manifestation, and, as long as the seeker waits for a sign, it is impossible for him or her to be sanctified.[53] Confidence in God alone, regardless of feeling or emotional state, will bring the victory. The following from Upham is quite clear:

> To give ourselves to God, in order that we may receive him as our life, and at the same time not to believe in him as actually becoming our life in accordance with his promise, is virtually to annul our consecration; because it is impossible for us sincerely to consecrate ourselves to a being in whom we have not perfect confidence that he will do what he has promised to do.[54]

The slant of Upham's emphasis is closer to Palmer's consecration than it is to the Methodist bishops' perseverance until the witness of the Spirit.[55] But Palmer placed a much greater emphasis on the prayer promises than Upham did, and this emphasis made her faith far more bibliocentric.[56] Upham was more philosophical. There is a natural confidence in the uniformity and consistency of God before consecration ever takes place.[57] At this point, Upham stands much closer to Butler's <u>Analogy of Faith</u> than he does to Wesley's prevenient grace.[58] From the propositional truth one can reason that God <u>is</u>, that he is knowable, and that relational laws between God and man are antecedent to the promises of God. Though faith has to take over when reason fails, a person can be aided in his faith as much by observing the ways and providences of God as by observing the promises.[59] Reason as well as faith teaches us that we may know God fully.

> But if we are so constituted, that we naturally and necessarily know something of God, it is still true, that we may know him more. If it is a conceded fact, that we know him in a small degree, it is equally true that we may also know him much. If we may know him as the God of nature, we may also know him as the God of the Bible, as the God of providence, as the God of the New Covenant, as the God of the promises.[60]

The excerpt above hints at the second influence on Upham and removes him farther from the Methodist bishops than even Palmer was removed. Upham and Palmer were both saying this: if the grace of God enabled a person to give his all and a person could be conscious that his all had been given, that person would be considered sanctified. For Palmer, this was an argument from analogy and propositional truth (scripture); for Upham, it was an argument from consciousness. His system of mental philosophy, which presumed a postulate of immediate intuition, was the background for his experiential theology. Scottish common-sense philosophy was relied on rather than a strict adherence to the direct witness of the Spirit.

How do we know that our faith is resting on the word of God? Our consciousness tells us so, just as it lets us know about any other state of mind.[61] Intuition is almost as important as the direct voice of the Spirit. The appeal to consciousness relates more to Wesley's indirect witness of the human spirit than to the direct witness of the Holy Spirit, but Upham was certainly not alone in this intuitive standard of epistemology as it relates to the possession of grace. In speaking of love (which Wesley and Upham both identified as the essence of sanctification), George Peck appealed to personal consciousness in order to be able to "distinguish between the genuine workings of this heaven-born principle and the operations of unsanctified affections."[62] The following from Upham is synonymous with Wesley's indirect--not direct--witness.

> The man thereby who is really in the outward truth in the matter of good fruits or good doing will know himself to be in the inward or essential truth because his consciousness cannot testify to falsehood.[63]

Wesley was not so confident as Upham and clearly postulated the direct witness as necessary for full assurance of faith (even though at times--as we have already hinted--there seemed to be a wavering in the matter). But Upham did not take that concept of assurance, which was postulated on consciousness, nearly so far as Finney. The Holy Spirit can illuminate the law to man's mind, but only consciousness can testify that man is walking in that illumination.[64] Finney taught that consciousness was entirely sufficient to inform man as to his acceptance with God.[65] If consciousness could testify to the love of God, it could testify to whether we love God with our whole heart.[66] Consciousness is the highest evidence of our true character, and there is no need for the safeguard of the witness of the Spirit to prevent individuals from being deceived in regard to their true spiritual condition.[67] Finney went to the logical anthropocentric extreme in his use of Scottish sense realism. Using it, he made the Word and the Holy Spirit almost superfluous as bulwarks to faith.[68]

> And if a man does not by his own consciousness know whether he does the best that he can, under the circumstances--whether he has a single eye to the glory of God and whether he is in a state of entire consecration to God he cannot know it in any way whatever, and no testimony whatever, either of God or man, could, according to the law of his being, satisfy him, and beget in him either conviction of guilt on the one hand, or self-approbation on the other.[69]

Keeping of the Law

Upham was certain that a man may be blameless but not necessarily faultless. Individuals were to be judged by the heart, the "intentions which prompt, rather than by the success which attends them."[70] One may be judged not by outward observable actions, but by motives, which only God knows.[71] Wilson Smith stated that "the coupling of duty to the intention by this sort of theorizing and the accompanying distinction between right and wrong intention by means of man's innate sense were the hallmarks of the antebellum moral philosophy textbooks."[72] Of course, the concept of pure love governing the intention was central to Wesley's idea of sanctification.[73]

In actuality, Upham was not theologically precise when he dealt with the difference between evangelical and legal perfection. As a philosopher, prescriptive application and adherence to the letter of the law had little concern for him. Upham's language concerning love and virtue was closer to Edwards' language than it was to Finney's. As it evolved in later holiness circles, Upham's language was primarily that of obeying God's commands. It was the mystical language of union with God and of fulfilling the law by means of loving an object according to the object's intrinsic value. Upham clearly did not believe in Adamic perfection; for him, Adam's knowledge was not marred by sin. In commenting on Christ's command to be perfect, Upham calls for an absolute adherence to the inward law and a relative adherence to the outward law.[74]

Upham's biblical theology is not explicit enough to give us a clear distinction between the relation of law to the old dispensation as compared with the gospel. Neither did Upham make the careful distinction between sins of ignorance, willful sins, or "involuntary sin," as Wesley did. The truth that binds Mahan, Finney, Wesley, Palmer, and Upham is the constant need for the mediatorship of Christ.[75]

Progressive Sanctification

The crisis theology of Phoebe Palmer somewhat eclipsed Wesley's emphasis of sanctification, both as a process and as an instantaneous work. Wesley was quite clear on the matter. But at times he left the issue open to question, as he did in the most important doctrinal message he ever preached, "The Scripture Way of Salvation."[76] Apparently, he was not lucid enough to prevent a doctrinal war from occurring during the latter part of the century. The holiness movement waited until the printing of J. A. Wood's Purity and Maturity in 1899, before issuing a definitive statement. Wood wrote that holiness, or purity, was instantaneously complete in regards to extent or quality. The degree or quantity of holiness could increase through growth in grace, power, and natural capacity.[77]

Wood and Phoebe Palmer were not without strong Wesleyan precedent. Adam Clarke had put strong emphasis on the instantaneous, which John Peters claimed was more dogmatic than Wesley's emphasis.[78] But we should not imply that either Palmer or those under her tutelage completely precluded the need for growth in sanctification.

Dr. Walter Palmer wrote the biography of the bishop closest to him, Leonidas Hamline. In it he used an agricultural analogy to describe the maturing process:

> Growth in sanctification may be illustrated thus: the weeds being uprooted from the field, there still remain certain methods of improvement. One is by enriching the soil. This is the privilege of the moral husbandman. When the Holy Ghost has cleansed the heart, or crucified its unholy affections, we may enrich the soil by the acquisition of knowledge. The heart is cleansed by faith in the blood of Christ; but we are exhorted to add to our faith virtue, or strength, and knowledge. Another method of growth is to mature the spiritual crop. The field may be cleared of weeds while the tender blade is springing up, and months will be necessary to grow the grain. So the heart may be cleansed from sin while our graces are immature, and the cleansing is a preparation for their unembarrassed and rapid growth.[79]

Upham believed that within the total process a definite turning point existed. He depicted, as crucial, a person's crossing over from a life of desire to a life of faith.[80] All desires are harmonized to the will of God; there is complete acquiescence to the providence of God.[81] A definite transition occurs when a person changes from a life of serving God out of obligation to a desire to promote God's glory and a delight in the character of God in all respects.[82] At this point, all opposition between the will of God and the will of the individual is gone.[83] Perfect love does not exclude perpetual development.[84] The worst enemy human beings have to their psychological and spiritual growth is selfishness. Because the soul focuses on God, the limitations of self are gone, and development is according to the rule of the infinite.[85]

Maturity can take place in a person who has given his will to God, both through discipline and by denial in both the minor and major areas of life.[86] Even after sanctification, there is still the pull of former habits and tendencies. As these are disciplined, they will have less and less effect.[87] Just as a person is totally depraved and can grow worse, a person who is holy can grow better. Repetition and practice of holy habits will strengthen the moral character of the individual.[88] The following reflects the process that must be carried on within the state of holiness. The statement hints at changes that still need to take place within the unconscious:

> The last state of mind may assume a new character, and may present the union of the will in a new aspect by becoming invigorated and perfected by habit. It may ultimately become so well established and strong that the effect of antecedent evil habits, which generally remain for a long time and greatly perplex the full sway of holiness in the heart, shall be done away entirely.[89]

Key to Upham's theory of growth is the way in which the intellect relates to the sensibilities and to the will. The more we understand the character of God, the more we will love God. Love to God and knowledge of God go together and can never be satisfied without constant increase.[90] Upham would agree with George Peck that perfect knowledge is not necessary for perfect love,[91] but as the perfect knowledge increases, the latter will grow in intensity though it may have already gained priority above all other desires.

At this point, Upham is much more explicit than Peck. A person cannot love an object without knowing it to some degree, and, as the intellectual basis expands, the affectionate basis can proportionately expand, too. "And accordingly, every new manifestation of God's character, every new exhibition of his attributes, every additional development of his providences will furnish new occasions of love."[92] Upham concluded his chapter "On Growth in Holiness" by claiming unequivocally, that the crucial differential between growth and nongrowth in holiness is increase in knowledge.[93]

While Upham was more psychologically astute in his understanding of the crisis-growth relationship than his contemporaries were, at the same time he was not so mechanical or dogmatic. Thus, in comparison to the Phoebe Palmer altar theology and the subsequent justification-sanctification dichotomies that developed in the later holiness movement, a deficiency would appear. The message of a crisis experience was there, but it would possibly have not been experientially clear enough for the decision process involved in the altar calls of the subsequent camp-meeting movement. Upham was not apt to use such graphic imagery as the "virus of inbred sin--holy expunged from the soul" or "the lingering man of sin breathes out his last."[94]

Above all, Upham would not have been guilty of

"abstracting" the term sanctification from its comprehensive meaning and reducing it to a single moment, thus robbing the word of its rich biblical connotation; this, however, is what Mildred Wynkoop accuses the modern holiness movement of doing.[95] Upham's language appealed more to a metaphysical mentality than to a thought process that wants everything in neat dichotomies. The Guide to Holiness referred to the "intricacy of the plan" in reference to Upham's Interior Life.[96] Upham's spiritual works did not point to "either-or" distinctions but to intricate spiritual roadmaps that tantalized those who believed that the mind was not to be divorced from the heart. That Upham was not a campmeeting evangelist may account for the contrast between his multidimensional dialectic and Phoebe Palmer's linear syllogisms.

Humanity and Spirituality

In terms of spiritual experience, there was plenty in Upham's writings to counteract fanatic irrationality. His teachings on the propensities assert that a person, after sanctification, will retain a strong sense of self. Appetites and desires are legitimate in themselves; it is only when self-interests and love of self are not controlled by the Holy Spirit that they become inordinate. Upham tersely reminds us that "the scriptures require us to become Christian; but they do not require us to cease to be men."[97] He exemplifies the person who understands the humanity of Christ--Christ, who "was tempted in all points as we are, and yet without sin."[98] In the following statement Upham seems to be trying to differentiate between sensuality and sensuousness:

> We are at liberty to take to ourselves the pleasure which naturally results from the use or gratification of the sense, such as eating and drinking, when such use or gratification occurs in the providence of God and with the divine permission; but if in our thoughts we unnecessarily anticipate pleasures, or, when they are past, recall them to recollection in a sensual manner, it is a melancholy evidence that God is not the full and satisfying portion of our souls, and that our heart is not wholly right with him.[99]

Self-annihilation does not mean that a person loses his or her distinct personality; it means the soul is turned from habitual reflection on its own joys and instead seeks the wants and happiness of others.[100] The person loses his consciousness of self-possession and senses himself owned and sustained by God, "a living fountain that takes its rise from God."[101] The holy being no longer operates from the compulsive power of conscience, but according to the impulse of love.[102] There is a spontaneity in cooperation with the laws of God rather than a compliance to duty or obligations.[103] The unsanctified person will not have a fixedness to the will of God, a rootedness in the absolute, and thus his views will be limited as to the absolute truth, the absolute good, and the absolute right.[104] "On the strong rock of the perpetual identity of the divine will, and not on the uncertain quicksands of a will which is liable to change, the holy man rests his head in place."[105]

While not as explicit as some of his contemporaries, and certainly not as systematic, Upham viewed sanctification as a critical change in the spiritual nature of an individual. He was concerned with keeping the human personality intact. The process was one of aligning man with God's original plan, i.e., that the human characteristics (all that make individuals human) would be subordinated to and controlled by divine grace.

Upham may have seen the process as being more complicated than a single altar call. His writings depict a God who does delicate corrective surgery (but nevertheless surgery), rather than one who impatiently accomplishes instant spiritual authenticity with an ax. The tree needs pruning, but maybe not entire uprooting; "...it is a more difficult thing, and requires more reflection and more religious principle to regulate the appetites and propensities, than it does to destroy them."[106] Nevertheless, selfishness is to be destroyed[107] because it "infuses perversion into all that is right and legitimate."[108] Upham was not so sophisticated that he refused to use the language of "excision and crucifixion."[109] He also realized that regenerated man needs the radical transformation that comes from divine purging.

> It is not till the flame has come upon us, and we have passed through the fire of the inward crucifixion, which consumes the rottenness, and the hay

> and stubble, of the old life of nature, that we speak, in a higher sense of the new life, and say Christ liveth in me.[110]

But Upham was much more careful than some of his contemporaries in pointing out exactly what God wanted to conserve. Even more important, perhaps, he saw that certain elements in the human psyche were not to be destroyed but simply cleansed and rejuvenated.

Conclusion

This chapter has not attempted to cover all of the issues involved in nineteenth-century holiness theology. The main focus was centered on the methods Upham used to resolve some of the more central issues, such as the relationship of the witness of the Holy Spirit to the assurance of sanctification; the definition of entire sanctification in terms of the law; the question of the instantaneous work as it relates to spiritual growth and progress.

The approaches of Upham and other holiness exponents have not been differentiated as to substance but as to matters of emphasis, tone, structure, metaphor, and symbol.[111] It must be remembered that degrees of difference for one generation become miles of separation for the next; such was the case of the "instantaneous" exponents and the "progressive" theorists. And, nuances of language do make a difference. Some weary seeker may have gotten more realistic and satisfying results from the reading the astute metaphysician, who spoke with moderation, than from listening to the camp-meeting speaker, who advocated rooting out the stump (sanctification) after the tree had been cut down (justification).

Notes

1. Palmer's account of Upham's sanctification is given in Faith and Its Affects, pp. 146-156. Phoebe Palmer, Faith and Its Effects (London edition: no year given; first printed in America, 1854).

2. John Wesley, A Plain Account of Christian Perfection (London: The Epworth Press, reprinted 1952), p. 8.

3. John Wesley, Sermon LXXVI, "On Perfection," Works, Volume VI, pp. 411-424.

4. Wesley, A Plain Account of Christian Perfection, p. 30.

5. Ibid., p. 107.

6. Wesley, "Working Out Our Own Salvation," Works, Volume VI, p. 509.

7. Phoebe Palmer, "The Methodist Ministry," Guide to Holiness, Volume XXVI (July 1854), pp. 1-2. Throughout the remainder of this book, the Guide to Christian Perfection, which became the Guide to Holiness, will be designated as the Guide. For a history of the Guide, see George Hughes, "Fifty Years of Holiness Publishing Work, 1839-1889," Fragrant Memories of the Tuesday Meeting, Part II (New York: Palmer and Hughes, 1886).

8. Ibid., p. 4.

9. Richard Wheatley (ed.), Life and Letters of Mrs. Phoebe Palmer (New York: W. C. Palmer, Jr. Publisher, 1876), p. 64.

10. Abel Stevens, Life and Times of Nathan Bangs, D.D. (New York: Carlton and Porter, 1863), p. 351.

11. Ibid., p. 357.

12. Charles Jones, Perfectionist Persuasion: The Holiness Movement and American Methodism, 1867-1936 (Metuchen, N.J.: The Scarecrow Press, Inc., 1974), pp. 2-3. A history of the "Tuesday meetings" is given in George Hughes' Fragrant Memories of the Tuesday Meeting (New York: Palmer and Hughes, 1886).

13. Guide, Volume I (1840), pp. 234-236.

14. Ibid., p. 236.

15. Ibid.

16. Palmer, Faith and Its Effects, p. 150.

17. Upham's testimony can be found in the Advocate of Christian Holiness, Volume XII (January 1880), pp. 76-78; Phoebe Palmer (ed.), Pioneer Experiences (New York: W. C. Palmer, Jr., 1872), pp. 91-97; Guide, Volume IV (September 1842), pp. 49-54; Olin Curtis, Forty Witnesses (New York: Phillips and Hunt, 1888), pp. 271-282.

An account of the revival at Dartmouth which Upham refers to, is given in the "Appendix" of William B. Sprague's Lectures on Revivals of Religion (Albany: Packard and Van Benthuysen, 1832), p. 112: "...a general and almost instantaneous solemnity prevailed. Almost before Christians became aware of God's presence, and increased their supplication, the impenitent were deeply convicted of sin, and besought instruction of their officers. The chapel, the recitation room, every place of meeting became a scene of weeping, and presently of rejoicing; so that in a few weeks about sixty students were supposed to have become regenerate. A revival of such rapidity and power has been rarely known, and perhaps never one of such unquestionable fruits. Not one of the number of apparent converts, at that time, is known to have forfeited a Christian standing. Most of them are ministers of the gospel, a few are missionaries, and all are using their influence for Christ."

18. Testimony in the Guide, Volume IV, p. 49.

19. Ibid., p. 50.

20. Ibid., p. 51.

21. Ibid.

22. John Wesley, "Spirit of Bondage and Adoption," in Wesley's Doctrinal Standards, The Sermons, ed. N. Burwash (Salem, Ohio: Convention Bookstore, 1967), p. 81.

23. Testimony in the Guide, Volume VI, p. 52.

24. Ibid.

25. Ibid., p. 53.

26. Ibid.

27. Ibid., p. 54. In an article from the Guide, Volume II (August 1840), pp. 25-28, Upham listed as the "Marks or Characteristics of Perfect Love": 1) Love of the Bible above all other books; 2) Exhibition of a trait of permanency and perseverance under trying circumstances; 3) Love to God in spite of circumstance; 4) Love of the brethren with peculiar strength. Before listing the inferences above he stated, "This, then, is the true mark of perfection in Christian love, viz., an entire coincidence of our own wills with the will of God, a full and hearty substitution of the divine mind in the place of our own minds; the rejection of the natural principle of life and the adoption of the heavenly principle of life; the expulsion of self from the heart and the enthronement of God there as its everlasting sovereign." This was written within six months after his sanctification experience.

28. Palmer, Faith and Its Effects, p. 152.

29. Ibid.

30. Ibid., p. 154.

31. Wheatley, p. 242.

32. In a manuscript being prepared for publication on the life and thought of Phoebe Palmer and sent to this writer for review, Charles White argues that though Phoebe Palmer was quite Wesleyan and biblical in her thought, she was also somewhat nonsystematic and ambiguous in her thinking.

33. Hughes, p. 28.

34. Ibid., p. 42.

35. Phoebe Palmer, *Entire Devotion to God* (Salem, Ohio: Schmul Publishers, no year given, original 1855), 14th edition, p. 90.

36. This ecumenicity was expressed by George Hughes in *Days of Power in the Forest Temple* (Boston: John Bent and Company, 1873), p. 108. The work is an account of the early years of the National Campmeeting Association for the Promotion of Holiness.

37. This concept was spelled out in all of Palmer's writings. Concerning her own testimony, she wrote: "And by the determination to consecrate all upon the altar of sacrifice to God, with the resolve to 'enter into the bonds of an everlasting covenant to be wholly the Lord's for time and eternity,' and then acting in conformity with this decision, *actually laying all upon the altar*, by the most unequivocal Scripture testimony, she laid herself under the most solemn obligation to *believe that the sacrifice became the Lord's property; and by virtue of the altar upon which the offering was laid, became 'holy' and 'acceptable'*" p. 63. Phoebe Palmer, *Notes by the Way* (New York: Lane and Scott, 1850). This was her first work and was first printed in 1843.

38. Melvin E. Dieter, *The Holiness Revival of the Nineteenth Century* (Metuchen, N.J.: The Scarecrow Press, Inc., 1980), p. 31.

39. Palmer, *Entire Devotion to God*, p. 15.

40. Ibid., pp. 83-85.

41. Ibid., p. 83. (Emphasis is mine.)

42. Ibid., p. 95.

43. See Charles Jones' comments, *Perfectionist Persuasion*, p. 6.

44. Upham stated in his testimony, "I would take the liberty to say to her that I do not consider consecration and sanctification the same thing. Consecration is the incipient, the prerequisite act. It is the laying of ourselves upon the altar; but it is not till God has accepted the sacrifice, and wrought upon us the consuming work of the Holy Spirit, that we can be said to be sanctified," Olin Curtis, pp. 276-277.

45. Thomas C. Upham, *Principles of the Interior or Hidden Life* (New York: Harper and Bros., 1865), pp. 41-55.

46. Ibid., p. 281.

47. Ibid., p. 47.

48. Ibid., pp. 64-68.

49. Ibid., p. 31.

50. Ibid., pp. 96-109. "Of a Life of Special Signs and Manifestations, As Compared with a Life of Faith."

51. Ibid., p. 108.

52. Ibid., p. 106.

53. Ibid., p. 105.

54. Thomas C. Upham, Treatise on Divine Union (Boston: George C. Rand and Avery, 1856), p. 360.

55. See Jesse Peck, "Entire Sanctification and Its Condition," The Guide, Volume XXVII (1855), p. 81; and Nathan Bangs, "Christian Perfection: How to Attain It," The Guide, Volume XXVII (1855), pp. 168-169.

56. Palmer stated, "You cannot dishonour your Saviour more than by doubting whether He will fulfill His promises." Faith and Its Effects, p. 23.

57. Thomas C. Upham, Life of Faith (Boston: Charles H. Pierce, 1847), p. 114.

58. For Upham, reason and consciousness were placed almost on the same level as the witness of the Spirit; in the whole order of salvation. The following quote is typical of Upham: "And the apostle Paul also, in the Epistle to the Romans, asserts that 'the Spirit itself,' who always harmonizes with the truth 'beareth witness with our spirit'"; in other words, concurrently testifies, in such ways as are known to himself to the affirmation of our consciousness, "that we are the children of God." The implication is that consciousness, or the indirect witness, comes before the direct witness. Thomas C. Upham, Absolute Religion (New York: G. P. Putnam's Sons, 1873), p. 271.

59. The person who walks by faith will not be oblivious to the events around him. He will interpret them as best he can, in order to detect and follow the will of God. God speaks through His providences. "But we cannot doubt that the true life of God in the soul must be sustained in a very considerable degree, by means of that specific form of faith which recognizes God as present, not only in every moment of time, but as present, either permissively, or causally, in every event that takes place." Upham, Principles of the Interior or Hidden Life, p. 89.

60. Upham, Life of Faith, p. 116.

61. Ibid., p. 131.

62. George Peck, The Scripture Doctrine of Christian Perfection (New York: Carlton and Phillips, 1854), p. 442.

63. Upham, Treatise on Divine Union, p. 271.

64. Charles G. Finney, Views of Sanctification (Oberlin, Ohio: James Steele, 1840), p. 150.

65. Ibid., p. 151.

66. Ibid.

67. Ibid., p. 155.

68. Ibid.

69. Ibid., p. 154. Daniel Steele noted that Upham, Finney, and Mahan, who demonstrated that human consciousness and God's presence could be as sure as the apprehension of the external, were the "conspicuous exceptions" among the psychologists of Christian experiences. "The Christian can give as sure an account of his experiential knowledge of Jesus Christ, as the philosopher can give of his knowledge of the external world." Daniel Steele, Love Enthroned (Salem, Ohio: Schmul Publishers, 1961), p. 163.

70. Upham, "Religious Maxims Having a Connection with Holiness," Guide, Volume VII (June 1845), p. 123.

71. Upham, Life of Faith, p. 234.

72. Wilson Smith, Professors and Public Ethics (Ithaca, N.Y.: Cornell University Press, 1956), p. 36.

73. Wesley, A Plain Account, p. 8.

74. Upham, Interior Life, p. 270.

75. All of the evangelical perfectionists maintained this principle of Wesley, i.e., a constant ongoing dependency on the intercession of Christ. "None feel their need of Christ like these; none so entirely depend upon Him. For Christ does not give life to the soul separate from, but in and with, Himself." Ibid., p. 123.

76. Wesley, Standard Sermons, p. 435. "Perhaps it may be gradually wrought in some; I mean in this sense, they do not advert to the particular moment wherein sin ceases to be. But it is infinitely desirable, were it the will of God; that it should be done instantaneously..."

77. J. A. Wood, Purity and Maturity, abridged by John Paul (Kansas City: Beacon Hill Press, 1950), pp. 64-70.

78. Peters, Christian Perfection and American Methodism, p. 106.

79. Walter Palmer, Life and Letters of Leonidas L. Hamline, D.D. (New York: Carlton and Porter, 1866), p. 99.

80. Upham, Divine Union, p. 52.

81. Ibid., p. 53.

82. Upham, "Marks or Characteristics of Perfect Love," the Guide, Volume II (August 1840), p. 26.

83. Ibid., p. 27.
84. Upham, *Absolute Religion*, p. 123.
85. Upham, *Madame Guyon*, Volume II, p. 197.
86. Upham, *Divine Union*, p. 164.
87. Ibid., p. 162.
88. Upham, *Interior Life*, p. 115.
89. George Peck, p. 215.
90. Upham, *Interior Life*, p. 115.
91. George Peck, p. 215.
92. Upham, *Interior Life*, p. 270.
93. Ibid., p. 273.
94. Claude Holmes Thompson, "The Witness of American Methodism to the Historical Doctrine of Christian Perfection," unpublished Ph.D. dissertation (Madison, N.J.: Drew University, 1949), pp. 343-372.
95. Mildred Bangs Wynkoop, *A Theology of Love* (Kansas City, Mo.: Beacon Hill Press, 1972), pp. 303-304.
96. *Guide*, Volume XIV (1848), p. 24.
97. Upham, *Interior Life*, p. 211.
98. Ibid., p. 254.
99. Thomas C. Upham, *Religious Maxims* (Boston: Waite, Peirce, and Co., 1846), pp. 56-57.
100. Upham, *Absolute Religion*, p. 264.
101. Ibid.
102. Upham, *Divine Union*, p. 133.
103. Ibid.
104. Ibid., p. 148.
105. Ibid., p. 151.
106. Upham, *Interior Life*, p. 186.
107. Ibid., p. 191.
108. Ibid., p. 210.
109. Ibid., p. 213.
110. Ibid., p. 214.
111. See Rob Staples, "Sanctification: A Phenomenological Analysis of the Wesleyan Message," *Wesleyan Theological Society Journal*, Volume VII (March 16, 1972), pp. 3-16, where he explains the difference between structure and substance. "By 'substance,' I refer to the essential content of sanctification, the 'what' of holiness. By 'structure,' I refer to the 'how' and the 'when.' Substance refers to what holiness is; structure to the process involved in attaining it" p. 24. Staples contends that Wesley based the substance of holiness on the teachings of scripture and that Wesley was dogmatic in his description. But because

Wesley derived the structure from empirical observation or experiential psychology, there was room for different interpretation.

The quote which Staples uses, is taken from Wesley's sermon "On Patience" from Works, Volume VI, p. 490. "Does he work it gradually, by slow degrees; or instantaneously, in a moment? ...The scriptures are silent upon the subject; because the point is not determined, at least not in express terms, in any part of the oracles of God. Every man, therefore, may abound in his own sense, provided he will allow the same liberty to his neighbor" p. 8. This writer asks: Is Wesley's phrase "in his own sense" similar to Upham's "assurance via consciousness?"

Chapter IV

THE QUESTION OF WESLEYAN THEOLOGY

It is commonly accepted that Wesley was not a systematic theologian.[1] This does not mean that Wesley did not exhibit an admirably consistent and comprehensive understanding of theology. It does mean that Wesley's theology was worked out in the exigencies of preaching, pastoral care, administration of the societies, and maybe, above all, in the tensions with whomever he found himself at odds throughout his long career: Moravians, Quietists, Predestinarians, and the Church of England. Add psychological and spiritual disturbances within Wesley's own breast to all this, and you have a man who, in the eighteenth century, was the most prolific writer on experiential theology.[2]

The task will not be to compare the motives behind Wesley's and Upham's writing but simply to state that if Wesley was not systematic, Upham was even more nonsystematic. This assertion does not mean that Upham lacked all sense of system in his writing; it merely says that there is no orderly, systematic statement of fundamental doctrine there. Thus, an inductive method is needed to draw from Upham those theological points that will help us gain a comparative understanding between him and Wesley.

The Hamartiology of Wesley and Upham

Wesley wrote his longest theological treatise on sin, and rightly so; sin and its remedy was at the heart of his thought.[3] As to his understanding of the innate condition of man, Wesley is at one with the Reformation. He wrote: "Our nature is deeply corrupted, inclined to evil and disinclined to all that is spiritually good; so that, without supernatural grace, we can neither will nor do what is pleasing to God."[4]

The reason for every man sinning is that there is a propensity or bent to sin inherited from Adam. As to why Adam sinned, Wesley--unlike Kierkegaard--did not attempt a psychological explication.[5] Sin came from Satan who "was self-tempted to think too highly of himself. He freely yielded to the temptation; and gave way; first to pride, then to self-will."[6] It is sufficient explanation for Wesley that Satan caused Adam and Eve to sin, and in turn, Adam's sin was inherited by all of his posterity. Paul's phrase, "all are made sinners" means that "all have sinned," and that all men are subject to the judicial sentence of death.[7]

For Upham there is, within individuals no inherited bent to evil that is the source for evil acts. To affirm sin in a newborn child seemed to Upham to make God the creator of sin.[8] Upham would not say that God caused the fall, but he did say that liability to sin was a necessity if God was going to make a man free.[9] Upham was in agreement with Nathaniel Taylor in saying that for man to be the best of all possible creatures and live in the best of all possible worlds, the fall and sin of man must take place. But Upham was more interested in the psychological integrity of man as a free human being than he was concerned with theodicy. Wesley and Upham both saw the root of sin as pride, but Upham was inclined to look on the healthy side of pride and saw how pride served man's own preservation and welfare. Sin is pride, which is a gift from God gone wrong. God has purposely so made man that man will naturally come in conflict with authority and any demands that call for personal self-sacrifice. Neither Upham nor Wesley was concerned about strict theological formula; it would have been unusual for Upham's philosophical mind to allow for a "mechanical biological" interpretation such as genetic transmission. The following excerpt illustrates Upham's anthropocentric approach to man's inevitability to sin and, in a strange sense, postulates sin on the imago Dei.

> The law and the facts of his being are such, that while they constitute the necessity and the glory of his existence, they draw the lines of separation, and place him, in the first instance, not only in the isolation of self-hood, but for a time at least in practical antagonism with everything else. He stands up in the conscious greatness of his individualism, which is only another name for his

> self-hood; and in the power and in the just pride of self-affirmation, his first utterance is necessarily an interrogation of the universe. He says, I am a man; let no one touch me; let no one violate the sphere of my activity; let no one attempt to control me. That proud voice which in affirming itself and ascertaining its own position, interrogates all depths, and proclaims the birth of a deific son. God himself stands aside, as it were, in deep reverence and love of his own mighty work; and will not, and in fact cannot, without a self-contradiciton, act adversely in the violation, in any degree whatever, of that divine attribute of freedom which He has given never to be recalled.[10]

Upham reflected much of Taylor's and Bellamy's reasoning by saying that we could never have any real understanding of the holiness of God without suffering the existence of sin.[11] Even though Wesley believed that Adam's sin brought good to the universe, he did not agree with Nathaniel Taylor's belief that Adam's sin was necessary for the highest good of the universe.[12] Upham consistently used the word "permit." In so doing, he protected Wesley's essential belief that the excellence of holiness is the best of all possible worlds. Upham did not defend a dualism, but hinted at it when he taught that evil was necessary for the existence of a moral universe,[13] and that the possibility of vice is dictated by the concept of virtue. The fact that all traits of virtue have their corresponding vice and make for a harmonious whole "is all for the best."[14]

Personal responsibility, punishment, offense--all the principles of the moral universe--are eternal with the mind of God in keeping with his wisdom and are incomprehensible to man's finiteness.[15] Upham did not go so far as to say that God willed the fall.[16] He also stated quite clearly that every man is born with something amiss in his moral character, but that this "something" is more of a deprivation than an actual constitutional deformity. He was at one with the loosely-defined Congregational tenet, "We believe that mankind are fallen from their original rectitude, and are, while in a state of nature, wholly destitute of that holiness which is required by the divine law."[17] The following from Upham is his clearest statement that the possibility of sin is a necessity but not sin itself.

> But the question is sometimes asked, whether this view does not make God the author of sin; in other words, whether all moral evils of whatever nature may not be laid directly and exclusively to his account? The fact supposed to be involved in such inquiries, is as far as possible from the truth. It is true that God cannot establish a moral universe in which the highest and most glorious results may be realized without admitting the possibility of sin. But it is also true, both on philosophic and scriptural principles, and also as shown by the history of his dealings with the world, that God takes all possible measures short of a violation of man's freedom, which cannot be violated without man's ceasing to be a man, to instruct man, to protect him against evils and to guide him to truth and to good. So far from being the author of sin, God shows himself both by his nature and his works to be the enemy of sin; and also looking at the subject in another aspect, that he is the friend of all good or holiness, the assertion that God is the author of sin in the sense in which the suggestion is evidently made, is not only an error but a wrong, a contempt of the highest goodness as well as a dishonor to unchanging able truth.[18]

A "positive taint" and a "filling of all manner of evil" were shibboleths for Wesley but not for Upham. Similarities of language did exist in that both men spoke of self-love, pride, and self-will; but a different imagery was evoked. Wesley's "image of the beast" and "image of the devil" as evil archetypes are somewhat more static than Upham's inordinately intense propensities, excessive appetites, and acquiescence to the lower principles of existence. The preceding inclinations are contradictory to what should be a Christian's supreme principle--that of unalloyed love to God.[19] To the extent that this chief regulative principle of the individual's existence is diminished, the other perfectly legitimate traits within themselves will gain ascendancy. Critical is the assignment of correct value to all of man's frames of reference. Love to God keeps all other loves in their proper place.

Upham agreed with Jonathan Edwards that depravity is not anything infused or planted; nor is it a positive fountain of evil in the heart.[20] Every man's sin occurs just as Adam's did; love for self-interest became insubordinated to love of God.[21] In the view of Edwards, man put something out of his heart--God or Satan did not implant something within--and every man, from the fact of human existence, repeats man's "privative original."[22] Upham wrote: "Only God's withdrawing, as it was highly proper and necessary that he should, from rebel man, being, as it were driven away by his abominable wickedness; and men's natural principles being left to themselves, this is sufficient for his becoming entirely corrupt, and bent on sinning against God."[23]

The above excerpt indicates that Wesley's description of sin as two-fold in its nature may not be so clear in Upham's writings. Modern Wesleyan holiness teachers argue that the doctrine of entire sanctification is predicated on sin being defined as a principle as well as an act.[24] Upham's psychological and philosophical approach, which depicted sin as inordinate, natural drives, was not easily adapted to an instantaneous eradication theory of holiness. Merne Harris and Richard S. Taylor cautioned against the "gradual erosion of a clear-cut doctrine of inbred sin."[25] They warned against defining sin as the "natural drive toward self-fulfillment of the normal personality, which is not in itself an evil, but needs to be made a 'living sacrifice' to the service of God."[26] This may be a partial explanation of the ready acceptance of Upham's writings by the "Keswick" holiness movement. The latter did not sense itself in direct lineage to Wesley's theology; neither did it teach a theory of entire sanctification which emphasized the cleansing from sin as a principle.[27]

Unlike Wesley, Upham did not believe that a child is born guilty. Not even Wesley believed that the guilt incurred by every human being at birth made individuals morally accountable before God. Even though an individual is liable to punishment, the grace of God protects a person until he or she has made a rational, conscious act against God.[28] At this point, the difference between the innocent state explained by Upham and Wesley's original, sinful condition, becomes one of theoretical importance, not of practical significance. Both men emphasized that to actually incur God's displeasure, one has to sin against God. Leo Cox wrote concerning Wesley:

> His use of the term "guilt" in the second sense, as inherited from Adam, is very different however from Calvinistic use. It cannot result in eternal death until a free agent (knowingly and willingly) accepts and makes it his.[29]

Culpable condemnation did not spring from our inheriting Adam's sin; it derived from the voluntary, repetition of Adam's disobedience.

Prevenient Grace

The bottom line is that, for Upham, a person begins life in a much better condition than he or she does in the Wesleyan scheme. For both Wesley and Upham, natural man has obstacles to overcome and also the problem of freely following and obeying God. According to Wesley, the problem of freedom is the more acute difficulty. Wesley took the theological route of prevenient grace while Upham argued for a clever, philosophical system. As the answer to original sin, prevenient grace is extended unconditionally to all men and is the source of any and all good deeds or thoughts that come from man. "The light that lighteth every man" is effected in every individual as soon as he is born. If properly nourished, the light will grow and result in entire sanctification in the present life, glorification in the next; but the light can be stifled and denied. Wesley wrote:

> Salvation begins with what is usually termed (and very properly), preventing grace; including the first wish to please God, the first dawn of light concerning his will, and the first slight transcient conviction of having sinned against him. All these imply some tendency toward life, some degree of salvation; the beginning of a deliverance from a blind, unfeeling heart....[30]

For Wesley, the ability to discern as well as to do right rather than wrong was a supernatural--not a natural--gift of God.[31] Pointing to the doctrine of prevenient grace, Wesley could maintain the reformation doctrine of total inability and at the same time embrace the tenet of free will; yet the latter was not a true theory of self-determination.

Wesley was optimistic about the spiritual prospects of man, but his optimism was thoroughly theocentric. All persons are able to grow into perfect stature, but the beginning of that quest arises from common preventing grace and not from any innate spark of righteousness that simply needs to be properly fanned.[32] Lycurgus M. Starkey, Jr. succinctly stated: "The Wesleyan bridge between nature and grace is the preliminary work of the Holy Spirit."[33]

Upham relied on supernatural grace, but in his work the relationship of supernatural grace to the order of salvation is not so clear as it is in Wesley's writings. Upham appealed more to natural reason as well as to the external evidences of God's order and benevolence. A natural affinity exists between the governed and the governor, between the controlled and the controller, between existing creatures and the source of their existence. The human's spiritual proclivity is not so removed that it cannot come to an initial realization of God. Sometimes, it is difficult to perceive whether innate intuition of the divine needs to be qualitatively assisted, additum to nature, or simply quantitatively extended.

A natural light needs to be attributed to God; if dependence is recognized, then God will increase what is already there.[34] Even if we do allow for a natural faith in the beginning,[35] there will need be additional grace from God if there is to be a perception of salvation.[36] Antecedent to believing for salvation is the unfolding light of nature that lets man know of his lost condition.[37] Man can awaken himself through reason, but only grace can awaken the sinner to the possibilities of salvation. "The Holy Ghost prepares his own habitation. He strikes the first blow in this spiritual work, he inspires the first breathings and the very beginnings of the life of faith; and as the contest thickens, he gives greater and greater strength to faith...."[38]

Upham believed that man is totally dependent, not on his own natural ability but on grace. A question arises that relates to the emphasis on the natural perception of God as opposed to the emphasis on light that comes from only God. As a moral philosopher, there was a uniformity in nature analogous to the consistency of moral principles among all men, even those outside of Christianity.[39] A natural conscience exists that leads to, at the very least, a darkly-veiled God, or to the hypothesis that God exists and even to the character of God. All men think of God in terms of right, equity, or justice.[40]

For the philosophic mind, immutable, moral laws exist that are co-eternal with an immutable moral God. Upham argued that the moral law could not be subsequent to God or simply based on his volition, because God would have been amoral before the volition.[41]

Faith and morality come subsequent to a rational understanding of God as revealed in nature.[42] Man cannot believe in something he has no knowledge of at all.[43] Faith is necessarily based upon antecedent acts of intelligence. "God has not left himself without a witness in the structure of the human mind;... It is a psychological fact, ... that the human mind, ... always develops the idea of a God."[44]

The essence of Upham's teaching demands that we begin with reason, continue for a while with faith and reason, and then ascend to grace and revelation over reason. In the words of Fenelon, there must be a "faithful use of all the natural light of reason, as well as the higher and spiritual light of grace."[45] The place for reason in Upham's *ordo salutis* is never depreciated. From the very beginning of salvation, faith is predicated upon a confidence in the capacity of the mental powers to perceive and believe correctly.[46]

One wonders if Upham, like Wesley, would have disliked the term "natural free will."[47] For Wesley, freedom to give oneself to God was due totally to prevenient grace. This central teaching of Wesley's theology is not so applicable, however, when Upham writes "that the consecration of ourselves to God which is so inseparable from the progress and perfection of the divine life; should be made deliberately. A consecration made in this manner, viz., with calmness and deliberation, is due to our own characters as *rational* and *reflective* beings."[48]

But it is clear in Upham that as the Christian matures, reason must give way to faith. In the end, there is the qualitative leap beyond speculative evidence. "Religious faith, that faith which recognizes and realizes the existence and perfection of God relating as it does to things which must always be beyond direct human cognizance, is and must be a gift of God."[49] Thus Upham is not as far removed from Wesley at the end of the grace process as he is in the beginning. Both differed from Finney's moral suasion theory that emphasized natural ability and taught that the preaching of the truth is, alone, what produces willingness. For Upham, human intelligence and keeping an eye on the providence of God could go a long way in perceiving God and His character, but only divine grace could quicken the possibility of personal knowledge as revealed through soteriology.

Synergism

For both Upham and Wesley, human cooperation is integral throughout the ordo salutis.[50] William Cannon argued, and I believe rightly so, that because man can resist saving grace and can kill the voice of the natural conscience (prevenient grace), he, in this negative way, is the absolute master of his fate and the captain of his own salvation.[51] Cannon believed that Wesley went beyond Arminius not only by saying that man is free to resist grace but by stating that this freedom is a positive power, an active nature "which exercises itself and which reaches out actively to claim the gift of faith."[52] Man has an active part, i.e., he is an active factor in his salvation because of his willingness to receive the gift of salvation, which is a necessary condition for justification. Cannon's perception that Wesleyan theology represents a synergism, a cooperation between God and man for the latter's salvation, is certainly contrary to any conception of complacency or sheer passivity on the part of the believer:

> Once you grant to man a power great enough to make itself felt as a deciding factor in the acceptance or rejection of the means necessary for the bestowal of saving faith, you lift him, whether you will or not, out of a state of mere passivity into one of activity and of cooperation or non-cooperation with the grace of God.... The usual conception of divine initiative and human response is of course descriptive of Wesley's teaching; but, if understood properly the conception of human initiative and divine response is believed descriptive of his teaching and is not alien to his theology.[53]

To be sure, the above assessment would be an overstatement according to some, but it can, nevertheless, find support from Wesley himself. (Wesley was likewise prone to overstatements.) It was recorded in the minutes of the 1770 conference:

> We have received it as a maxim that a man is to do nothing in order to [receive] justification: Nothing can be more false. Whoever desires to find favour with God should cease from evil and learn to do well, so God himself teaches by the prophet, Isaiah, Whosoever repents should "do works meet for repentance." And if this is not in order to find favour, what does he do them for?[54]

Perhaps an "active response to the grace of God" would be the most accurate descriptive summary--a reception by faith that God is willing and wanting through the merit of Christ to save individuals and to save them now. But it is a particular kind of faith, a faith marked by the fruit of repentance. The fruit of repentance will not avail or earn salvation but will be psychologically necessary for the person to accept it. One must always differentiate between works and repentance as a condition, between works and repentance as merit. Wesley clarified: "Some infer that repentance and faith are as mere gifts as remission of sins. Not so: for man cooperates in the former, but not in the latter."[55]

For Wesley, works and repentance, in a sense, are indirect conditions of salvation in that they are a condition of faith. Faith cannot take place without repentance,[56] and a person cannot be saved without genuinely appropriating faith. Without the sincerity of repentance, man will be demonstrating only an intellectual faith.[57] Wesley resolved the conditional and unconditional elements in the following manner: "...repentance and its fruits are only remotely necessary; necessary in order to faith; whereas faith is immediately and directly necessary to justification. It remains, that faith is the only condition, which is immediately and proximately necessary to justification."[58]

Upham worked out the theological discrepancies between the sovereignty of God's grace and the part that human agency plays in the salvation scheme. A moral responsibility is present in salvation that involves an individual's "free and positive action," an act of the will that renounces self and harmonizes with God.[59] Personal effort is unavailing in and of itself but, nevertheless, must be present if faith is going to be effective.[60]

Man's destiny is in his own hands because he has the freedom to choose life or death; the only thing predetermined is where he can find life.[61] Human consent must take place initially and continue moment-by-moment for God's life to remain in the soul. The nature of God, which has been willfully adopted, is destroyed when consent ceases.[62] Cooperation is always the key word in the human-divine encounter. God has condescended to allow man to be His coworker.[63]

In the process of salvation, cooperation is progressive. As man actively receives light from God, God proportionally increases the light.[64] James' proposition that "if we draw nigh to God, He'll draw nigh to us" (James 4:8) is accepted quite literally. God meets man where he is; but in a very real sense, man--each according to his ability--needs to move to where God is.[65] As man uses his spiritual insight and mental vision, God will increase these two qualities. God, increasingly, will be a God "afar off," or a God "objective" but will become a God "subjective," a God "inward," a God "interior," "a real dweller in the saved and spiritual home of holy thoughts and holy disposition."[66] God is the stimulus; man is the respondent, but the process does not compare to an instrument being played by a musician or to a brush being held by an artist. Rather, it is an active acquiescence to the imagination of God--what God wills, desires, and says.[67]

All God looks and asks for is consent. In that one requirement, God can allow man to retain moral responsibility while at the same time He can exclude moral merit.[68] This view is synonymous with Wesley's evangelical synergism, of which Starkey says: "This evangelical synergism gives to man the full dignity of his creation, recognizable in common experience: that man is a creature of choice with the capacity of self-criticism and self-transcendence."[69]

Grace or favor, for Upham, implied a suitable subject for the reception of grace. If God bestowed it upon a person who willfully rejected the free Gift--a subject without the faith or intelligence to accept it as such--that person could never experience or realize the love of a merciful God.[70] The harmony between the infinite and finite must, according to the nature of the creator and the creature, always be based on the willful compliance of the latter. The following clearly states Upham's synergism:

> Man's moral agency, when he exists in full union with God, either in his original creation or in his restoration to God through Christ, is felt, not so much in guiding himself as in harmonizing with God's guidance; not so much in originating knowledge and holy affections, as in rejecting all confidence in himself and accepting God as his teacher: in a word, not so much in willing or purposing to do whatever he may be called to do by an independent action, as in ceasing from everything which is not God, and in desiring and willing to let God work in him.
>
> At the same time it is true, that God, in thus taking possession of the mind and becoming its inspiration, harmonizes with the mind, not less really than the mind harmonizes with himself; namely, by originating thought, feeling and purpose, through the medium of their appropriate mental susceptibilities and laws. That is to say, if it is true that God acts, and thereby constitutes a vital principle, it is also true that God acts in the moral and responsible man; not only acts in the man, as the locality and the subject of action, but also by means of the man, as the voluntary and concurrent instrument of action.[71]

A Crucial Difference in the Free Will Argument

The words used to explain man's ability to freely consent to God constitute, for Upham, a philosophical and psychological argument, not a theological one. Outler claims that Wesley's manner and method in his essay "Thoughts Upon Necessity" carried him "as far into the arcanum of speculative theology as he ever got."[72] For Wesley, it is essentially the moral choice based on free will that separates man from inanimate objects.[73] Necessity makes God the author of sin and destroys the basis for rewards and punishments as stated in the scriptures. Similarities exist between Wesley's and Upham's arguments against determinism and the former's appeal to consciousness as a support for free agency. Even though Wesley did not understand the will as separated from the sensibilities, he continued to argue that motives did not automatically dictate a specific action--this sounding similar to Upham's separation of desires and obligations within the sensibilities.[74]

Curiously, however, the essence of Wesley's argument was the opposite of the essence of Upham's. Wesley believed God could intervene and break the power of determinism inherent in nature--the connection between vibrations and sensations, between sensations and reflections, between reflections and judgements, and between judgements and passions or actions.[75] According to Wesley, determinism could be broken only through miraculous, loving, prevenient grace, i.e., the intervention of God. In contrast, Upham did not need a miracle, simply a recognition of the already existing harmony between man, the universe, and God.

Man enjoys freedom by subjecting himself to God's law, a law that was created for man's highest actualization, and it is at the point of man's highest harmony with God's order that man is most conscious of liberty.[76] Certainly, full liberty is not attempting to run God's machinery without giving careful heed to the operating manual, which guarantees maximum output. Without laws of causality between God and his creation, between mind and action, between moral order and deeds, there would be

> chaos, an universal breaking up of the established system of things, a complete and utter embroilment, the reign of chance and tumult, of confusion and discord, like the jarring of the infernal doors, "grating harsh thunder."[77]

Living with lack of causality would be like trying to operate life without an instruction booklet of cause and effect; that, in itself, would be fatalistic. Man would never be able to get to the state of entire sanctification because he would constantly end up on a dead-end street. In a sense, then, the road to spiritual actualization is more naturalization in Upham than it is in Wesley. The journey begins with an innocent man who is more harmoniously healthy in his original state than Wesley's diseased misfit is. And Upham doesn't emphasize the inanimate world as having been cursed as Wesley does. Upham did believe that man was born with a selfish nature and that, in a sense, he naturally sins. But for Upham, the holy life is the truly natural life.[78] At this point, Upham is accenting not only his mental philosophy but the mystical teaching that redemption is not so much supernatural as it is a law of life. Upham certainly does not rule out the supernatural, but because God does not act upon the creature contrary to the powers of nature, there is a depreciation of the miraculous.[79]

Believing that holiness and God's law are compatible with the nature of things was certainly not foreign to Wesley's thinking. Both Upham and Wesley recognized a law that is reasonable to the creature. Harold Lindstrom wrote: "Wesley, too, can look at the law as an expression of God's will as an eternal, reasonable scheme of things, and at religion as founded on and fully in harmony with eternal reason."[80] The classic statement from Wesley is found in his Appeals: "Why this is the very religion we preach; a religion evidently founded on, and every way agreeable to eternal reason to the essential nature of things. Its foundation stands on the nature of God and the nature of man, together with their mutual relations."[81]

Love

For Wesley, the essence of entire sanctification is love. He wrote that a religion worthy of God should be conceived as love, the love of God and of all mankind--the loving of God with all our heart, and soul, and strength, as He, who having first loved us, is the fountain of all good we have received. Love is the first and great commandment,[82] "the royal law of Heaven," the sum and substance of all the other commandments.[83] Reaching Christian perfection demands that no wrong temper--none contrary to love--remains in the soul; and that all the thoughts, words, and actions, are governed by pure love.[84]

Entire sanctification meant a subjective, relative perfection, not an absolute objective, prescriptive, legal standard. Unlike the Oberlin perfectionists' view of Him, this view has God judging man by the purity of man's intention. Purity of intention could be perfectly compatible with infirmities, mistakes, faults, failures, and all kinds of irregularities in the emotions, understanding, and deportment. A person with purity of intention does not always demonstrate propriety of language or actions, or even act with mature Christian judgement.[85] A man could have both pure motives and much defect of character. Entire sanctification is meant to recover the heart and affections of man, not the pristine state of Adam's physical and mental constitution.[86] In 1765, Wesley referred to Jeremy Taylor's Rules of Holy Living and Dying and to Thomas a Kempis's Christian Pattern.

> I was exceedingly affected; that part in particular which relates to purity of intention. Instantly I resolved to dedicate all my life to God, all my thoughts, and words, and actions; being thoroughly convinced, there was no medium; ... I saw, that giving even all my life to God (supposing possible to do this, and go no farther) would profit me nothing, unless I gave my heart, yea all my heart, to him. I saw that "simplicity of intention, and purity of affection," one design, in all we speak or do, and one desire ruling all our tempers, are indeed the wings of the soul, without which she can never ascend to the mount of God.[87]

In a sense, only the soul is moral. But, in another sense, all of man is a moral unit made up of dependent components. Actually, the carefulness Wesley demonstrated in circumscribing his definition of Christian perfection and the meticulousness he evidenced in defining sin, refutes Flew's contention that Wesley's understanding of moral character was simplistic, especially as it related to the unconscious.[88] Wesley did not teach that a work of grace could ever undo all that had been done by an individual's ancestors or all that had been accumulated in the individual's own moral attic during his lifetime. What he did teach, was that grace existed which could enable the individual to couple his will with God's will and to live a life free from "voluntary known transgression of the will of God."[89]

As Harold Lindstrom observed, love is the highest

value on both the human and divine ethical scale. Through love, all other human elements are evaluated, whether they be outward acts or inward tempers.[90] Love needs to be not only the impetus but the telos for all human activity. Upham, likewise, conceived of perfection as involving the intentions. For another life, he reserved the absolute perfection of judgement, expression, and manner;[91] in this world, men may possess love that desires the happiness of all creatures.[92]

Upham did not use happiness in a hedonistic or utilitarian sense. he related it to what, according to the divine mind, is best for the creature. The sanctified heart is one in which the "love of its true centre" has displaced attachment to disordered objects. It is the heart that has rid itself of inordinate degrees of love for legitimate objects.[93] Sanctification and restoration by God is primarily a restoration of the affections.[94]

Free and full acceptance depends on one's ability to love God with all the heart despite any physical or intellectual defects.[95] The only true criterion for judging a person is knowing the motive of the heart; hence, judgement is the prerogative of God alone.[96] The following excerpt illustrates Upham's historical understanding of the matter:

> And accordingly, it will be found to be a historical truth, which will be the more evident the more carefully the subject is examined that the doctrine of perfect love as advocated by Mr. Wesley, by Mr. Fletcher, and other distinguished and pious men of modern times, is the same in all, leading and important respects, with the doctrine of pure love as advocated by Fenelon, and as it had been advocated and illustrated before him in the life of Catherine of Genoa.[97]

The Will

The resignation of the will of man to the will of God is of extreme importance to Wesleyan theology and holiness thought.[98] Phoebe Palmer was thoroughly Wesleyan in her teaching that consecration called for complete yielding of the will, and that a person could be conscious of making a commitment.[99] But Upham's theory requires closer examination. As we have already said in the last chapter, Upham constantly wrote that self-annihilation and loss of the will did not psychologically mean man no longer had a will.[100] Is this language too radical for Wesleyan theology or, more accurately, did Upham teach an unrealistic view of sanctification with respect to the will?

Historically, Wesleyans had no problem equating unreserved consecration with the eradication of self-will.[101] Upham stated that those who aim at the highest results of the divine life ought not to have and cannot have a will of their own that is distinct from and is at variance with the divine will.[102] The aspect of the human will that needs to die is the part that is "resting in the origin of its movement on the limited and depraved basis of personal interest, and out of harmony with the will of God."[103] Upham's language places the will at the heart of Madame Guyon's sanctification experience. She not only desired to be holy but resolved to be holy. "Her will was in the thing,--the will, which constitutes in its action the unity of the whole minds action, and which is the true and only certain exponent of the inward moral and religious condition."[104]

Upham took the spiritual development of the will one step farther. The affections can be so sanctified that doing the will of God is somewhat automatic, "a life springing up and operative within," the will of God done "quietly, freely, naturally, continually."[105] In a sense, the sanctified will no longer needs "the constraints of conscience, because being moved by perfect love, it fulfills the will of God, and does right without constraint."[106] The sanctified individual does not so much rely on conscience but is said to act by nature and not by constraint. The person acts from a self-moved life at the centre, and not by a compulsive instigation which has no higher office than to guard and compel the centre.[107] Even thus expressed, the language can be described, safely, as consistent with Wesleyan teaching. In speaking of someone justified but not sanctified, Wesley wrote:

> His will was not wholly melted down into the will of God: But although in general he could say, "I come not to do my own will, but the will of him

> that sent me," yet now and then nature rebelled, and he could not clearly say, "Lord, not as I will, but as thou wilt." His whole soul is now consistent with itself; there is no jarring stirring.[108]

But when the human will becomes so absorbed in the divine that man becomes oblivious to natural desire, the case is overstated. One wonders if Upham is consistent with the Wesleyan position that sin is primarily an act of the will. He wrote: "The life of faith, which cherishes the love of God, as the supreme inward principle allows of no desire, no emotion, no passion, which is inconsistent with this love."[109] Upham did not censor Madame Guyon when she said that "nothing entered into my imagination but what the Lord was pleased to bring."[110]

Upham implied that our natural desires are so automatically fulfilled doing the will of God that we are not even conscious of human or earthly needs.[111] He often made the distinction between legitimate self-love and selfishness (unlike Hopkins), but, at other times, he implied that there is an indifference to self as well.[112] Circumstances of life--whether oppressive or delightful, adverse or favorable--all seem the same;[113] the significance of desires is depreciation. In describing the sanctified life: "Whether he suffers or does not suffer, the throne of peace is erected in the centre of his soul. Wretchedness and joy are alike. He welcomes sorrow, even the deepest sorrow of the heart, with as warm a gush of gratitude, as he welcomes happiness, if the will of God is accomplished."[114]

The above language sounds like those rash statements Wesley made at the beginning of his ministry; it does not resemble his more mature assessments of spiritual experience, which he made in later years. In 1741, Wesley wrote that the sanctified are "free from self-will, as desiring nothing but the holy and perfect will of God, not supplies in want, not ease in pain, nor life, or death, or any creature; but continually crying in their inmost soul, 'Father, thy will be done.'" In 1777, he commented on the above: "This is too strong. Our Lord Himself desired ease in pain. He asked for it, only with resignation: 'Not as I will, I desire, but as thou wilt.'"[115]

Temptation

Upham's depreciation of the desires in favor of an assimilation of the human psyche into the divine mind, lent a non-Wesleyan understanding to his theory of temptation. Upham was in agreement with the Wesleyan and Oberlin perfectionists that man, in whatever spiritual state he may be, is susceptible to temptation. In an article on "Peculiar Dangers Attending a State of Holiness," Upham discussed increased vulnerability to temptation because of lack of awareness.[116] He gave a helpful psychological suggestion for overcoming temptation, i.e., instead of giving direct resistance to the temptation, keep the mind focused on God in prayerful trust.[117] There is also a helpful distinction between evil thoughts and thoughts of evil; the latter are not sinful because no consent or feeling is added to them.[118]

But Upham said that when temptation moves past the intellect into the affections and the least amount of desire exists for that object which is out of God's will, it is sin. Taking this stand, Upham made a serious blunder: "if the temptations advance in their influence beyond the intellect, and take effect in the desires and will, prompting them to action when they should not act at all, or prompting them to a prohibited and inordinate degree of action when they are permitted to act, they are always attended with sin."[119]

Upham explained the temptation of Christ by saying that the offers of Satan were merely propositions, and no desire in the mind of Christ attached to them. Upham's intellectual theory of temptation, when compared to most concepts of inner spiritual warfare, is no temptation at all. Temptation for Upham did not mean that an actually appealing act or object had to be presented to the mind; temptation means there is a possibility for the will to make a choice in regards to the proposition.[120] Caldwell Merritt correctly pointed out that the practical application of Upham's theory is that the automatic horror at objects of temptation rules out the spiritual contest and there is "no other alternative but loathing or sin."[121]

An article in the Methodist Quarterly Review, which responded to Joseph Butler's ideas on temptation as explicated in his Analogy of Religion, called Upham's theory a mere abstraction, saying that it differed from those impulses which men usually call temptation, at least as much as the "cold and motionless statue differs from the living and breathing form."[122] The article agreed with Butler that excitement of the emotions and stimulation of the desires were necessary to our correct concept of temptation. The author even used Upham's explication concerning the mind's ethical operation to demonstrate how all moral conflict, before it reaches the will, is a battle between desire and obligation.[123] In other words, Upham's theory of temptation does not make sense in view of his psychology on conscience.

> The class of mental states, which are termed emotions, are followed not merely by desires, but also by another class, distinct from desires, and yet sustaining the same relation of proximity to the will, which, for want of a single term, we have been obliged to denominate feelings of obligation. Desires are founded on the natural emotions, or those which involve what is pleasurable or painful, while obligatory feelings are exclusively based on emotions of a different kind, viz., moral emotions, or emotions of moral approval and disapproval. The obligative states of mind, although they are easily distinguished by our consciousness from desires or the decisive states of mind, agree with the latter in being in direct contact with the voluntary power, and not unfrequently these two classes of mental stand before the will in direct and fierce opposition to each other.[124]

Upham was a better psychologist than theologian, but in this instance expertise in psychology did not enhance expertise in theology. Upham envisioned a sanctified state in which the desires and affections would be "thrown into the conscious attitude of repellency."[125] Ronald Knox described this ultra-supernatural spiritualizing of the human desires: "every action whose conscious nature is something other than love of God, and desire of this glory, is an action not inspired by grace, and therefore, worthless or worse."[126] Not that Wesleyan perfectionism did not support sanctification of the desires, but Upham's definition of divine union somehow destroyed the metaphysical distinction between sin and enticement to sin. He described divine union as "a state or condition of mind extending to the most interior depths of our nature, in which the human affections and the human will are fully harmonized, and made one with the heart and will of the infinite."[127]

Upham partially removed from the Christian pilgrimage the liability of sinning. On certain occasions, Wesley exhibited superhuman security in the matter as when using the illustration of a solicitous woman to clarify how temptation is concurrent with sanctification: "But in the instant I shrink back and I feel no desire to lust at all; of which I can be as sure as that my hand is cold or hot."[128] At other times, he seemed more realistic and demonstrated progression of thought. In 1741, when describing the sanctified life, he stated: "They are in one sense, freed from temptation; for though numberless temptations fly about them, yet they trouble them not."[129] He later responded in 1777: "Sometimes they do not; at other times they do, and that grievously."[130] The historical Wesleyan interpretation has been that temptations are not real unless affinity is present between the enticement and natural desire and unless there is an ensuing struggle between the desire and the moral ought.

A Third Stage

There is a third stage of spiritual experience beyond justification and sanctification. From it, Upham derived a spiritual security not found in Wesley's thought. This higher stage of sanctity not only brings the will in submission to God; the "secret influences of former evil tendencies and habits are fully done away."[131] At this point, the person who has found ultimate union with God differs qualitatively from the sanctified person who still is influenced by scars and habits imbedded within the unconscious.[132] There are two degrees of sanctification: holy resignation to the will of God and, beyond that, a holy indifference which has already been alluded to.[133] The divine mind brings the human mind into a state that is free not only of desires and passions but of unnecessary and wandering thoughts.[134]

Nowhere did Upham state his belief in a third stage of spiritual experience more precisely than in the following:

> Divine union is to be regarded as a state of the

> soul different from that of mere sanctification both because it is subsequent to it in time and sustains the relation of effect; and also because its existence always implies two or more persons or beings, who are subjects of it.[135]

Unlike Wesley's individual who has defects in knowledge and makes errors in judgement, this person can be assured that his inward decisions and judgements are God's voice or answer.[136] Consciousness of thoughts and volitions are swallowed up in the divine impulse so that cognizance of human inclination is at a low ebb or entirely obliterated. As a drop of water loses its identity in the ocean, so does an individual whose thinking, feeling, and acting have fully blended become one with the divine mind. Human consciousness has been immersed into divine consciousness so that "Another mind, the mind of Christ, may be said to have taken inward possession, and so close is the union, which has now been formed between himself and God, that he finds himself perplexed, and at a loss to discover the nature and operation of what he was formerly wont to call his own mind."[137]

Although neither Upham nor Wesley ever taught permanent sanctification, Upham claimed an attainment of grace of which Wesley, at least in his later years, would have been leery. The state of divine union is a static concept that does not lend itself either to a reliance on Christ or to a dynamic ongoing relationship with Him. Wesley saw a danger in thinking that spiritual experience was a plateau that once reached could, once and for all, be conquered. A minute of the 1770 Conference is crucial for retaining a concept of dynamic sanctification and for correcting any misconception that a single work of grace, wrought in a moment of time, will unconditionally validate one's spiritual security:

> Does not talking ... of a justified or sanctified state, tend to mislead men; almost naturally leading them to trust what was done in one moment. Whereas we are every moment pleasing or displeasing to God, according to our present inward tempers and outward behaviour.[138]

The Discipline of Christian Living

For Upham, reaching maturity during one's Christian journey meant maintaining a contemplative repose in God, which increases knowledge; as knowledge increases, the possession of God increases.[139] In this assertion, Upham was not dismissing the importance of discipline. But his discipline consisted not so much in trying to interpret and effect the principles of Scripture as it did in assisting the Christian to gain an understanding of his mental propensities as well as of his biological desires.[140] To be sure, the wisdom of man has to rely on the wisdom of God, but there is still a good deal of autonomous rationalistic morality in this regulation. Upham paraphrases Fenelon:

> The rules of holy living would require them every moment to make a faithful use of all the natural reason, as well as the higher and spiritual light of grace to guide them in accordance with the requisitions of the written law and of natural duty.[141]

As we shall see in the next chapter, much of the pruning and disciplining of Christian life is, for Upham, a waiting for God's providence to remove not only unwholesomeness from the individual but "happiness founded on false principles."[142] Reliance on sovereignty is somewhat different than incessant application of specific rules found in Wesley's own spiritual life and in the disciplining of the societies. There must be an avoidance of evil of every kind, and Wesley was not above meticulously enumerating those evils.[143] William Cannon observed that Wesley was pedantic in his enumeration of do's and don'ts; Wesley "assumes an extreme form of outward discipline in the performance of duty and in the conduct of personal life."[144]

Upham focused on the duty and obligation grounded in philosophical authority, the laws of common sense and intuitive ethics, and the premise that honest intentions are "ever in accord with the immutable moral laws of God."[145] Upham was not as concerned with Judeo-Christian prescriptive ethics as he was with the assurance that moral-sense theory is compatible with revealed theology and human intuition--both of which Francis Wayland taught were the proper guides to correct actions.[146]

Paul McNulty pointed out that Wesley's rules presupposed not only the morality embraced by the Ten Commandments but a knowledge of right and wrong as well. What the rules do is "pinpoint Christian morality at stressful places in a methodological, practical, biblical way."[147] McNulty went on to say that Wesley, as an Englishman, "was more interested in morality than with metaphysics, and his sermons clearly show it, for they abound in implicit and explicit ethics."[148] Also, Wesley was more concerned than Upham with "biblical injunctions"; these injunctions seemed not to be nearly so strategic to Upham's concept of growth in grace.

Soteriology and Sanctification

Persons maintain moral responsibility in both justification and sanctification; free will continues to be inviolated by the sovereignty of God.[149] But works do not merit the grace of God any more in sanctification than they do justification.[150] Upham turns a critical eye to Christians who attempt to bolster feelings of acceptance and assurance through works.[151] In addition to the process of volitional consecration and renunciation, there must be a cutting loose of all reliance ... on merit and self-congratulation.[152] Upham clearly explained that the greatest danger in possessing gifts and graces comes from the subtle process of attaching merit or personal worth to them.[153] In the words of Madame Guyon, "We are to be dead to them (virtues), considered as coming from ourselves; and alive to them only as the gifts and the power of God."[154] Upham was eager to put the asceticism of the mystics, especially Madame Guyon, in the best light. Her austerity and mortification had more to do with the laws of human nature and discipline than they did with atonement or expiation.[155] She attributed nothing to herself that belonged to God.[156]

Consecration prepares the mind for salvation. Even though God views consecration as a preparatory and necessary condition, it does not place God under obligation to save or sanctify because of the merit of consecration.[157] It is also in keeping with uniformity of law that God will not act accidentally. In the divine mind are reasons why God, in response to consecration, will give that which he would not give otherwise. Sanctification is not earned. It results "from an antecedent fact, some preparatory condition, in connection with which this great blessing takes place."[158] The following leaves no doubt as to the non-efficacy of works in obtaining holiness:

> It is undoubtedly trying to unsubdued and selfish nature, to attach no value, considered as its own works, to what it fondly calls its good deeds; such as its outward morality, its attendance upon the institutions of worship, its study of the Scriptures, its visits to the sick, its charities to the poor, and other things of a similar nature. These things, it is true, are all good and desirable. We would not, by any means, speak lightly of them. It is perhaps difficult to value them too highly, if we ascribe them, as we ought to do, to the mere favor, and grace of God, and ascribing them to his own merit, it is easy to see that a man may make an idol of his good works, whatever may be their nature; and that he may, in the perversity of his spirit, fall down and worship them. We must be willing, therefore, to account our good deeds as nothing, and to regard ourselves, when we have done all in our power, as unprofitable servants, in order that Christ may be to us all in all.[159]

The assertion that Christ may be to us all in all, leads to the last and most important area that can well be commented on in this chapter. Wesley wrote to Mary Bishop: "Nothing in the Christian system is of greater consequence than the doctrine of the Atonement. It is properly the distinguishing point between Deism and Christianity."[160] Though there is no specific theory of the atonement advocated by Wesley,[161] the death and mediatorship of Christ is of crucial importance. In comparing Wesley and Upham's theories of sanctification, the doctrine of atonement is crucial to each man's interpretation of evangelical holiness. For both, holiness was attainable only through the merits of Christ's death.

Christ is the end and fulfillment of both the Adamic and Mosaic law. Because man is impaired, he needs Christ as a prophet for light, Christ as a king for supply of holiness, and Christ as a priest for atonement.[162] The sanctified constantly need the mediatorship of Christ, "not only as the continuance of their every blessing depends on His death and intercession," but because they have fallen short of the law of love.[163] The concept that the atoning death of Christ is the ongoing meritorious cause of man's sanctification, was consistently at the heart of Wesley's theology. In his exhortation to Alexander Coates in 1761, Wesley makes the most succinct expression of this truth. "Practical religion is your point; therefore keep to this: repentance toward God, faith in Christ, holiness of heart and life, a growing in grace and in the knowledge of Christ, the continual need of his atoning blood, a constant confidence in Him, and all these every moment to our Life's end."[164]

No one could accurately make the accusation that Upham was not Christocentric. The only way to please God and be his friend is through Christ.[165] No other influence or intercession is needed but the credentials of having been purchased by the blood and sustained in union with God by the merits of Christ. One could hardly be more Christocentric than Upham in this quote from his Madame Guyon:

> Oh, let us labor for his present coming, not for a Christ in the clouds, but for a Christ in the affection; not for a Christ seen, but for a Christ felt, not for a Christ outwardly represented; but for a Christ inwardly realized.[166]

Upham asserted that Madame Guyon's experience of faith and forgiveness was in Christ alone,[167] (whether he was right in his interpretation or not will be discussed in the next chapter). Complete surrender to God is entirely dependent on the ongoing application of Christ's blood.[168] Upham constantly portrayed Madame Guyon as turning those that she influenced away from ceremonial merit and toward salvation in the cross of Christ. Ceasing sinful activity can be accomplished only through recognizing "the great truth, that our life is from God" and through accepting "his appointed way of return through Christ, our mediatoral sacrifice."[169] Sanctification and purification for heaven would be impossible but for the atoning blood of Jesus.[170] Christ is not only our eschatological hope; He is life itself. The true life of the soul is derived from Christ much as a branch is connected to the root.[171]

CHRIST IN THE SOUL

If God is LOVE, and God and Christ are One,
Then Love becomes the Life-power of the Son;
And Love and Christ in essence are the same,
One central life, with difference of name:

And thus it is, when selfishness is dead,
And living Love is planted in its stead,
And doth the inmost faculties control,
That Christ is said to dwell within the soul;

CHRIST IN THE SOUL becomes the name and sign
Of inward life, eternal, and divine;
The life, descending from its home above,
The life of PURE AND UNIVERSAL LOVE.[172]

Conclusion

In this chapter, differences and similarities between Upham and Wesley have been analyzed. The discussion has included such areas as: prevenient grace, freedom of the will, the essence of entire sanctification, temptation, spiritual security, spiritual discipline, and Christology. Upham's divergencies are accredited to a naturalistic optimism that Wesley's more definite concept of depravity did not allow him to share. Upham does not present a clear, precise hamartiology. Wesley's constant reference to sin as a "being" led Sugden to comment that "He never quite shook off the fallacious notion that sin is a thing, which has to be taken out of a man, like a cancer or a rotten tooth."[173]

In Upham's theory of sanctification, there is more of an emphasis on the positive aspect of union of God than there is an emphasis on cleansing. Upham was not so concerned with treating disease as he was with seeing that man reached his full potential in terms of the laws of God written in the human mind--and in all of creation--for man's benefit. Upham treated the patient more as a physical therapist or a rehabilitationist would, who attempts to strengthen what is already God-given.

But it must be kept in mind that Upham was not primarily a theologian. John Wesley, the born debater, made much finer theological distinctions than did Thomas Upham. In this sense, fresh creativity is more recognizable in Upham than it is in Wesley, the latter needing to satisfy an inner compulsion to defend, rationally, every critique. For Upham, the cornerstone in building a holiness theology was molded from metaphysics, a philosophy that inspired the Christian to operate at optimum capacity, afforded by the natural affinity between the creature and the Creator. Wesley began by "circumcising" from the heart, a disease. Lindstrom succinctly caught the Wesleyan thrust: "As sin is thus regarded as an illness, it follows, that salvation will be seen primarily from a subjective medical rather than an objective judicial angle."[174]

The holiness movement maintained a strong "eradication" emphasis throughout the rest of the century and into the next. In so doing, they either were not astute enough to discern this deficiency in Upham's thought or they rejected it. Elmer Clark correctly stated in his discussion of the perfectionist sects that they adhered to the older theology that "original sin is necessary to their main doctrine of sanctification."[175] Thomas Upham was an exception.

Notes

1. Skevington Wood states that "as a preacher, Wesley was content to declare the doctrine of holiness, from scripture and confirmed by Christian experience, without entering into a theological debate about the precise formulation of its contents; as a result, he left a number of ends untied and it would be quite impossible to reduce his teaching to a neat consistent scheme." A. Skevington Wood, The Burning Heart (Minneapolis: Bethany Fellowship Inc., 1978), p. 66.

Albert Outler states that Wesley "was by talent and intent, a folk-theologian; an eclectic who had mastered the secret of plastic-synthesis, simple profundity, the common touch. He was an effective evangelist guided by a discriminating theological understanding, a creative theologian practically involved in the application of his doctrine in the renewal of the church." Albert C. Outler (ed.), John Wesley (New York: Oxford University Press, 1964), p. 119.

2. Wesley created theology not only from psychological introspection but from empirical observation and

excessive "clinical" questioning. Maximin Piette wrote: "Since practical experience and experimentation had been triumphant in the field of natural science, Wesley was led to transport it to the religious domain--to the field of the supernatural life. Around his own personal experiences, and those he was familiar with in his disciples, he gathered and polarized all his theological writings." Maximin Piette, John Wesley in the Evolution of Protestantism (New York: Sheed and Ward, 1937), p. 436.

In his "Plain Account of Christian Perfeciton," Wesley wrote: "This is the doctrine which we preached from the beginning, and which we preach at this day. Indeed, by viewing it in every point of light, and comparing it again and again with the words of God on the one hand, and the experience of the Children of God on the other, we saw farther into the nature and properties of Christian Perfection." Works, Volume XI, p. 385. (Emphasis is mine.)

Wesley collected much of his data for formulating his theology in the letters which he wrote. Notice March 16, 1770, Works, Volume XII, p. 494. Compare with the letters to Jane Hilton, Letters to John Wesley, Volume V, ed. John Telford (London: Epworth Press, 1931), p. 98., and to Ann Bolton, Volume V, p. 319.

Wesley was possibly even more psychologically objective in his investigation than Upham.

3. Wesley wrote: "All who deny this, call it original sin, or by another title, are but heathens still, in the fundamental point which differences Heathenism from Christianity. They may, indeed, allow that men have many vices;.... But here is the shibboleth: Is man by nature filled with all manner of evil? Is he void of all good? Is he wholly fallen? Is his soul totally corrupted? or to come back to the text, is 'every imagination of the thoughts of his heart only evil continually'? Allow this, and you are so far a Christian. Deny it, and you are but an Heathen still." Colin W. Williams, John Wesley's Theology Today (Nashville: Abingdon Press, 1960), p. 47.

4. Works, Volume IX, p. 273. Harold Lindstrom states: "At one with the Reformed outlook, he insists here on the total corruption of natural man, grounding the tenet on the doctrine of original sin." Harold Lindstrom, Wesley and Sanctification (London: The Epworth Press, 1956), p. 20.

5. Soren Kierkegaard, The Concept of Dread, trans. by Walter Lowrie. (Princeton, N.J.: Princeton University

Press, 1944). Kierkegaard theorized that the first man sinned because of the anxiety caused by the possibility of sinning.

6. Works, VI, p. 271.
7. Ibid., IX, p. 255.
8. Upham, Absolute Religion, p. 105.
9. Ibid., p. 116.
10. Ibid., p. 120.
11. Ibid., p. 155.
12. "Wesleyanism and Taylorism," Methodist Quarterly Review, Volume XLII (1860), pp. 656-669. The author argues that Wesley's belief that Adam's sin as the occasion of greater good to man, is not an identical proposition as "sin is the necessary means of the highest good of the universe" p. 656. Wesley's exact statement on the matter is found in his sermon: "God's Love to Fallen Man." Works, Volume, VI, pp. 231-240.
13. Upham, Absolute Religion, p. 155.
14. Ibid., p. 160.
15. Ibid., p. 162.
16. It was Taylor's argument that God willed the fall, so that God's sovereignty would be protected. Upham and Wesley were both more interested in protecting God's holiness. Thus, they believed that the "excellence of holiness is the best of all possible worlds."
17. Thomas Upham, Ratio Discipline or The Constitution of the Congregational Churches (Portland, Me.: William Hyde, 1844), p. 67.
18. Upham, Absolute Religion, p. 161.
19. Upham, Mental Philosophy, Volume II, p. 226.
20. Ibid., pp. 230-232.
21. Ibid., p. 231.
22. Ibid., p. 232.
23. Ibid.
24. George A. Turner, The More Excellent Way, p. 76. "In the minds of many, the Wesleyan doctrine of Christian perfection stands or falls with the traditional doctrine of in-dwelling sin with which entire sanctification is supposed to deal."

William Arnett says "Indeed, the doctrine of entire sanctification rises or falls on whether or not sin is basically two-fold in nature; sins as acts or deeds, and sin as an attitude or disposition, a principle or instinct of indwelling corruption." William Arnett, "Entire Sanctification," the Asbury Seminarian, Volume XXX (October 1975), p. 33.

The two sermons which expound sin as a principle and the need for cleansing in a second work of grace subsequent to justification were on "Sin in Believers" and "The Repentance of Believers." "Though we watch and pray ever so much, we cannot wholly cleanse either our heart or our hands. Most sure we cannot till it shall please our Lord to speak to our hearts again, to speak the second time, Be Clean; and then only the leprosy is cleansed. Then only the evil root, the carnal mind is destroyed, and inbred sin subsists no more. But if there be no such second change, if there be no instantaneous deliverance after justification, if there be none but a gradual work of God (that there is a gradual work none deny), then we must be content, as well as we can, to remain full of sin till death; and, if, so, we must remain guilty till death continually deserving punishment." Wesley, Sermons, ed. Burwash, p. 134.

25. Merne Harris and Richard S. Taylor, "The Dual Nature of Sin," The Word and the Doctrine, Kenneth E. Geiger (ed.), (Kansas City, Mo.: Beacon Hill Press, 1965), p. 116.

26. Ibid.

27. The Keswick movement was thoroughly Calvinistic in its teaching of inbred sin. But it did not teach the cleansing or eradication theory of entire sanctification. "On the contrary, it was always most carefully guarded by an insistence on the fact that sin remains in us to the last and that though Christ will by His Holy Spirit's power keep the true believer moment by moment from falling into known and unknown sins, yet that every thought, word, and deed of the Christians--to the last moment on earth--is tainted by the fact of indwelling sin or corruption, and that therefore, the blood of Christ is needed, every moment of our lives to cleanse us from guilt and keep us acceptable in the sight of the Holy God." Rev. Preb. H. Well Peploe, M.A., The Rev. E. W. Moore, M.A., The Keswick Convention--Its Message, Its Method and Its Men, Charles F. Harford, M.A., M.D. (ed.), (London: Marshall Brother, 1907), p. 39.

28. In commenting on Wesleyan-Arminian theology, H. Orotn Wiley wrote: "But the term 'guilt' ... needs to be carefully guarded. It may mean, as we have shown, either culpability (reatus culpoe), or mere liability to punishment (reatus poenoe). In this case, the culpability belonged solely to Adam, and resided in the first sinner as the natural head and representative of the race. The

consequences of his sin were passed on to his descendants as the reatus poenoe, or liability to punishment." H. Orton Wiley, Christian Theology, Volume II (Kansas City, Mo.: Beacon Hill Press, 1952), p. 26.

29. Leo Cox, John Wesley's Concept of Perfection, (Kansas City, Mo.: Beacon Hill Press, 1964), p. 49.

30. Wesley, "Working Out Our Own Salvation," Works, Volume VI, p. 509.

31. Wesley, Works, Volume VII, p. 187.

32. C. K. Berkower, Faith and Sanctification (Grand Rapids, Mich.: W. B. Erdman Publishing Company, 1952), p. 92.

33. Lycurgus M. Starkey, Jr., The Work of the Holy Spirit: A Study in Wesleyan Theology (Nashville: Abingdon Press, 1962), p. 45.

34. Upham, Life of Faith, p. 117.

35. Ibid., p. 115.

36. Ibid., p. 118.

37. Ibid., p. 119.

38. Ibid., p. 367.

39. Upham, Mental Philosophy, Volume II, p. 257.

40. Ibid., p. 347.

41. Ibid.

42. Upham, Life of Faith, pp. 40-41.

43. Ibid., p. 37.

44. Ibid., pp. 38-39.

45. Upham, Madame Guyon, Volume II, p. 105.

46. Upham, Life of Faith, p. 46.

47. Wesley, Works, Volume X, pp. 229-230. "But I do not carry free-will so far: (I mean, not in moral things), Natural free-will, in the present state of mankind, I do not understand: I only assert, that there is a measure of free-will supernaturally restored to every man, together with that supernatural light which 'enlightens every man that cometh into the world'."

48. Upham, Interior Life, p. 34.

49. Upham, Divine Union, p. 59.

50. See Adolf Koberle's argument against synergism in the process of sanctification from a Lutheran standpoint. Adolf Koberle, The Quest for Holiness (Minneapolis: Augsburg Publishing House, 1936).

51. William Cannon, The Theology of John Wesley (Nashville: Abingdon Press, 1946), p. 114. Compare with George Croft Cell, The Rediscovery of John Wesley (New York: Henry Holt, 1935), pp. 255-256.

52. Cannon, p. 107.

53. Ibid., pp. 115-116. A contrasting view to Cannon's description of an active Wesleyan theology is, Robert Moore's argument that Wesley psychologically adapted himself by adopting a theology of passivity. "Yet with the development of the theology of passivity his denial of initiative and rationalization of the intensively active modes of his overt behavior had found a systematic framework and a historical and biblical foundation which enabled them to function far more successfully in facilitating ego activity, and with it, purposive movement toward the fulfillment of his ego-ideals. The rejection of the decrees of predestination had affirmed that any real authority in the divine realm had to be fair, and that the spiritual 'race' was human initiative and affirmation of the divine had insured that he would not only avoid immobilizing assaults by the super-ego, but that through submission he would be empowered by the grace of God to work toward ends both sanctioned by the super-ego and representative of ego-ideals. The resigned self had found a theology which could energize his quest for exaltation."

Robert L. Moore, John Wesley and Authority: A Psychological Perspective (Missoula, Mont.: Scholars Press, 1979), p. 79.

54. Wesley, Works, Volume VIII, p. 337.

55. John Wesley, Explanatory Notes upon the New Testament (London: Epworth Press, 1976), p. 412. This is Wesley's comment on Acts 5:31: "Him hath God exalted a Prince and a Saviour with his right hand, to give repentance to Israel, and forgiveness of sin."

56. "God does undoubtedly command us both to repent, and to bring forth fruits meet for repentance; which if we willingly neglect, we cannot reasonably expect to be justified at all: therefore both repentance, and fruits meet for repentance, are, in some sense, necessary to justification. But they are not necessary in the same degree; for those fruits are only necessary conditionally; if there be time and opportunity for them. Otherwise, a man may be justified without them, as was the thief upon the cross ..." Wesley's Sermons (ed. Burwash), p. 167.

57. Ibid., "Salvation by Faith," p. 5.

58. Ibid., p. 432.

59. Upham, Life of Faith, p. 61.

60. Ibid., p. 218.

61. Upham, Divine Union, p. 22.

62. Ibid., p. 181.
63. Ibid., p. 362.
64. Upham, Absolute Religion, p. 165.
65. Ibid.
66. Ibid., p. 66.
67. Upham, Madame Guyon, p. 168.
68. Upham, Catherine Adorna, p. 187.
69. Starkey, p. 152.
70. Upham, Catherine Adorna, p. 19.
71. Upham, Divine Union, p. 29.
72. Albert Outler, p. 472.
73. Ibid., p. 482.
74. Ibid., p. 498.
75. Ibid., p. 490.
76. Upham, Will, p. 233.
77. Ibid.
78. "Thoughts on Holiness: The Naturalness of a Truly, Holy Life," Guide, Volume XIV (1848), p. 26.
79. Inge argues that this concept is explicit in both William Law and Jacob Bohme. "'There is nothing that is supernatural,' he says very firmly, 'in the whole system of our redemption. Every part of it has its ground in the workings and powers of nature, and all our redemption is only nature set right, or made to be that which it ought to be. There is nothing that is supernatural but God alone.... Right and wrong, good and evil, true and false, happiness and misery, are as changeable in nature as time and space. Nothing, therefore, can be done to any creature supernaturally, or in a way that is without or contrary to the powers of nature; but every thing or creature that is to be helped, that is, to have any good done to it, or any evil taken out of it, can only have it done so far as the powers of nature are able, and rightly directed to effect it." William Ralph Inge, M.A., Christian Mysticism (London: Methuen and Company, 1899), pp. 283-284.
80. Lindstrom, p. 181.
81. Wesley, Works, Volume VIII, p. 12.
82. Ibid., p. 3.
83. Wesley, Sermons, (ed. Burwash), p. 167.
84. Wesley, Works, Volume XI, p. 394.
85. Wesley, Sermons (ed. Burwash), p. 394.
86. Leo G. Cox, "The Imperfection of the Perfect," Kenneth Geiger (ed.), Further Insights into Holiness (Kansas City, Mo.: Beacon Hill Press, 1963), p. 179.
87. Wesley, Works, Volume XI, pp. 366-367.

88. R. Newton Flew, The Idea of Perfection in Christian Theology (Oxford: Clarendon Press, 1934), pp. 332-333.

89. Wesley, Letters, Volume V, p. 255.

90. Lindstrom, p. 172.

91. Upham, Life of Faith, p. 189.

92. Thomas C. Upham, "On the Three Forms of Love: Namely, of Benevolence, of Complacency, and of Union," the Guide, Volume XV (1849), p. 97.

93. Ibid., p. 97.

94. Upham, Life of Faith, p. 265.

95. Ibid., p. 436.

96. Ibid., p. 234.

97. Upham, Catherine Adorna, p. 131.

98. The subjective hymnology of Fannie Crosby largely displaced the objective verses of Charles Wesley within the holiness camp-meeting movement. A popular hymn penned in 1875 was "I Am Thine, Oh, Lord."

> Consecrate me now to Thy service, Lord,
> By the power of grace divine;
> Let my soul look up with a steadfast hope,
> And my will be lost in thine. (Emphasis is mine.)

99. The psychological explication of the commitment of the will in the following, sounds very much like Upham's appeal to consciousness: "I am conscious to myself of one more property, commonly called liberty. This is very frequently confounded with the will; but is of a very different nature. Neither is it a property of the soul; as well as all the motions of the body.... And although I have not an absolute power over my own mind, because of the corruption of my own nature; yet, through the grace of God assisting me, I have a power to choose and do good, as well as evil. I am free to choose whom I will serve; and if I choose the better part, to continue therein even unto death." Wesley, Works, Volume VII, p. 228.

100. Upham, Interior Life, p. 356.

101. Ibid., p. 378.

102. Upham, Life of Faith, p. 211.

103. Upham, Divine Union, p. 157.

104. Upham, Madame Guyon, Volume I, p. 109. It is almost superfluous to say that Upham had a mystical concept regarding the commitment of the will even before he met Phoebe Palmer:

Thou Sweet, beloved will of God,
My anchor ground, my fortress hill,
My spirit's silent, fair abode,
In Thee I hide Me, and am still.

Thy beautiful sweet will, my God,
Holds fast in its sublime embrace,
My captive will, a gladsome bird,
Prisoned in such a realm of grace.

Thy wonderful grand will, my God,
With triumph now I make it mine;
And faith shall cry a joyous "yes!"
To every dear command of Thine.

Harford, p. 50; penned by Madame Guyon.

105. Upham, Madame Guyon, Volume I, p. 186.
106. Upham, Divine Union, p. 391.
107. Ibid., p. 392.
108. Wesley, Works, Volume VI, p. 489.
109. Upham, Life of Faith, p. 456.
110. Upham, Madame Guyon, Volume I, p. 338. Palmer was of the firm opinion that Upham was too extreme in his treatment of the will. She thought his "death of the will" to be an overstatement--and unrealistic in view of true spirituality and scriptural teaching. Wheatley, pp. 518-523.
111. Upham, Madame Guyon, Volume II, p. 165.
112. Ibid., p. 228.
113. Ibid., p. 366.
114. Upham, Interior Life, p. 109.
115. Wesley, Works, Volume XI, p. 379.
116. Thomas C. Upham, "Peculiar Dangers Attending a State of Holiness," Advocate of Christian Holiness (July 1872), p. 13.
117. Upham, Life of Faith, p. 431.
118. Upham, Interior Life, p. 161.
119. Ibid., pp. 157-158.
120. Ibid., p. 159.
121. Caldwell Merritt, p. 141.
122. "Theory of Temptation," Methodist Quarterly Review, Volume XXIV (1842), p. 151.
123. Ibid., p. 153.
124. Ibid.
125. Upham, Interior Life, p. 159.
126. Ronald Knox, Enthusiasm--A Chapter in the History of Religion (New York: Oxford University Press, 1950), p. 219.

127. Upham, Absolute Religion, p. 223.
128. Wesley, Works, Volume XI, p. 419.
129. Wesley, Works, Volume XI, pp. 379-380.
130. Ibid., p. 380.
131. Upham, Madame Guyon, Volume II, p. 110.
132. See Kenneth Grider's argument that instantaneous sanctification does not influence and cleanse the subconscious. "Entire sanctification is not a panacea; it does not right the sundry derangements due to aberrating experiences that have happened during this life. These become fully corrected only when our 'mortality puts on immortality' only when the sanctified are glorified." J. Kenneth Grider, Entire Sanctification: The Distinctive Doctrine of Wesleyanism (Kansas City: Beacon Hill Press, 1980), p. 127.
133. Upham, Madame Guyon, Volume II, p. 214.
134. Wesley was not so confident of the possibilities for mental tranquility and composure that Upham claimed for mystical divine union. Wesley, Standard Sermons, ed. Burwash, pp. 412-413.
135. Upham, Catherine Adorna, p. 236.
136. Ibid., p. 213.
137. Upham, Interior Life, p. 158.
138. Wesley, Works, Volume VIII, p. 338.
139. Upham, Interior Life, pp. 267-273.
140. Ibid., pp. 176-192. Upham has six chapters on regulation of desires, appetites, curiosity, etc.
141. Upham, Madame Guyon, Volume II, p. 241.
142. Ibid., p. 102.
143. Wesley, Works, Volume VIII, p. 270.
144. Ibid., p. 236.
145. Wilson Smith, p. 36.
146. Ibid., p. 40.
147. Frank John McNulty, "The Moral Teachings of John Wesley," unpublished S.T.D. Thesis, Washington, D.C.: Catholic University of America, 1963, p. 67.
148. Ibid., p. 84.
149. Upham, Catherine Adorna, p. 61.
150. Ibid.
151. Upham, Interior Life, p. 369.
152. Upham, Interior Life, p. 216.
153. Ibid., p. 229.
154. Upham, Madame Guyon, Volume II, p. 101.
155. Upham, Madame Guyon, Volume I, p. 187.
156. Ibid., p. 196.

157. Upham, Interior Life, p. 75.
158. Ibid.
159. Upham, Interior Life, p. 216.
160. Wesley, Letters, Volume VI, p. 297.
161. William Arnett documents Wesley extensively claiming that "it is an oversimplification to identify Wesley with one particular theory of the atonement, and to limit his view to any certain position or theory." From William Arnett's "John Wesley's Doctrine of Jesus Christ and Redemption," Doctrine 29--course taught at Asbury Theological Seminary, Wilmore, Kentucky.
162. Wesley, A Plain Account, p. 73.
163. Ibid.
164. Wesley, Letters, Volume IV, p. 159. (Emphasis is mine.)
165. Upham, Madame Guyon, Volume II, p. 14.
166. Ibid., p. 75.
167. Upham, Madame Guyon, Volume I, p. 57.
168. Ibid., p. 106.
169. Ibid., p. 323.
170. Upham, Life of Faith, p. 164.
171. Upham, Interior Life, p. 2.
172. Upham, Christ in the Soul, p. 116.
173. Sugden, Volume II, p. 456.
174. Lindstrom, p. 41.
175. Elmer Clark, The Small Sects in America (Nashville: Abingdon Press, 1949), p. 60.

Chapter V

THE INFLUENCE OF MYSTICISM

More than it did from any other source the intense spirituality that marked Thomas Upham's writings derived from the thought patterns of seventeenth- and eighteenth-century European mysticism. Upham drew from the French Quietists Francois de Sales, Francois Fenelon, Madame Guyon, and the Italian Catherine Adorna.[1]

Despite its cropping up in either general theological conversation or informal writings, Christian mysticism is a term implying poorly-laid and not easily-agreed-upon ground rules. On the one extreme, mysticism connotes an immediacy or immanence that disregards historical roots, sacraments, original sin, scriptures, means of grace--everything worthy of a sane Christian gospel. At the other extreme, it connotes that element of contact with God by which genuine worship and life are differentiated from dead formalism.[2] How did the above writers and others influence Upham? How did he interpret what they said? What departure from Wesleyan holiness, if any, did they introduce to his theology. These are questions that will be dealt with in this chapter.

Assessment of Upham's Interpretation

Ronald Knox' accusation that Upham imposed nineteenth-century evangelicalism on French Quietism, merits immediate attention because it focuses on the critical question that concerns Upham's utilization of his resources. According to Knox, the three Protestant eggs that have been laid by Upham in the wrong nest are assurance of faith, personal reliance on Christ for salvation, and justification by faith rather than works.[3]

At worst, Upham was fighting the wrong battle in the wrong camp or, at least, had misjudged the skirmish line. According to Knox, he was not well-enough versed in the theological jargon of Catholic mysticism to realize how its tensions are essentially different from those resolved in the Reformation, and indeed extend to the whole of evangelical Protestantism. Knox argued that the respective differences between Quietism and evangelical Protestantism are: reverence for Christ as the redeemer of the human race, rather than individual appropriation of the atonement; spiritual trial after surrender to God, rather than acute mental suffering before justification; and indifference to assurance as opposed to "an act of confidence in the promise of salvation."[4]

A careful reading of Madame Guyon's Autobiography, A Short and Easy Method of Prayer and Spiritual Torrents demonstrates Knox to be essentially right. At no point did Madame Guyon give a clear statement as to Christ being the meritorious and procuring cause of man's salvation. In his attempt to put Madame Guyon in the best light, Upham was led to an incorrect evaluation: "She had now a clearer perception both of what God is, and of what he requires, and especially of the way of forgiveness and salvation by faith in Christ alone."[5]

The emphasis in Madame Guyon is not on a justification and regeneration by faith. It is not on sanctification that continues by faith but on suffering inflicted by the sovereignty of God, which brings purification. Wesley called this the capital mistake, the one that runs through all of Madame Guyon's writings.[6] If one were reading the autobiography of a Protestant reformer, careful attention would have to be paid to the language used before justification as opposed to the language used afterward, but there is no such conversion point in Madame Guyon, and the language is consistently the same throughout. If there are milestone spiritual experiences for Madame Guyon, they consist in the following: first of all, the realization that the kingdom of God is within[7] and that a divine spark exists within that needs to be cultivated,[8] and; secondly, that suffering should not be self-inflicted--God will apply it according to his own wisdom and providence. Madame Guyon wrote:

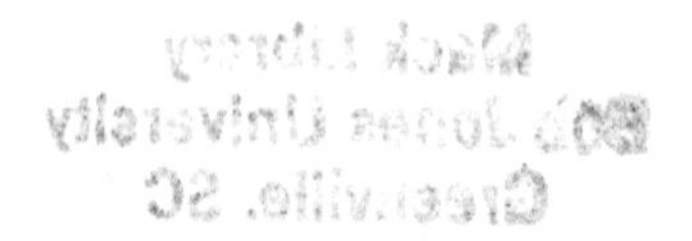

> So eager was I for the cross, that I endeavored to make myself feel the utmost vigour of every mortification and felt then to the quick: Yet this only served to awaken my desire of suffering, and to show me that it is God alone that can prepare and send crosses suitable to a soul that thirsts for a following of his sufferings, and a conformity of his death.[9]

Christology

For Madame Guyon, the cross was not so much a vicarious sacrifice to atone for man's sin and to be appropriated by faith as it was a pattern to be followed. The secret to spirituality is not the seeking of particular crosses, but acquiescence, "always new and unexpected," to the crosses that God gives.[10] Suffering that is sought and applied by the individual only tends toward pride and self-love and self-preoccupation. As Fenelon wrote: "It does not consist, however, in upsetting ourselves, tormenting ourselves, being constantly preoccupied with ourselves, rather than lifting our eyes to God, our only help against ourselves."[11] But even though there is no clear teaching on sanctification through the merits of Christ, just as safely it can be observed that for Madame Guyon no holiness existed but that which came from God through Christ.

> It is being truly sanctified in all holiness to have none of our own but the holiness of Jesus Christ. Let him alone be all in all in us, that the work of sanctification may be carried on through the experimental knowledge of the divine truth.[12]

But at times there is enough hint at merit to make a Luther, a Calvin, or even a Wesley uncomfortable. Reference to merit made Upham uncomfortable also, which is the reason he tried to camouflage Madame Guyon's works-righteousness. Madame Guyon stated: "As for me, I only glory in my infirmities, since they have merited for me, such a Saviour."[13] She believed that her suffering was instrumental in procuring not only her salvation but the salvation of others.

Her own pattern pointed to the pattern of Christ.[14]

Even though Fenelon perceived the futility of meriting salvation by great deeds, a high sense of self-sufficiency is still important to him.[15] But neither Fenelon nor Madame Guyon perceived the highest state of sanctification as a self-mortification or a self-infliction of meriting penance. Pervading their work is always an emphasis on immediate relationship to God, not through mere ceremony but through Christ.

Sanctification Through Suffering

That providence will make the cross, or suffering, relevant to our specific situation is one of the keys to sanctification; the greatest spiritual profit, therefore, will be effected by God's ingeniousness.[16] Abandonment to divine prescience rather than to self-mortification will bring the correct "austerities of grace."[17] The suffering that truly sanctifies, must not result from a prescribed plan of human ingenuity. Madame Guyon testifies:

> God knows well, in the admirable economy he observes, how to render the crosses more weighty, conformable to the ability of the creature to bear them; giving them always something new and unexpected. Hereby my soul began to be more resigned and to comprehend that the state of absence and of wanting what I longed for was in its turn, more profitable to that of always abounding; because this latter nourished self-love. If God did not get there, the soul would never die to itself. That principle of self-love is so crafty and dangerous, that it cleaves to everything.[18]

Throughout Upham's writings is evidenced a notable accordance with the mystics' concept of sanctification through suffering. "The crucifixion of our inward nature cannot take place without the experience of suffering."[19] Attractive objects that draw our attention from God must be removed from our lives by the divine, sovereign, sanctifying process.[20] Physical suffering and weaknesses are to be welcomed as "a means of growth and grace" and "as the forerunners of increased purity and happiness."[21] Upham said of Catherine Adorna that "she held with great truth, that it is by means of such temptations and afflictions accompanied by the influence of the Holy Spirit that God, as a general thing, destroys those depraved tendencies, which constitute 'what is denominated the life of nature'."[22]

Upham's definition of sin lies at the heart of his sanctification theory of suffering. Sin consists primarily of desires and affections attached to wrong objects. God sovereignly changes our value structure by destroying and removing those objects upon which we place inordinate value.

> And this is done by a course, the reverse of that which sin has previously prompted it to take, namely, by the substitution of a right faith for a wrong one, by taking the desires from wrong objects, and by suppressing all their inordinate action. But this is a process which is not ordinarily gone through without suffering.[23]

Throughout Madame Guyon's biography, Upham stayed true to Madame Guyon's own account that suffering is crucial to the sanctifying process. This is how Madame Guyon understood her unhappy marriage, mistreatment by her mother-in-law, her physical illnesses, and attacks by the church; Upham understood them no differently. Both were in agreement with John Tauler that God would sooner "send an angel from heaven, to refine his chosen vessel through tribulations, than leave it without sufferings."[24] Commitment, consecration, and love to God can be best nursed by sorrow, earthly loss, and earthly pain.[25] Suffering is the means of testing consecration and assuring us of its sincerity. Sanctification is enhanced by the crucifixion of every psychological and material prop, which depreciates reliance upon divine grace. Upham quoted from Lady Maxwell: "Put a thorn in every enjoyment, a worm in every gourd, that would either prevent our being wholly thine or any measure retard my progress in the divine life."[26] Upham expressed in verse the mystical understanding of the cross and suffering:

> LOVE OF THE CROSS
>
> O Father! Let me bear the Cross,
> Make it my daily food,
> Though with it Thou dost send the loss
> Of every other good.

Take house and lands and earthly fame;
To all I am resigned;
But let me make one earnest claim;
Leave, leave the Cross behind!

I know it costs me many tears,
But they are tears of bliss;
And moments there outweigh the years
Of selfish happiness.

The Cross is Love, to action given;
Love "seeking not its own;"
But finding truth and peace and heaven,
In good to others shown.

The Cross doth live in God's great life,
In Christ's dear heart doth shine;
And how, without its pains and strife
Shall God and Christ be mine?[27]

Acquiescence

Upham consistently maintained that both acquiescence to providence and to the sovereignty of God in the sanctification process gives validity to suffering. He defended Fenelon: "That quietude is bad which is the result of the ignorant and unbelieving pride of self; but it is not so with the quietude which is the result of an intelligent and believing acquiescence in the will of God."[28] Complacency and confidence in the character and administration of God are crucial for complete acquiescence in the will of God in all things.[29] Growth in sanctification is to a great extent evidenced by one's ability to accept, cheerfully, greater and greater crosses and burdens. Acquiescence purifies the tendencies of the will to rebel against the providence of God, which is a mark of a sinful disposition.[30] Right feelings about adverse circumstances are unmistakable indications of the extent of our sanctification.[31]

For Upham, acquiescence to the laws of providence was just as important as obeying the law of scripture; the two are in agreement.[32] We cannot lay claim to the God of scripture without accepting the arrangements of providence, of which God, excepting sin, is the chief and only originator. God's direction applies to all events, except sin, and at that point there is simply divine permission. "We must then sacrifice the riches, privileges and gifts, both spiritual and temporal, to the arrangements of Providence, in order that we may retain and enjoy, what is infinitely more valuable, the God of Providence."[33]

Even though sin does not come from God, God directly uses the wickedness of others as the instrument of individual suffering, just as if God were inflicting the blow.[34] A sovereign will is in control of all events--great or small, and affection for those events--positive or negative--is tantamount to affection for the God behind them.[35] At the heart of the resignation principle are the words of Jesus: "where your treasure is, there will your heart be also." (Luke 12:34) The treasure may consist of friends, land, health, etc.; a ready acceptance of their dispensability at the hand of God is proportionate to one's love to God and an indicator of the unsanctified impurities that may still detract from that love. Upham clearly stated the relationship of providence and holy affections:

> The law of Providence requires this modification of the feelings as strictly and as truly as the written law; so that we may lay it down as a principle, that the law of Providence must regulate, to a considerable extent, not only our outward acts, but our affections. It is Providence which places before us the objects we must love; and, what is more, it indicates the degree of our love, and the ways of its manifestation. And, on the other hand, the same Providence indicates to us the objects which should excite our disapprobation, and also the degree and manner of our disapprobation.[36]

Wesley, too, emphasized the necessity of providential suffering. Though it may not always be understood, providential suffering promotes spiritual keenness and growth; it may be a form of chastisement, and can always be used for profit. To Lady Maxwell in 1769, Wesley wrote: "You have accordingly found pain, sickness, bodily weakness, to be real goods; as bringing you nearer and nearer to the fountain of all happiness and holiness."[37] Pain serves the purpose of cleansing from us remaining sinful affections, and for stifling temptations that would otherwise prevent the perfect work of holiness. The indication likewise exists that this infliction is directly imposed by God because of his determination to honor that person through his hallowing purpose.[38] One of the most lucid, most concise statements of the relation of suffering to Christian perfection was written to Mary Bishop in 1777:

> We have now abundant proof that very many are made better by sickness; unless one would rather stay in sickness. This is one of the grand means which God employs for that purpose. In sickness, many are convinced of sin, many converted to God, and still more confirmed in the ways of God and brought onward to perfection.[39]

Indifference

Complete acceptance of providence is total indifference to one's state of affairs, whatever those circumstances may be. The scriptural principle is found in Paul's testimony: "I have learned in whatsoever state I am, therewith to be content" (Phil. 4:11). Fenelon wrote: "we worship, we praise, we bless God for all things."[40] But indifference implies something more, a state of spiritual and psychological obliviousness to circumstances. Madame Guyon believed that the soul could be so consumed by the fire of God's love, that "it is utterly dead, and nothing affects it either from without or within, that is, it is no longer troubled by any sensible impressions."[41] The individual that can accept every moment as divine light from God, "is already in the sweet peace of Paradise."[42] She wrote: "I had a perfect indifference to everything that is here and a union so great with the good will of God, that my own will seemed to be entirely lost."[43] No statement of indifference is more succinct than the following: "I love my chains. Everything is equal to me, as I have no will of my own, but purely the love of him who possesses me."[44]

Upham tempered the doctrine of indifference by distinguishing between sorrow and complacency.[45] When we consider an event as having been ordered by God, such as the death of a family member, there will be sorrow, but at the same time, there will be acquiescence and patience in God's wisdom.[46] But at other times, Upham hinted at the possibility of a state of grace, which perceives an event or circumstance, no matter how good or bad, with an unrealistic optimism. Upham tried to maintain the best of both worlds, i.e., human emotions and heavenly constancy, and risked contradiction.[47]

He was careless with language when he used such phrases as "unelated by joy," "undepressed by sorrow," and "unaltered by temptation." The following paragraph may be the most exemplary of Upham's attempts to maintain both a Quietistic indifference and a healthy psychological view of man.

> God makes the arrangement; but the disposition with which we shall receive that arrangement, he leaves to ourselves. And let this satisfy us. In every arrangement which he makes, his own is our highest good; but whether it will result in our highest good, depends upon the spirit in which we accept it. He never violates our moral liberty; and if, in the exercise of that liberty, we put our thoughts and our feeling in his keeping, he will give a heart so correspondent to our habitation, that our cottage will be beautiful in our sight as a palace, and the darkness of our dungeon as bright as the open day.[48]

Disinterested Benevolence

Inherent to the idea of indifference is that of disinterested benevolence, which essentially means an unconditional giving, without regard for return of our love or service. The Quietists espoused this doctrine as consistently as any other single group within the history of the church.[49] The translator of Madame Guyon's Autobiography claimed that her doctrine of "the pure disinterested love of God" was the chief reason for her imprisonment and for the imprisonment of Father La Combe. God could be sought for himself without regard to his attributes, gifts or graces. Personal interest was to be set aside. Madame Guyon wrote that "there must not only be a death to the joys of sense and emotion, but a death to the joy that God gives."[50] Fenelon was in agreement: "Seek God for Himself only, not for the pleasure which comes from the search."[51]

Disinterestedness was to extend even to our regard for eternal rewards or punishments.[52] Madame Guyon further wrote: "I believe that if such a soul were taken to hell, it would suffer all the cruel tortures of its fate in a complete contentment, because of the beatitude of its transformed centre; and this is the cause of the indifference which they feel towards all conditions."[53] Rufus Jones explained it in this way:

> The soul must get beyond the state of enduring crosses, and suffering because it wants God to see its devotion and its love, and it must learn to love and suffer and be crucified without knowing or asking whether He sees its devotion or whether He cares.[54]

Upham stated that God must be loved for what He is in Himself, but admits that this cannot exclude what He has done for us because His actions are a part of His whole character.[55] The philosophical premise behind Upham's disinterested love is that "right love is love precisely conformed to its object in all the facts and relations of the object, so far as the object is susceptible of being known."[56] God contains everything that is loving or perfect and thus is deserving of pure love.[57] It will be a love that terminates in the object loved, rather than in the person who loves.[58] Upham argued that perfect love is not truly self-sacrificing if it has any regard to its reward.[59] It never thinks of what consolation may come in the relationship of divine union, because "it thinks more of what God is than what God gives."[60] Upham would have agreed with Evelyn Underhill, who wrote:

> The mystic does not enter on his quest because he desires the happiness of the beatific Vision, the ecstasy of union with the Absolute, or any other personal reward. That noblest of all passions, the passion of perfection for love's sake, far outweighs the desire for transcendental satisfaction.[61]

The essence of disinterested benevolence is that the truly sanctified do not have any unfulfilled desires. Complete union with God means that a person is hardly conscious of personal or individual desire.[62] Fenelon tempered this view by saying that there may be desire for houses, lands, etc., but non-desire means not desiring anything out of God.[63] Fenelon did not teach that desire can be eliminated; he taught that we can serve God out of nonutilitarian motivation. The proper disposition should be service that comes not from a desire of personal happiness or eternal deliverance but from fulfillment of God's pleasure, this resulting in his glory because he himself desires and wills what we should desire and will.[64] That detachment and poverty of spirit is what brings true liberty. St. John of the Cross said it best:

> That you mayest have pleasure in everything, seek pleasure in nothing.... That thou mayest know everything, seek to know nothing. In detachment the spirit finds quiet and repose, for coveting nothing, nothing wearies it by elation, and nothing oppresses it by dejection, because it stands in the centre of its own humility. For as soon as it covets anything, it is immediately fatigued thereby.[65]

Inactivity

The above aspects of complacency, passivity, disinterestedness, and indifference, lead to the essence of Quietism, i.e., inactivity. Activity denotes a desire to change the relationship between the individual and the circumstances that surround him. If a person experiences indifference, then that person is active neither in the initiating nor in the prevention of change. There is an entire passivity toward whatever God may send.[66] Complacent prayer takes precedence over meditative prayer because the latter denotes activity of the mind and petition for God to act in a particular way.

Madame Guyon taught that actions are the gate to perfection, but if they are not laid aside they will become clogs, preventing those who adhere to them, "from ever arriving at the end of their course."[67] Inge characterized contemplation as negative, "being occupied with no sensible image, no distinct and nameable idea ... it stops only at the purely intellectual and abstract idea of being."[68] Knox defined contemplative prayer as prayer in which one deliberately gives up "trying to make acts or to elicit emotions in your prayer; you remain simply attentive to God's presence, or if you could be said to show any sign of activity, it was only that general bearing of the soul to him which you meet within."[69]

Fenelon tempered the above definition by pointing out that true contemplation is not really cessation of activity but cessation of self-interested activity.[70] Acceptable activity is not activity of the person but activity of God in the person--a passive activity of the Christian initiated by God. As for Madame Guyon, Fenelon, and others, the difference between the contemplative way and the active meditative way likely was more theoretical than practical; one could hardly charge the seventeenth-century mystics with inactivity. As Knox writes: "But the motto of Quietism was not _laissez-faire_, it was _laissez-faire Dieu_; and the whole of her life, except when she was shut up in prisons or convents, was a round of ceaseless activity--God's, she said, not hers."[71] According to Madame Guyon, the only thing that gives actions meaning comes not from any inherent virtue but is wrought out of the divine plan.[72]

The phrase that best describes the above is "reposeful activity."[73] Upham corrected the idea that contemplation supposes rest in God to be the same thing as inactivity of nature.[74] Stillness or silence is actually a cessation of those workings of self that choose the wrong time and place. Stillness is also cessation from the impulse of worldly passions and the tumult of unsanctified anxieties.[75] Georgia Harkness suggests that the word "passive" is entirely out of place in speaking of Quietism's complacency. "There is nothing passive about the endeavor to quiet one's mind and conflicting emotion so that one can hear the voice and feel the presence of God."[76] Fenelon wrote: "Holy indifference is not inability. It is the farthest possible from it. It is indifference to anything and everything out of God's will, but it is the highest life and activity to anything and everything in that will."[77]

The Moment

Everything in the will of God means a perfect reconciliation to the "moment," the "now." Quietism does not live in the past or future, because living in the past would mean regret and living in the future would mean unfulfilled hopes and anxiety. Upham taught that the moment must not be anticipated before it arrives because anticipation implies a premature decision.[78] But a decision must not be delayed until after the departure of the divine moment.[79] In order for right action to take place in the moment, preconceived notions must be ruled out because no moment in which action is required can give all the facts requisite to right decisions.[80]

Saying this, Upham did not mean that approximate decisions or probable opinions could not be formed before the moment arrives. But there must be no preconceived plans of action that cannot be changed by the momentarily revealed will of God. Upham wrote:

> No man lives in the will of God, who anticipates the divine moment of actual duty, by making up a positive decision before it arrives, or by delaying a decision until after its departure. We must meet God there, and stand in his will there, or meet him nowhere, and stand out of his will everywhere. If, therefore, we would live in the will of God, we must conform to that beautiful and sacred order, in which his will is made known. In other words, if it is our sincere desire to live in the divine will, it seems to follow that we must live by the moment.[81]

God does not reveal himself in a broad future prospective but only in successive moments.[82] God is in all instances, and it is in the present instant that we find Him. If we are living in the past or the future, i.e., out of the present moment, we miss something of God.[83] If we accept the present moment, God will see to it that the right internal emotion corresponds to the present event.[84] Because we find God in all events, all times, all places, we meet him as both immutable and changing. Every moment presents a different experience with God and this God is always fresh "affording new elements of knowledge, new tests of strength, and new foundation and appliances of growth and happiness."[85] God's habitation is with all moments, and with all events and circumstances he comes bringing inspiration for the task at hand.[86] The philosophical and psychological disposition of living in the eternal "now" is at the heart of Upham's realized eschatology (which will be discussed in the next chapter). No passage in Upham would have been more pleasing to Emerson, Parker, and Thoreau--along with the other nineteenth-century transcendentalists--than the following:

> And thus looking for God, finding Him not thousands of years hence in time, but as He is revealed in the correlated and correspondent facts and incidents of each successive moment, we shall know experimentally what He becomes now, and that in the continuous application and issue of this great principle, He becomes always a presence and a power, a source of goodness to ourselves and of goodness to others, and with a recognized dwelling place, which has its center in our own hearts and its circumference in the objects and events, including their necessary relations, which the present moment reveals.[87]

A Theology of Vocation

One man's moment is just as important as any other man's moment, whether he be king or peasant, clergy or laity, because that particular moment is God's particular moment for that particular person. Every moment for every individual is of equal importance; thus, we have a theology of vocation that is prominent in both the mystics and Upham. As Fenelon so accurately observed: "Most people, when they wish to be converted or reformed, expect to fill their lives with especially difficult and unusual acts of their conditions."[88] Fenelon's observation was none other than a paraphrase of the scriptural maxims. "Whatsoever thy hand findeth to do, do it with thy might," and "Whether therefore ye eat or drink..., do all to the glory of God." (Eccles. 9:10, I Cor. 10:31). The commonest acts are turned into sacraments, and, as Inge pointed out, all of life for the mystic is a sacrament.[89] There are no inherently lesser or greater acts done in God's will; they directly receive their importance as they are done with the intention of conformity to God's will."[90]

Madame Guyon emphasized that we should be delighted with all duties, even in playing cards with a spouse. The greatness of a work is inconsequential because "the divine plan makes all things one and all things God."[91]

Upham indicated that bearing the Saviour's image means the opposite of withdrawal. The sanctified person will not be any less a good neighbor or a good citizen, and "he cannot think less or work less when he is called to do it."[92] The dominant theme through Upham's American Cottage Life, is that

> farmers and others, who may seem to some to do menial tasks, are just as suredly doing God's will as the more esteemed of our society. Among those who cultivate the soil especially in the more retired, rural districts, there is very generally a recognition of God, a love for the Sabbath, and the Bible, and much of the Spirit of humble prayer.[93]

Upham and Emerson were one with the mystics in elevating to a new prominence and hope those who

> are united in a common love of truth, and love of its work. They are of all conditions and constitutions ... without pomp, without trumpet, in lonely and obscure places in solitude, in servitude, in compensation and privation, trudging beside the team in the dusty road or drudging a hireling in other men's cornfields.[94]

One of the evidences of a truly holy man is that he will be happy in his work--in fact man cannot be happy without work; "his work is his recreation, his labor is his play."[95] Whatever we do, if God requires it, it is the highest worship and homage we can pay to God.[96] Upham saw minimum tension and ambiguity in simultaneously carrying out the duties of this life and being a citizen of the kingdom of God.[97] The religious character of daily performance does not rest upon the place of a person's employment or type of activity but upon "the question whether God calls him to do it, and whether he acts from a true inward life."[98] Upham is one with the early church fathers, the reformers Calvin, Luther, and Wesley, and the Quietists, who believed not as those of the medieval church believed that a rigid dichotomy exists between the secular and sacred but that a spiritual transfiguration is required of the tasks relative to every day life.[99]

Critical Distance from the Mystics

Despite his association with mysticism, Upham does keep a critical distance from the mystics. He often explained or qualified exaggerated or overly simplistic language. Concerning Madame Guyon he wrote:

> I am aware that some of the methods she took seem to imply an undue degree of violence to principles of our nature, which are given us for wise purposes, and which in their appropriate action are entirely innocent.[100]

Such corrections are in keeping with Upham's understanding of the psychological drives and human propensities. These can be used for the glory of God and, at the same time, can maintain their distinctive purposes. When Madame Guyon spoke of a will lost or annihilated, Upham argued that if such language actually were fact, moral agency would be destroyed. At this point, Upham was expressing, in psychological language, the Wesleyan assertion that the "bent to sinning" that clings to our will can be crucified. The will's

> original life such as it had when it came from the hand of God is not necessary to destroy; but it is necessary, indispensably necessary to destroy all that fake and vitiating life, which sin, availing itself of the immense influence of the law of habit, has incorporated so strongly with the will's original nature that they now seem to be one.[101]

Upham asserted that any union between God and man that would imply physical union would endanger our personality and moral accountability.[102] A modified interpretation is needed for those passages of scripture that speak of the union of the regenerated with the mind of God.[103] What is to be recognized is not a union of substance or essence, but of morality, spirituality, and religion.[104] On the other hand, a person can testify to self-annihilation, though not literally because he "knows enough of himself as an individual to know that he is not his own, that his soul has become, a living fountain which takes its use from God, and flows out to all the boundless variety of existences."[105]

Upham denied that Madame Guyon's claim to increased power of the intellect is always the case in sanctification.[106] Her declaration should at times be received in a modified sense because apparent contradictions exist in various explanations of her experience.[107] As to her theory of divine grace, i.e., that spiritual power or influence flows from one person to another, Upham wrote that she described things as they seemed to be and not as they really are.[108] At this point, Upham interjected that though Madame Guyon exhibited great intellectual power she was somewhat defective in education.[109] Upham did not say "defective in Biblical exegesis," which would have been a much more satisfying criticism for Asa Mahan or B. B. Warfield.

Upham was most often correcting or qualifying Quietists' statements concerning loss of desire or of the will. He paraphrased Catherine Adorna's claim that she was without desire, by saying "that the sanctified or holy soul is a soul so united to God by conformity with the divine will as to be without desire; that is to say without any desire of its own, or any desire separate from the will of God."[110] In fact, as human beings we do not even have the right to not desire our own good or to act in a way which would be destructive to our well-being.[111] Loss of will does not differentiate us from our fellow men in essence; neither does it mean that we cannot have a strong energetic will, but only that our will cannot be at variance with God's will.[112] The will shall cease to act on the depraved basis of personal interest but itself will remain because it is psychologically essential to human existence.[113]

A Third Stage

Even a mere perusal of the mystics will clue us as to why Upham suggested a third stage of spiritual experience, or work of grace. In Madame Guyon's *Spiritual Torrents*, she described three ways of faith. In the fourth way exist four degrees that consist of progressive loss of gifts, grace, favors, virtues, etc., so nothing of the creature--and all of the creator--remains. The third way is passive. The degrees of stripping or dividing within the third way will free the pilgrim from hidden love of self, esteem for his own position, a secret desire to attract attention, an affected modesty, a faculty in judging others, and a preference for private devotion rather than domestic duties.[114] John Tauler spoke of three phases of personal life--the sensuous nature, the reason, the third way--the spiritual life or pure substance of the soul.[115] The number three dominates the writing of Hugo of Saint Victor. As for contemplation, there are three kinds: suspense, silence, sleep. Silence has three stages (which sounds similar to Madame Guyon): the silence of lips, the silence of thought, and the silence of reason.[116] Ignatius of Loyola explicated the three states of humility. The third state is the way of the perfect in which the Christians' wills are "completely set upon one object, for which they easily abandon everything else, 'to make their lives harmonize with the life of Christ.'"[117]

For Upham, the integral truth was not so much related to the number of critical spiritual experiences attained by the seeker but to the core definition of the ultimate in spiritual experience, i.e., union with God. Mysticism conditioned Upham to stress one aspect (while not entirely excluding others) of the Wesleyan doctrine of entire sanctification--this route, as opposed to cleansing, separation, righteousness, and purity. All of these concepts can be found within his writings, but none are so prominent as "divine union." Absorption into the divine was the goal--not the essence--of sanctification. Taken as a whole, Upham's writings give the impression that a step or distance exists beyond the second work of grace. In fact, divine union is such an involved and lofty spiritual aspiration, the tendency to reduce the hallowing process to a single spiritual exercise (as in the nineteenth-century holiness movement) does not exist.

Conclusion

Melvin Dieter's defense of Upham, in the face of Phoebe Palmer's criticism, needs to be further explicated. Concerning Palmer's charge that Upham's "divine union" moved beyond the clear teachings of scripture, Dieter stated: "A careful reading of Upham's writings does not seem to bear out the intensity of these fears or the continuing charge of 'heresies'."[118] Exception was taken not so much with heresy (though Upham was charged with it) as with extremism of language that needed to be qualified.

At times, Upham was contradictory when he tried to be both psychologically true to reality and simultaneously faithful to mystical language. For the most part, the contradictions can be reasoned away. But the mentality that wants theology meticulously, consistently, and systematically presented, may call for Upham to do a lot of explaining. Indeed, the concepts of indifference, inactivity, absorption, etc., may have been too extreme for nineteenth-century holiness exponents, even though tempered with a lot of qualifying. Upham left himself open, but then again he was not all that concerned about being on guard.

Even though Wesley abhorred much of the mystics' practice, he inherited an intimacy with God and a discipline of devotion from them, which he never lost. Experiential piety and a faith beyond philosophical speculation were streams that flowed from the mystics to Wesley, and subsequently to the holiness movement. The radical "death" and "crucifixion" language used by Wesley and the American exponents of entire sanctification was not unlike the spiritual descriptions of the seventeenth-century European mystics. Upham fused them together in ways that demonstrated agreement and compatibility. In a sense, Upham's writings are Wesley's spiritual discoveries from the mystics (1725-1738), coming home to roost. Whether John Wesley would have been somewhat chagrined to read them, is another question.

At the core of both Wesleyan perfectionism and Guyon mysticism was the religion of the heart--this as opposed to sheer rationalism. Upham's introspective psychology was easily adapted to both. Each aimed at total commitment of the "will" to God and each strived for an intimacy with God, which was beyond nominal Christianity. The holiness movement, at least for Upham, epitomized in contemporary form that which he had read about in a century gone by.

Notes

1. Upham quotes from other mystics: William Law, George Fox, Thomas á Kempis, and Jacob Boehme.

2. "No deeply religious man is without a touch of mysticism; and no mystic can be other than religious, in the psychological, if not in the theological sense of the

word." Evelyn Underhill, Mysticism (New York: E. P. Dutton and Company, Inc., 1961), p. 70.

3. Ronald A. Knox, Enthusiasm (New York: Oxford University Press, 1950), p. 236.

4. Ibid., pp. 237-238.

5. Upham, Madame Guyon, Volume I, p. 57.

6. Wesley, Works, Volume XIV, p. 277.

7. "Some of those who are thus exercised having never been taught that they must seek to have God within them, and not expect to find Him in outward righteousness, give themselves up to meditation, and seek without what can only be found within." Madame Guyon, Spiritual Torrents, translated from the Paris edition of 1790, by A. W. Marston (London: H. R. Allenson, Ltd., no date), p. 29.

8. The kingdom of God already within points to mysticisms defectiveness concerning the doctrine of original sin. Wesley criticized William Law at this point, i.e., "every man hath the spirit of God, the spirit of Christ is in the soul." Wesley, Works, Volume IX, p. 501.

9. Madame Guyon, The Exemplary Life of the Pious Lady Guion, translated from her own account by Thomas Digby Brooke (Philadelphia: Joseph Crukshank, 1804), pp. 95-96. (Will be referred to as Madame Guyon's Autobiography.)

10. Ibid., p. 135.

11. Francois Fenelon, Christian Perfection (New York: Harper and Brothers, 1947), p. 99.

12. Madame Guyon's Autobiography, p. 443.

13. Ibid., pp. 175-176.

14. Ibid., p. 378.

15. Derek Stanford (ed.), Fenelon's Letters to Men and Women (London: Peter Owen Ltd., 1957), p. 58.

16. Fenelon, Christian Perfection, pp. 16-18.

17. Madame Guyon, A Short and Easy Method of Prayer, translated from the French by Thomas D. Brooke. Included in Madame Guyon's Autobiography, p. 462.

18. Madame Guyon's Autobiography, p. 135.

19. Upham, Life of Faith, p. 244.

20. Upham, Divine Union, p. 168.

21. Ibid., p. 394.

22. Upham, Catherine Adorna, p. 179.

23. Upham, Divine Union, p. 168.

24. Upham, Madame Guyon, Volume II, p. 365.

25. Upham, American Cottage Life, p. 127.

26. Upham, Interior Life, p. 222.

27. Upham, Christ in the Soul, p. 35.
28. Upham, Madame Guyon, Volume II, p. 330.
29. Upham, Interior Life, p. 147.
30. Upham, Divine Union, p. 166.
31. Ibid.
32. Ibid., p. 196.
33. Ibid., p. 210.
34. Upham, Madame Guyon, Volume II, p. 43.
35. Upham, American Cottage Life, p. 176.
36. Upham, Divine Union, p. 197.
37. Wesley, Letters, Volume V, p. 134.
38. Ibid., Volume I, p. 103.
39. Ibid., Volume VI, p. 279.
40. Fenelon, Christian Perfection, p. 77.
41. Madame Guyon, Spiritual Torrents, p. 101.
42. Upham, Madame Guyon, Volume I, p. 315.
43. Madame Guyon's Autobiography, p. 197.
44. Ibid., p. 211.
45. Upham, Catherine Adorna, p. 149.
46. Upham, Divine Union, p. 197.
47. Ibid., pp. 377-379.
48. Ibid., p. 209.
49. This was similar to Samuel Hopkins' thought, but Hopkins did not inherit it from Quietism but from the logistics of Calvinism. His biographer wrote: "Samuel Hopkins' well-known doctrine of disinterested benevolence for instance, which required self-denial (even to the point of being willing to be damned for the glory of God and the good of the universe), was far from simply an abstract theological argument that was unconnected to social reality" (Conforti, p. 6).
50. Upham, Madame Guyon, Volume I, p. 121.
51. Fenelon, Letters, p. 170.
52. Wesleyan holiness did not go this far with disinterestedness. Note Randolph Foster's Christian Purity, p. 196.

Meister Echart wrote: "Cast me into Hell: His goodness forbids! But if He did cast me into hell, I should have two arms to embrace Him. One arm is true humility, that I should lay beneath Him, and be thereby united to His holy humanity. And, with the right arm of love, which is united with His holy divinity, I should so embrace Him that He would have to go to hell with me. And I would rather be in hell and have God, than in heaven and not have God." Underhill, Mysticism, p. 209.

53. Madame Guyon, Spiritual Torrents, p. 152.

54. Rufus Jones, New Studies in Mystical Religion, p. 49.
55. Upham, Interior Life, p. 110.
56. Ibid., p. 111.
57. Ibid., p. 113.
58. Ibid., p. 111.
59. Ibid., pp. 149-150.
60. Ibid., p. 156.
61. Underhill, Mysticism, p. 96.
62. Upham, Madame Guyon, Volume II, p. 194.
63. Ibid., p. 215.
64. Ibid., p. 213.
65. Underhill, Mysticism, p. 206.
66. Madame Guyon's Autobiography, p. 240.
67. Ibid., p. 493.
68. Inge, p. 238.
69. Knox, p. 247.
70. Inge, p. 239.
71. Knox, p. 262.
72. This particular premise was problematic for Wesley. He believed that virtue in itself was sufficient reason for action. Thus, he criticized the Quakers "waiting on God." Wesley wrote in "A Letter to a Person Lately Joined with the Quakers": "He (God) moves him by his understanding, as well as his affections; by light, as well as by heat. He moves him to do this or that by conviction, full as often as by desire. Accordingly, you are as really 'moved by the Spirit' when he convinces you you ought to feed him that is hungry, as when he gives you ever so strong an impulse, desire, or inclination so to do." Wesley, Works, Volume X, p. 81.
73. William Marshall Urban wrote: "The really fundamental character of all mystics is ... that they are able to make certain syntheses which the non-mystical find impossible.... The synthesis of perfect activity and perfect repose may be called a synthesis of apparent opposites, although even in our experience of ourselves we can sometimes find ourselves dwelling upon something in a condition which we might want to describe as one of reposeful activity." Illtyd Trethowan, Mysticism and Theology (London: Geoffrey Chapman Publishers, 1974), p. 109.
74. Upham, Catherine Adorna, p. 101.
75. Ibid., p. 203.
76. Georgia Harkness, Mysticism: Its Meaning and Message (Nashville: Abingdon Press, 1973), p. 31.

77. Upham, Madame Guyon, Volume II, p. 214. No one expressed more clearly the mutual double movement of activity and rest than John of Ruysbroeck: "God comes to us incessantly, both with means and without means; and He demands of us both action and fruition, in such a way that the action never hinders the fruition, nor the fruition the action, but they strengthen one another. And this is why the interior man (i.e., the contemplative) lives his life according to these two ways; that is to say, in rest and in work. And in each of them he is wholly and individedly; for he dwells wholly in God in virtue of his restful fruition and wholly in himself in virtue of his active love. And God, in His communications, perpetually calls and urges him to renew both this rest and this work. And because the soul is just, it desires to pay at every instant that which God demands of it; and this is why each time it is irradiated of Him, the soul turns inward in a manner that is both active and fruitive, and thus it is renewed in all virtues and ever more profoundly immersed in fruitive rest.... It is active in all loving work, for it sees its rest." Underhill, Mysticism, pp. 435-436.

78. Upham, Life of Faith, p. 414.

79. Ibid.

80. Ibid., p. 410.

81. Ibid., p. 414. Compare Upham's language with Dr. Thomas Oden's discussion of boredom in his essay "The Tragedy of Our Gods." Oden points out that most people experience complete boredom because of some actualized value in the past or some absolutized value hoped for in the future or the inability to see the worthwhile values of the now. The answer to boredom is Christian responsiveness to the now action of God and the unique opportunities occurring moment-by-moment that are pregnant with meaning and historical self-determination, though I may not fully understand them. Instead, man is tempted to look ahead at limited causes and creaturely goods that he believes are ultimate sources of meaning and value. This is the process of enthroning our values, making gods out of them and trusting that they will render life meaningful. Oden poignantly stated "Absolutizing relative values, idolatry becomes the hub of much human anguish, the hidden root of dysfunctional anxiety and guilt." Thomas C. Oden, Structures of Awareness (Nashville: Abingdon Press, 1969), p. 238.

82. Upham, Absolute Religion, p. 300.

83. Ibid.

84. Ibid., pp. 301-302.

85. Ibid., p. 308.

86. Ibid., p. 311.

87. Ibid., p. 305. The Rev. Edward E. Hale, pastor of Boston's Congregational South Church, wrote of Finney's preaching in 1858: "The doctrine beneath (his) language is the doctrine from which old Calvinism is to meet its inevitable doom. It is the Quaker doctrine, the Methodist doctrine, the Transcendental doctrine--that God is, every moment, with every child, in a union so close that nothing can be compared with it." Taken from Timothy Smith's Revivalism and Social Reform, p. 97. Smith states Upham "joined Wesleyanism to mysticism in a dozen thoughtful books, which bridged the chasm between Christian piety and transcendentalism" (p. 41).

88. Fenelon, Christian Perfection, p. 8.

89. Inge, p. 258. For an excellent essay on the mystical understanding of sacraments, read D. Elton Trueblood's "A Sacramental World," A People Called Quakers. (New York City: Harper and Row Publishers, 1966), pp. 128-147.

Also see "The Quaker Vocation," "If we start with the central idea that Quakerism is nothing but 'Christianity writ plain,' we have an excellent beginning in the effort to know what the people called Quakers ought to do in the modern world. The task is to try to be faithful and intelligent Apostles of Christ, in the world, the particular emphasis being determined in the light of each particular experience." Trueblood, p. 268.

90. Fenelon, Letters, p. 124.

91. Madame Guyon, Spiritual Torrents, p. 108.

92. Upham, Madame Guyon, Volume II, p. 236.

93. Upham, American Cottage Life, p. 106.

94. From Emerson's editorial "Introduction" in the first issue of the Transcendentalist Dial in 1836, quoted in Frederick Ives Carpenter's essay "Transcendentalism," American Transcendentalism: An Anthology of Criticism, ed. by Brevin M. Barbour (Notre Dame, Ind.: University of Notre Dame Press, 1973), p. 29.

95. Ibid., p. 408.

96. Ibid., p. 433.

97. Ibid., p. 416.

98. Upham, Absolute Religion, p. 275.

99. See poem "Work Today" from Upham's Christ in the Soul, pp. 98-99.

100. Upham, Madame Guyon, Volume I, p. 84.
101. Ibid., p. 133.
102. Upham, Interior Life, p. 374.
103. Ibid.
104. Ibid.
105. Upham, Absolute Religion, p. 264.
106. Upham, Madame Guyon, Volume I, p. 259.
107. Ibid., p. 332.
108. Ibid., Volume II, p. 165.
109. Ibid., p. 371.
110. Upham, Catherine Adorna, p. 92.
111. Ibid., p. 93.
112. Upham, Life of Faith, pp. 210-211.
113. Upham, Divine Union, p. 157.
114. Madame Guyon, Spiritual Torrents, p. 39.
115. Inge, p. 183.
116. Récéjac, p. 56.
117. Underhill, the Mystical Way, p. 69.
118. Dieter, p. 53.

Chapter VI

CONSTRUCTING A HOLINESS ETHIC

Thomas Upham held the "Chair of Mental and Moral Philosophy" at Bowdoin College, which implies he was both a psychologist and an ethicist. In this chapter and the next, these areas will be investigated as to their influence on his holiness theology. Upham never wrote a textbook on ethics per se, but there is plenty of material in his writings that suggests that the field was one he investigated.

In a sense, Upham's mental philosophy was only a means to an end, i.e., an attempt to discover from the laws of the mind, the laws of ethical obligation. French reminds us that the understanding of God's moral order as derived from the investigation of the mind, "came to be increasingly accepted as the most important implication of mental philosophy...."[1] In the 1830s, academicians expressed renewed interest in this concept; from the beginning of Upham's writing for print, evidence exists that he was at the vanguard of this nineteenth-century endeavor. Concerning Upham's work on the moral nature of the sensibilities, his contemporary, Robert Vaughn, wrote that Upham

> has rendered the greatest service to mental science, by the original and masterly exposition he has given of man's moral nature. The connexion, the mutual dependence of these two great problems in mental and moral philosophy--what are man's moral susceptibilities, his moral nature? and the other, the determination of which constitutes ethics, properly, so called--what is right action? are admirably explained and illustrated. This connexion has been too frequently overlooked by theologians; they have attempted to sever mental and moral philosophy.[2]

Immutability of Moral Law

For Upham, an absolute moral law is written into the nature of the universe--a law that is as eternal as God himself. If moral law is dependent on the will of God, then God could have not been moral until he willed some particular command or moral premise.[3] Morality is not dependent on God's arbitrary enactment or volition but is written into the very nature of God, and God will never violate his character. God does not define love, honesty, justice, etc., but universal virtues define God. This does not mean that man cannot increase his understanding of these virtues by God's divine revelation, but the proposition that "It is right because God says it," had little meaning for Upham.

> For if God's will or mere enactment constitutes itself, and independently of everything else, all right and wrong, then the assertion that God is right or just, is obviously an identical proposition; and is the same as to say that he is what he is, and does what he does.[4]

The above view was certainly not unique to Upham. A review of Archibald Alexander's Outlines of Moral Science pointed out that God cannot deny the eternal standard of rectitude that is inherent to his existence.[5] Asa Mahan was adamant that God wished or performed an act because it was right and not vice versa.[6] James Fairchild, also "saw no virtue whatever in defining 'right' as whatever God wills."[7] Thus, it became a major objective of moral philosophers to construct an ethical system upon a theoretical basis that consisted of the objectivity and immutability of moral law.[8] The Wesleyan-Arminian theologians were in complete agreement. Richard Watson indicated that holiness was essential to the nature of God, and that rectitude must be the spring and guide of his own conduct.[9] Luther Lee argued that the position which premised right or wrong on God's will or declarations, "would make God's moral government, wholly an arbitrary matter, and render it responsible for all the moral wrong that exists."[10] No one stated it clearer than Thomas N. Ralston:

> As sweet and sour, straight and crooked, denote abstract qualities, having a real existence, independent of the physical substances to which they

> may be attached; so right and wrong, good and bad, denote abstract principles, having a real existence in themselves, independent of all internal emotion or external action to which they may be applied; hence, we conclude that rectitude is an abstract principle, eternal and immutable as the attributes of God. Indeed, it is a principle inhering in, and essentially pertaining to, the divine nature.[11]

Thus, among most academic philosophers and theologians of the nineteenth century, there was an explicit move against any kind of simplistic teleological utilitarianism that argued for determining the worth of action according to the results of said action. For Mahan and Upham, virtue--regardless of consequences--was intrinsically an abstract principle. Upham wrote that

> uprightness or virtue is an object to be contemplated in itself, and to be loved and practiced for its own sake. It is to be loved, and honored, and practiced, not simply because it is commanded, not simply because it may in its results be beneficial, but solely for itself, and out of regard to its own exalted nature.[12]

Ostensibly, the argument was opposed to Paley's utilitarianism; but, even more importantly, it attempted to counterbalance both the sacred and the secular currents that were swelling the mainstream of mid-nineteenth century popular evangelicalism.

Long before the formation of William James' pragmatism, the practical effects of nineteenth-century revivalism were being used to authenticate evangelistic activities. Finney's productive methodology and a capitalism that produced wealth and bigness were to win, in evangelical and holiness circles, what philosophical arguments in the classroom failed to achieve. Finney's teleological revivalism was to have a profound effect on the nineteenth-century holiness camp-meeting thrust, with which Upham did not identify. In answering criticism of his manner of preaching, Finney said:

> Show me a more excellent way. Show me the fruits of your ministry; and if they so far exceed mine as to give me evidence that you have found a more

> excellent way, I will adopt your views. But do you expect me to abandon my own views and practices, and adopt yours, when you yourselves cannot deny that, whatever errors I may have fallen into, or whatever imperfections there may be in my preaching, in style, and in everything else, yet the results justify my methods.[13]

Deontology

Upham's ethics, like the ethics of most of the contemporary moral philosophers, was decidedly deontological. The expedience of revivalism and commercialism had a greater appeal to the popular mind than did the immutability of moral distinctions. Had America paid more attention to Upham's cogent arguments, it might have escaped the developing sectarian and provincial interpretations of God's will.

A basic understanding exists in all languages of distinction between the term _right_ and that which represents mere personal good, interest or happiness, and "between the terms _utile_ and _honestum_."[14] In supporting his deontology, Upham argued that men are judged by their motives and not by their overt acts. He also asserted that civil law, in judging right from wrong, uses an external absolute standard.[15] Above all, the means never justify the end.

> In the discharge of those duties which are incumbent upon us, if our hearts are right with God, we shall consider it indispensably necessary to employ just means, as well as to aim at just ends. And however just and desirable the ends may be, in themselves considered, if the methods or means are such as we cannot rightfully employ, we must always regard the end as forbidden.[16]

Universal Law

Throughout Upham's writings, an intuitive appeal to universal law is present, which is prerequisite to any kind of supernatural revelation. Upham's Kantian optimism implies that the moral good is self-evident. The concept of God is universal; thus the concept of worship and the concept of law.[17]

The basis for all law is love, which is perceived, at least to some extent, by all people and can be universally observed.[18] An inherent law exists within individuals and tells them that God is love and that He is the universal embodiment of an immutable categorical imperative. "He was not at first, as some may be led to suppose, a mere precipient being, having all knowledge, who formed conjecturally an idea of love, came to the conclusion that it was a good and desirable thing, and then as an accessory to his original existence."[19] The love of God, which is apparent to the moral nature of human beings, defines the ought of the universe. The permanent and controlling element of his nature sustains the rectitude or right within the nature of things.[20] Harold Kuhn accurately described and, at the same time, criticized this kind of approach to ethical formulation:

> The metaphysical type of ethic assumes that the principles of right and good are embedded in the universe, and that the cosmos will support only what it is, and render certain and condign punishment for it. This takes for granted that man can properly and adequately read the moral cipher of the universe --an assumption which is difficult to support by an appeal to human history.[21]

The belief that benevolent affections were innate and at least partially understood, was in keeping with Scottish common-sense philosophy.[22] The obligation to love could be naturally understood, but only revelation could fill in the blanks and stipulate the minutia of ethical performance. Wilson Smith argued that American moral philosophers affirmed their own theology by attempting to demonstrate that the "intuitionism of a secular, moral sense philosophy was compatible with the dictates of revealed religion."[23] The primal law of love has been imperfectly revealed to every heart, but only Christ can clarify its forms and practical applications. Smith wrote:

> It is the basic law of the universe; and Christ came not merely to announce it as a principle, but to fulfill it as a fact, in order that men seeing with their own eyes that love is ready to pour out its heart-blood for the good of others, might understand and know, as they otherwise could not do, the moral basis on which the universe stands.[24]

Upham offered an extensive argument regarding why he believed in humanity's innate moral conscience and the universality of absolute law. In children, decisive feelings exist toward cruelty and crime on one hand and toward benevolence or virtue on the other.[25] Man respects the conscience of his fellow man and deals with him according to fair play.[26] Every language has terms and distinctions; these indicate "that the foundation of moral emotions and of feelings of moral obligation is actually laid in the human constitution."[27] There are universal ideas of moral merit and demerit, of reward and punishment.[28] Savages evidence a natural conscience, demonstrate a desire to do good to their fellow man, and show a regard for kindness, truth, and justice.[29] There are universal traits of similarity in civil or political form and similar principles of regard for conduct and character that run through the literature of historians of all ages.[30] Upham concluded his argument with scripture:

> For when the Gentiles, which have not the law, do by nature the things contained in the law, these, having not the law, are a law unto themselves; which show the work of the law written in their hearts, their conscience also bearing witness, and their thoughts the meanwhile accusing, or else excusing one another.[31]

Use of the Bible

Both mysticism and metaphysics tended to remove Upham from the Bible-centered arguments that were common to nineteenth-century holiness exponents. Nothing even close to an extensive Biblical argument for Christian perfection can be found anywhere in Upham's writings. This void is somewhat strange, taking into consideration that Upham studied under Moses Stuart, a fanatical exegete of the scriptures who wrote: "The Bible is a revelation by *language*. To know what it teaches, *language* must be studied and understood."[32] Upham did know languages, but virtually no exegesis can be found anywhere in his writings. He quotes verses for two reasons: to support the spiritual experience of his biographical subjects or to lend weight to philosophical arguments.

In his attempt to demonstrate that holiness was The Central Idea of Christianity, Jesse Peck was staying true to his Wesleyan heritage when he wrote:

> The great idea, which originated the several parts of this amazing scheme, is to be ascertained, not by accidental reading or limited study of the Bible, but by the strictest attention to its drift. Principles, in the abstract and in the concrete, must be collated with the utmost care. The minutest particular, as well as the most prominent and extensive, must be viewed in their relation to each other, and the grand scope of the whole divine teaching ascertained.[33]

One of the practical results of the above, was that Upham was not nearly so prescriptive in ethical application as was Wesley. Scripture for Wesley was used to enforce a lifestyle that included rules for drinking, cursing, Sabbath-breaking, fighting, unaccustomed goods, usury, etc. Concerning the "General Rules of the United Societies," Wesley wrote: "If there be any among us who observe them not, who habitually break any of them, let it be made known unto them who watch over that soul as they must give an account."[34]

No sort of pedantic exhortation can be found in Upham. Perhaps a partial explanation for this absence is that, unlike Wesley, Upham was not charged with the care of souls. Upham's exposition of an ethical norm, based upon a mystical relationship with God, was to have no effect on the later legalistic pronouncements of the holiness movement. The movement's conflict with the established Church and the psychological need for identity both called for institutionalizing a manner of dress, prohibition of jewelry, rules against smoking, and regulations for the Sabbath. Charles Jones demonstrated how the experience of entire sanctification came to be associated with prohibitions against certain items of behavior or practice:

> While adoption of new terms signalled no significant theological change, new terminology pointed to a new method of determining the loyalty of individuals within the holiness camp, a method, which ultimately delineated social requirements for admission to the

> holiness group. Identifying inward purity for decorous conduct, holiness evangelists often confused the two. In the belief that extravagant dress indicated inward haughtiness, some condemned ruffles, feathers, jewelry, (including wedding rings), and corsets.[35]

Upham's explanation of keeping the Sabbath is a case in point of his nonlegalistic casuistry. Actually, the Sabbath is not holier than any other day; we are to be holy on all days and do those things that will bring glory to God. The emphasis is not on prohibitions of different activities, but on the necessity on the Sabbath for proclaiming the gospel message, the need for bodily rest, and a season for moral and religious reflection and worship. The emphasis is positive rather than negative, in that the Sabbath is "the great, the cheering hope of the human race."[36]

Upham came to the unique conclusion that, in a sense, the Sabbath is made for the non-Christian rather than for the Christian: "That is to say, the holy man, who has a perpetual Sabbath in his soul, could perhaps, do without it, while the unholy man could not."[37] The activities that are appropriate for glorifying God on the Sabbath are different from activities for the other six days:

> But it ought to be particularly remembered, while we admit that the requisition of holiness attaches itself to all days alike, and that one day is not and cannot be more holy than another; and they are alike by sameness of disposition, and not by similarity of outward acts.[38]

Liberty

Upham's ethic of love is a liberty above the law, but in no sense is it a license. Therefore, Upham could never be accurately accused of antinomianism. There is a freedom to do as one wants to, but that freedom exists only because one has passed from "ought to" to "want to." The sanctified does what he delights in because his delights have been correctly prioritized. There is rest from the enthrallments and appetites of the world; that is to say, the Christian is no longer tyrannized by the lower or appetitive part of his nature.[39] A person experiencing true liberty will not attach stronger affection to parents, family, country, political party, etc., than he or she does to God.[40] The individual will not be so enslaved to "disinclination," "aversions," and "refined mental habits," that he cannot minister to the profane, the poor, the outcast.[41] A holy person will be sufficiently distanced from his own judgements and presuppositions to be able to overlook the constitutional differences and taste preferences of others.[42]

A liberty or freedom circumscribed by law, which is at the heart of Upham's mental philosophy, became focal for his holiness theology. It is not unlike the spiritual freedom found in mysticism. Such acquiescence exists to the will of God that there is calmness in facing loss of time, loss of things, and adverse turns of events. Liberty of holiness means an inner transcendence over space-time limitations. In the performing of duty, the Christian at rest in God's will is able to leave the results of his or her actions in God's hands. Such submission exists in obedience that the anxiety of performance is gone; the Christian simply has to obey and allow God to effect the obedience in whatever way he sees fit.

> It may be laid down as a maxim, that he who asserts that he has left all things in the hands of God and at the same time exhibits trouble and agitation of spirit in relation to the results of those very things, (with the exception of those agitated movements or disquietudes which are purely instinctive), gives abundant evidence in the fact of this agitation of spirit, that he has not really made the entire surrender which he professes to have made.[43]

True Virtue

What is the essence of virtue for Upham? He was in total agreement with Jonathan Edwards believing that true virtue consists in love of existence or being in general. It does not consist of affections aroused by objects or by people, which have immediate influence on the subject.[44]

Upham, in his lengthy discourse on the benevolent affections, parental affections, filial affections, fraternal love for the human race, the philanthropic principle, patriotism, etc., argued they could all result from instincts and emotions, and therefore, were devoid of moral character.[45] He implied that, at times, pure instincts are not enough to carry out benevolent affections--even in the above relationships--during those times, the voluntary action of duty must take over.[46]

Upham illustrated this assertion by saying that a mother, in reviewing her responsibilities toward her child, may find herself wanting and thus makes a decision to improve the situation. The ensuing voluntary action is virtuous, and henceforth, moral.

Edwards would have disagreed. He was too interested in defining true virtue as a sui generis experience and making it completely independent of anything that smacked of self-love. The natural impulses of pity and gratitude, love between the sexes, love between parents and children, a sense of justice and sanction of virtue, all stem from the psychological factors of natural instinct, association of ideas, and secondary beauty--such as are found in a well-ordered society.[47] Edwards wrote

> that no affections toward particular persons of Being are of the nature of true virtue, but such as arise from a general benevolent temper, or from that habit or frame of mind, wherein consists a disposition to love Being in general.[48]

This disposition could only come through divine grace. Love of friends, sense of justice, desert, and gratitude actually derive from self-love, because all either consciously or unconsciously take into consideration how the self should be treated.[49]

Upham was not as clear as Edwards on the necessity of regenerating grace for perceiving the morally beautiful or sublime. True virtue, for Edwards, was a kind of beauty perceived not by the natural intellect or understanding but by a changed disposition and will.[50] The ability of a person to perceive has been thwarted by the principle of self-love.[51] Predestined grace is the only means by which man can perceive and perform true virtue.[52] In contrast, moral beauty, for Upham, is an innate abstract conception of the soul, which enables a person to envision and detect a beauty of a moral kind.[53]

> The ability to contemplate moral worth, wherever it exists, in the aspect of the beautiful, and to throw around it lustre, which has its origin in the fountains of the heart, is equivocally an important fact in the history of the mind.[54]

The reason why some people have a clearer perception of moral beauty than others is not due to sovereign grace but to differences in temperament[55] and also to the fact that some individuals have voluntarily yielded too great an ascendance to the lower principles of nature.[56] Upham did admit that the light of moral beauty as it relates to the Supreme Being can be fully realized only by hearts that are themselves morally pure.[57] Thus, there is a qualitative distinction between the supernatural and the natural (both Edwards and Wesley would have been pleased with this view).

Upham's defective view of the fall, however, later undermined his apparent orthodoxy. Moral sublimity does not differ from mere moral beauty in kind or quality so much as it does in degree.[58] Since in the particular passage under review, Upham was writing for a secular purpose, it may be that he was too reticent to point out how moral sublimity differs for Christian and non-Christian.

Despite the above difference, Upham's ethic of love is decidedly Edwardian laced with a touch of transcendentalism. In the true Edwardian fashion, Upham defined love as "a desire for the good or happiness of everything which exists."[59] In God, who unites and consolidates all things in himself, we love the infinitude of being, the life of the universe, the everywhere present, the silent but universal operator, the all in all.[60] This is the basis for all other kinds of love;[61] a love that extends to the animate and inanimate.

Upham could not understand how anyone bearing the divine image could "mar the face of nature by needlessly crushing a flower...."[62] Even more inexcusable was anyone's purposely marring or diminishing the happiness of a sentient being.[63] Upham was an adamant exponent of reverence for life and God's creation. But to love that which is unlovely and to love unconditionally that which is enmity, can only be accomplished by partaking of the divine nature;

> to separate between existence and character, and to attach affection to the mere reality of being simply because it is being; and, whatever may be its relations of harmony or of opposition to us or to others, to seek, to pray, and to labor for its redemption, to purity and to happiness, simply because it is susceptible of such redemption, and without thought of personal reward; this is love, of which reason, in being unable to explain it, can only say, it is of God.[64]

Self and Selfishness

The above can take place while the person retains a moral self-love, but it is not compatible with the heart of selfishness. Upham was always clear in distinguishing between the two. Neither Upham nor Edwards would agree with Hopkins that self-love is wickedness in disguise.[65] "A heart free from selfishness and filled with pure love will be precisely conformed to its object."[66] It will love God supremely above all other objects. But to not love self at all would be a love disproportional to its object because the creature recognizes self as having come from God. God will approve self-love and self-preservation as guiltless if, "in the pursuit of our own happiness, we have a suitable regard to the claim of all other beings, especially the Supreme Being."[67] Upham wrote: "It is the nature of perfect love in its forgetfulness of self, to array the object toward which it is directed in every possible excellence."[68] H. B. Smith said Upham taught that self-love in its "primeval, abstract, almost-ideal character" is innocent, but it is the perversion of self-love which is properly called "selfishness."[69]

Justice

Upham differed from Edwards in regard to justice. Edwards believed that justice, grounded as it is in how a person wants others to respond to him, turned love into a secondary principle. Upham believed that jutice regulated love and saved it from sentimentality, that, in turn, both justice and love regulate life.[70]

Even love itself, an element so essential to all moral goodness that it gives a character and name to God, ceases to be love the moment it ceases to be in conformity with justice. Love that is not just is not holy, and love that is not holy is selfishness under the name of love.[71] A belief that justice is an equally important attribute of God precluded Upham from arguing for any type of universalism. The belief certainly disallowed anyone's teaching that God predetermined a certain number to damnation in order to enhance the happiness of those who would experience holiness and subsequent bliss.[72] For Upham, justice fulfilled and complemented love and did not contradict it.

Wesley adopted this view as did the holiness movement. Adam Clarke wrote:

> God never acts from one of his attributes exclusively, but in the infinite unity of all his attributes. He never acts from benevolence to the exclusion of justice; nor from justice to the exclusion of mercy.... Even justice itself on the ground of its holy and eternal nature gives salvation to the violent who take refuge in Christ's atonement; for justice has nothing to grant or Heaven to give which the blood of the Son of God has not merited.[73]

Inviolability of Life

The above sentiments led to the basic principle that was to influence and be the ruling motif for all of Thomas Upham's practical ethics, the inviolability of life; for Upham, all life was sacred. At times, Upham's reverence for life bordered on sentimentalism. "It is no more possible for God to see the smallest insect crushed and put to death without feeling an interest in it, than it would be for him to witness the fall and destruction of the highest angel without feeling an interest."[74]

There could be no higher teleology than the protection and preservation of human life. Life defines love, and love defines life, and the two together are a unit, an end in itself. Whatever qualitatively and quantitatively enhances life is of intrinsic worth. If Upham maintained a categorical imperative, it is that the inviolability of life is an a priori ethical commitment.[75]

> Human life is sacred; it is the gift of God; it is that which nothing short of divine power can create; and no hand of man or angel, no principality or power of heaven or earth can lawfully touch it without the permission of that Being, who gave it existence.[76]

Pacifism

Immediately after writing his Treatise on the Will, Upham wrote as urgent an argument against war as he could possibly construct.[77] His scheme for an international court that would settle global disputes, was not an original idea. The President of Bowdoin, William Allen, had advocated the concept before the Phi Beta Society, September 5, 1833. Allen used the standard antiwar arguments: destruction of human agency, loss of wealth, innocent victims crushed, maimed, and homeless. Both Allen and Upham graphically painted the horrors of war. According to Allen, the central problem is that every nation is a judge in its own case and cause, without any internationally-established rules, courts, impleaders, recorders, or sacred halls of justice.[78] One cannot depend on the prevalence of the Gospel to automatically cure the evils of war. Means are necessary for ends, and moral changes among men must be effected by the toils and influence of men.[79] Allen demonstrated the usual millennial optimism:

> Questionless, the time is hastening on, when men will look back upon days of war with indescribable emotions of astonishment and horror, wondering by what demoniac frenzy their brethren were instigated, that they should array themselves against each other in battle, and deal about destruction with every instrument of death, and send each other's spirits into eternity to the judgement seat, while burning with malignity and rage.[80]

What direct influence Allen had on Upham is difficult to determine, but a crucial difference exists in their views. Allen justified an unavoidable defensive war, while Upham was a pure pacifist.

As magistrate of a town that was attacked by an alien

force, Upham would open the churches and exhort the people to pray for God to change the hearts of the alien invaders.[81] And, if God did not effect the change, it would be better to die "in the spirit of innocence, forgiveness, and love, praying like Stephen for your murderers, than to die succeeders and murderers yourselves."[82] Upham conceded the likelihood of losing his own life by total nonresistance, saying that the avoidance of war would spare his family and property.[83] By not retaliating, the victor of attack has the advantage whatever his fate. If he loses his life, less total destruction shall have been unleashed on life and property. But "if I succeed, what a contrast to his success."[84] Upham did not wrestle with those evils that some consider worse than death, such as loss of liberty or enslavement.

Ethical Optimism

The ambiguities of choosing a lesser evil for a greater evil did not seem to occur to the author. Implementation of the principles of Christ will always conquer in its contest with evil.[85] This view, then, was the mystical optimism that said love could exist without any mixture of self, and such purity of conscience could always distinguish clearly between right and wrong.[86] There is little sense of Richard Niebuhr's dualism, which mirrors the actual struggles of the Christian who "lives between the times" and, because of his conflict, "cannot presume to live by the ethics of that time of glory which he ardently hopes."[87]

Upham was influenced by an ideal view of the primitive church and by the conviction that the principles of the millenium could be implemented today. He gave little recognition to the necessity of God having to deal with man as he is at the present, i.e., in light of the "hardness of his heart."

For Upham no difference exists between the personal ethic and the national ethic. The private and corporate ethic are the same; they both "turn the other cheek." "If nations are treated as moral persons, it must be on the ground, that they have the character, attributes, and rights of persons; and that there is some analogy between them."[88] But Upham went beyond the teachings of Christ. If nations reject protecting themselves externally by arms, then no need exists for civil government to protect, internally, either itself or its citizens. Upham takes his pacifism to its logical conclusion: do away with law enforcement. "There are elements in human nature, which will infallibly secure the existence and advancement of society, if there is a suitable share of benevolence and justice in the administration of the concerns."[89]

Optimism that man can rationally settle his disputes with a priori commitments to equity and fairness, is the philosophical premise that undergirds the entirety of Upham's argument. High-raised battlements and moated gates can be replaced by the knowledge of rights, the spirit of justice, magnanimous temper and the "obligation of doing good to others as we desire them to do to ourselves."[90] The inability or unwillingness to recognize the fallen nature of man has reached its most practical implementation. Or was it Upham's projection of his own pacifistic psychological temperament of the world around him? "It is one of the honorable characteristics of the present age, that there is a universal disposition to substitute reason for violence, and the logic of good advice for that of blame and bloodshed."[91]

Minimal polarization exists between the city of God and the city of earth. In the words of Richard Niebuhr, there is resolute affirmation "that the God who is to rule now rules and has ruled, that His rule is established in the nature of things, and that man must build on the established foundation."[92] The gradual progress of the present dispensation of Christ has now brought man to the potential for love reigning supreme. Upham wrote:

> The necessities and sufferings of mankind, the inefficiency of existing means of redress, the experience of past ages, the deduction of reasoning, the prophetic anticipations of benevolence, the opinions of wise and learned men, the advancements in civilization and freedom, all seem to point in one direction; all seem to be verging to a common centre.[93]

The common centre is the overruling principle of the gospel of love, which Upham believed could conquer all evils. But his argument was more than a sentimental appeal to the brotherhood of man. It was a call for the rationale to give careful consideration to the logical and moral implications of war.[94] If we teach individuals to kill and destroy, such action will obscure their moral distinctions. Individuals are placed in situations where they are destitute of wholesome moral and religious influence, and the person who goes "from his father's hand a human being, endued with human feelings, returns with the guilt and stupidity and hardness of a monster."[95]

Upham was entirely pessimistic as to the effect of military chaplains. If they were men of deep religious feeling and had an earnestness to save souls, they would not put themselves in a situation "where there is so little prospect of doing good."[96] When Upham recognized the vanity of chaplains praying for the success of their own armies, he was hinting at the folly of a nation's being transcended over God. The presence of chaplains tends to sanction the error that the Gospel justifies war.[97]

Slavery

Upham sincerely believed that the problem of war could be conquered by men who live by the principles of the Gospel, "by [their] looking the great subject fearlessly in the face, not only in its outlines but its details."[98] Upham never admitted, that instead of illuminating the path to solution, understanding could create ambiguities and complexities. Thus, he was to be blind-sided by a dilemma that, if understood, he certainly never fully explicated.

No immediate way existed that could abolish slavery and, at the same time, remain pacifistic. Timothy Smith defended the holiness movement's lack of overt activity against slavery by arguing that they were inhibited by their love of the slaveholder.[99] Smith recognized that Upham and many others were caught in the middle; they "dared not forsake either the slave or the Golden Rule."[100]

Upham stated that the "great object of moral reform was to bring the code of nations in strict conformity with the code of Jesus Christ,"[101] but he never saw that if there were not conflicts within the code, at least the precepts were not worked out to perfectly satisfying and practical, non-conflicting implications.[102] Since the real problem was the depravity of man and the solution was redemption through Jesus Christ, grounds existed for abstaining from, in the words of Leonard Woods, Jr.: "violent and irritating operations, as directly injurious to his cause." The prudent reformer "seeks, even with reference to particular reform, to multiply and strengthen all those general influences of example, law, education, arts, and religion, by which the moral dispositions of mankind are regulated and improved."[103]

That Upham was a gradualist, does not mean he was inconsistent with his principle of human sanctity or had a defective view of natural rights. It also does not mean that, believing the system a necessary evil, he acquiesced to it or succumbed to a culture marked by inequities and perpetual uneasiness, conditions at variance with abstract conceptions of a perfect state. What it does mean is this: if an American could manage to recognize the divine image in every human being, he or she would no longer find it possible "to hold his brother man in slavery or to maltreat him or injure him in any way whatever."[104] But an implicit acquiescence to the providence of God can, in regards to the affairs of men, become complacency.[105]

This acquiescence occurred in spite of Upham's maxim that "no person can be considered as praying in sincerity for a specified object, who does not employ all the appropriate natural means which he can, to secure the object."[106] But on the whole, theologically and ideologically, Upham was forced to look for the bright side of all events, and slavery was no exception. He wrote:

> Is it not possible, that the Supreme Being, in permitting this race to be carried to America has done it with the design of giving them a knowledge of the English language, of modern acts, and civilization, of free political institutions, and especially of the Christian religion--in order that in due time and under the providence of God, they may carry back the arts, and freedom, and Christianity to benighted and suffering Africa?[107]

The "middle axiom" between radical immediatism and support of the slave trade was colonization. Upham was a lifelong member of the African Colonization Society, giving as much as $1,000 at one time for the cause. Despite, during the 1840s and 1850s, the growing realization of the society's impotence, Upham, like Lyman Beecher, did not give up on the cause as a valid alternative to the nation's number one problem.[108] But there was hardly more patience with pure "immediatism" and with Garrisonian outrage within the northeast and especially Congregationalists. In his argument against the effectiveness of Garrison and the American Anti-slavery Society, Gilbert Barnes wrote:

> Some general action by the Congregational Churches condemning the Boston abolitionists was inevitable; but that the action should close the Churches to their agents, and by unanimous vote as well, was fatal to the Boston movement.[109]

Upham's idealization of the primitive church,[110] and his visionary utopian hopes of the coming millennium, which would finally recognize that "all slave-holding is a sin,"[111] eclipsed the urgency of acting in the present. He was against using force to stop the slave trade; its demise would be effected by destroying the market at home.[112]

Upham's hesitancy to take urgent action does not mean that he closed his eyes to gross atrocities. "It shocks humanity to add that the wretched slaves, in a number of instances, have been thrown overboard alive, as they were mere ballast, and not our brethren, bone of our bone and flesh of our flesh."[113] But Upham was an institutionalist who saw no need of going through unaccepted channels while there remained an explicit conviction that republican government, based on a priori assumptions of natural law and inherent rights, would ultimately bring about equality. Upham's institutionalism was the same kind that marked John Wesley's reform and, as Francis McConnell implied, prevented him from exploding now and then against the English system.

Upham and Wesley both believed that one did not have to acquiesce to the evils of the system, but at the same time, the men saw no need for radical revolt.[114] Both were patient with working within the confines of the system, and both would have been in agreement with Leonard Woods, Jr.:

> These views of the true reformer respecting the nature of his work repress the visionary expectation

> of sudden and immediate change, and lead him even to prefer, that improvement should be made gradually.... That tender sense of justice too, which distinguishes the true reformer from the radical revolutionist, leads him to seek the general good with the least possible sacrifice of private rights, and therefore to allow time for the escape of those most nearly interested in the devoted system, and who would be overwhelmed with ruin, should its subversion be immediate...."[115]

Capital Punishment

The inviolability of human life extended to a categorical stand against capital punishment. Upham admitted that, because of the hardness of men's hearts, God suspended "Thou shalt not kill" in the Old Testament dispensation. But the same injunction in the New Testament is an unqualified, unequivocal commandment.[116] Neither communities nor individuals have the right to take a life.[117] Upham proceeded to show that execution does not fulfill the true ends of punishment: "reparation for injury done," "the reformation and good of the offender himself," "the direct protection of society against future attacks by the same individual," and the benefit of the example on other "evil disposed persons."[118] Execution cannot restore or make restitution for what has already been done.[119] If one uses the analogy that the civil government is a parent to society, it does not make sense that a parent would punish a child by execution.[120]

Upham expended a good deal of ink arguing that capital punishment is not an example, and therefore, does not serve as a deterrent to crime. Even though Henry VIII executed people at the rate of 2,000 per year, his actions didn't seem to have had any beneficial effect.[121] Of course, the problem always exists of establishing with absolute certainty whether one has indeed committed a crime.

Throughout his argument, Upham was optimistic that man can be reformed. Environment, he said, can be a determining factor in the formation of character and more effective than one's resorting to threats of retributive violence. Capital punishment serves only to harden society and to lessen the value of human life. Upham may have presented one of America's most cogent pre-Civil War arguments against capital punishment.[122]

> The more you raise the standards of character in the community, the more you can lower the scale of penal enactments. A mild criminal code will assuredly answer in a well-informed and virtuous community; and no legislature is at liberty to adopt a severe one, until it has tried every means to diffuse intelligence and uprightness.[123]

Redemption of Society

Contrary to what the preceding statement suggests, Upham did not believe the individual could be reformed by placing him or her in the proper surrounding. The redemption and elevation of society can take place only through the elevation and redemption of the individual.[124] Individual salvation through Christ happens first--and then the subsequent restoration of society.[125] Only when people are filled with the Holy Spirit and apply the principles of scripture can communities and nations be transformed.[126] The schedule a person must follow for restoration is the following:

> His first work is to perfect his own nature; or rather to let God do it by leaving himself in the hands of the divine operator. But in being perfected in himself, he is perfected at the same time in the relation he sustains to others. In being a better man, he is not only a better father and husband, but a better citizen;--and while he labors and prays for the new and perfected life of those immediately around him, he does what he can for the restoration of all others in all places.[127]

The above paragraph brought to light two very important implications for nineteenth-century perfectionism, at least as Upham represented it. First, Upham demonstrated a strong sense of collective responsibility--what might be called corporate sanctification. As the holiness movement matured throughout the century, sin was increasingly interpreted as an isolated individual act; hence, the need for individual or private sanctification. By the twentieth century, the holiness movement had become somewhat separatist and forgotten its solidarity with the evangelical mainstream--if not its link with the whole human race. The proliferation of camp meetings became somewhat escapist in mentality, and the later separation from the mainline denominations provided a sectarian emphasis for the movement. Entire sanctification became an intensely private matter experienced in a ritualistic manner as interpreted by the particular group of which one was a member.[128] In his Ratio Discipline, Upham pointed out the need for one's church expressing affections and interest in other churches, and "to assert and insist on the great principle of Congregationalism, that the churches are not independent of each other, but are bound by the principles of the Gospel, to exercise a mutual watch, love, and assistance."[128]

For Upham, the ethics of being "my brother's keeper" not only expanded within Congregationalism but extended to other denominations and the unregenerate as well. A realization that one is part of the problem leads to a belief that one needs to be a part of the solution.

Upham wrote: "And it remains to be added that men are not only judged in their individual capacity, but they necessarily take their share of the judgement which falls upon corporate bodies and associations and communities, of which they are members."[129] Because of our being part of the human family, suffering and punishment comes upon those who may have not individually deserved it and because of the great connective laws of nature, "there comes a common liability of error that extends throughout the whole human race."[130]

Upham faced many of the issues that concerned antebellum nineteenth-century evangelicals and especially theological perfectionists--peace, slavery, women's rights, and temperance.[131] The Upham story is one that, at least to some extent, supports Donald Dayton's thesis that "evangelical social ethics have been largely grounded in themes of sanctification."[132] Such themes usually lead to dichotomous thinking and are not slowed down by the ambiguities of moral issues. Absolutes--not compromises--are the framework for operation. An idealistic operationalism takes precedence over the institutionalized process of the establishment.

But sufficient adherence to the establishment existed, also enough sense of ambiguity, to prevent the kind of single-eyed reform that marked Oberlin. Timothy Smith wrote:

> All of the socially-potent doctrines of revivalism reached white heat in the Oberlin and Wesleyan experience of sanctification--ethical seriousness, the call to full personal consecration, the belief in God's immanence, in his readiness to transform the present world through the outpoured Holy Ghost, and the exaltation of Christian love.[133]

Upham believed in all of the above, but yet they did not stem from the "white heat" of revivalism. There was more of a restraint and a moderation and perhaps even a certain degree of academic and mystical detachment. Wilson Smith is at least partially right about Upham when he makes the following observation concerning the nineteenth-century moral philosophers: "In their textbooks, academic moralists never really did come to grips with problems of democratic politics--the new industrialism, immigration, urbanism, or a hundred and one other challenges of mid-nineteenth century America."[134]

Eschatology

A consideration of theological ethics deserves a brief notation on eschatology, eternal reward and punishment. Little that Upham asserted indicates that he conceived of the doctrines of heaven and hell as integrally motivating performance of duty. The mystical eternal now and the belief that the hope of future consolation somewhat undermined faith, did not allow for sharp dichotomies between this life and the next. In fact, the lack of clarity regarding the final abode of the "cursed" and the "blessed" would have made later nineteenth-century fundamentalists uncomfortable. Though Upham did not deny the reality of heaven or hell, he preferred to stress states of mind rather than localities.[135] Just as an inevitable distinction exists between right and wrong, so an infinite gulf stands between heaven and hell.[136] "So that happiness resulting from conformity with spiritual laws constitutes heaven, and unhappiness resulting from a violation of these laws constitutes hell."[137] The walls and gates of each are the laws that rule them, and the fitness of those laws determines where a man will spend eternity.[138] In other words, a man automatically goes, not where God sends him, but where he is in--not out of--place.

> Such is the nature and fixed relation of things, that it can be said in terms which admit of no uncertainty that the sinner is necessarily a sufferer; and that the doer of good is necessarily happy, and that neither the one nor the other, neither the good man nor the sinner, can fly from the heaven or hell that is appropriated to him any more than he can fly from himself.[139]

Upham did not believe in universalism. But, in a curious sense, hope even for the eternally doomed is never lost. Christ, who preached to the spirits in prison, continues to watch over and ever seek those who are in the lowest state of spiritual existence.[140] The essence of Upham's teaching is that the next life (<u>next</u> seems a poor term) is essentially an extension of this life even to the possibility of reformation of character. Unless man is free from the rule of self--selfishness--he will never know anything but hell either now or infinitely later.

The philosophical tendency to fuse time and eternity makes McConnell's statement concerning Wesley quite apropos for Upham, too, and for all nineteenth-century Wesleyan holiness. "To seek a life, however, because of the life itself, to follow it whithersoever it leads, to ask this, lifts all up into a genuinely moral realm and appeals to the highest and best in human nature."[141] Perhaps no single statement could fuse ethical commitment and eschatology more inseparably than Upham's request just before his death:

> I do not think of heaven, as rest or enjoyment,--my heaven will be to teach and raise the lowest. I want to go to the spirits in prison, in the darkness of their unbelief--and be a ministering spirit to help them.[142]

Conclusion

Upham was much more philosophical and naturalistic in

constructing an ethical norm than were the Wesleyans in creating their contemporary bibliocentric teachings of sanctification. The influence of Jonathan Edwards, as much as that of any other person, resulted in Upham's defining holiness ethics in terms of love and reverence for life. A categorical imperative, which elevates life, was what motivated social implementation of religious conviction; the establishment of legalistic moralisms was not responsible for that result. Yet, with Upham a case in point, the hallowing of life could not always be practically implemented in ambiguous moral conflicts.

Upham's understanding of corporate responsibility reflects an admirable inclusiveness and cosmopolitanism; this understanding was unlike the later separatist and individualist view of the holiness movement at the turn of the century.

Upham's catholic spirit did not dissolve into simplistic latitudinarianism or naive utopianism. At the same time, it was practical enough to be translated into many of the urgent issues of the day, such as temperance and women's rights. But a certain academic aloofness and moderation were present that prevented Upham from having the singleminded ethical enterprise that marked Oberlin. In the final analysis, Upham gave evidence to the claim that love, while inarguably an admirable and necessary pursuit, does not--at least in this life--conquer or solve all.

Notes

1. French, p. 269.
2. "American Philosophy," The British Quarterly Review, Volume XII (February-March 1847), p. 117.
3. Upham, Mental Philosophy, p. 350.
4. Thomas C. Upham, "The Immutability of Moral Distinction," Biblical Repository and Quarterly Observer, Volume VI (July 1835), p. 130.
5. "A Review of Archibald Alexander's Outlines of Moral Science," The Princeton Review (January 1853), p. 25.
6. Edward H. Madden, Civil Disobedience and Moral Law in Nineteenth Century American Philosophy (Seattle: University of Washington Press, 1968), p. 52.
7. Ibid.
8. French, p. 190.

9. Richard Watson, Theological Institutes, Volume I (New York: N. Banks and J. Emory, 1825), p. 488. But certainly, perfectionists did not have a corner on the objectivity of moral law. There was plenty of precedent within the American theological mainstream, which was mainly the result of Calvin's influence. It was written of Timothy Dwight: "For in common with most leading writers on this subject, he rightly argues that if, virtue be founded in the mere will of God, then if God should so ordain lying, theft, and blasphemy would be virtuous, a conclusion from which we instinctively revolt." Review of Archibald Alexander's Outlines of Moral Science, p. 19. Also of Joseph Bellamy: "He contended that right and wrong do not result from the mere will and law of God, nor from any tendency of things to promote or hinder the happiness of God's creatures. It remains, therefore, that there is an intrinsic moral fitness absolutely in things themselves" (p. 21 from the same).

10. Luther Lee, p. 334.

11. Thomas Neeley Ralston's Elements of Divinity was the second Wesleyan-Arminian systematic theology to be published in America, 1847. Quote is taken from the later edition, Cokesbury Press, 1924, p. 749.

12. Upham, Mental Philosophy, Volume II, p. 353.

13. Charles G. Finney, Memoirs of the Rev. Charles G. Finney (London: Hodder and Stoughton, 1876), p. 83. Since Wesley was often on the defensive against the established church, he frequently resorted to a teleological argument of results. He most often pointed to the changed lives of converts: "I will show you him that was a liar till then, and is now a lamb; him that was a drunkard, and is now exemplarily sober; the whoremonger that was, who now abhors the very garment spotted by the flesh. These are my living arguments for what I assert, viz., that God does now, as aforetime, give remission of sins, and the gift of the Holy Ghost, even to us and to our children, yea, and that always suddenly, as far as I have known, and often in dreams or in the visions of God." Works, Volume I, p. 195.

14. Upham, Mental Philosophy, Volume II, pp. 338-339.

15. Ibid., pp. 344-345.

16. Upham, Religious Maxims, pp. 77-78.

17. Upham, Absolute Religion, p. 21.

18. Ibid., p. 151.

19. Upham, Divine Union, p. 100.

20. Ibid., p. 101.

21. Harold B. Kuhn, "Ethics and the Holiness Movement," Insights into Holiness, ed. Kenneth Geiger. (Kansas City: Beacon Hill Press, 1962), p. 244.

22. French, p. 31.

23. Wilson Smith, pp. 36-40.

24. Ibid., p. 91.

25. Upham, Mental Philosophy, Volume II, p. 249.

26. Ibid., p. 250.

27. Ibid., p. 252.

28. Ibid., p. 254.

29. Ibid., p. 258.

30. Ibid., p. 261.

31. Ibid., p. 263.

32. French, p. 112.

33. Jesse D. Peck, D.D., The Central Idea of Christianity, (Louisville, Kentucky: Pentecostal Publishing Co., 1902 [original edition, 1858]), p. 9.

For an excellent discussion on Wesley's use of scripture in formulating the doctrine of Christian Perfection, see William Sangster's essay, "Texts on Which He Built." William Sangster, The Path to Perfection (New York: Abingdon Press, 1943), pp. 37-52. Dr. Sangster wrote: "In his Plain Account--the main source of our knowledge of Wesley's mind on this doctrine--he quotes the Bible one hundred and ninety-five times: twenty-three times from the Old Testament and one hundred and seventy-two from the New. Some of his pages are little more than a catena of quotations. He seems to have lived in the Scriptures so long that Bible phrasing has become second nature to him, and he swims from one citation to another with effortless ease. Ignoring the repetitive use he makes of certain texts, he quotes the Synoptic Gospels twenty-nine times, Paul seventy-four times and the Johannine writings thirty-four times. The most quoted book is the First Epistle of John, from which he culls twenty-texts, some of which he repeats frequently. After the First Epistle of John, Matthew and Romans are cited most, with eighteen varied quotations each" (p. 36).

Wesley wrote: "I am a Bible bigot. I follow it in all things both great and small." Journal, Vol. V, p. 169. "The scriptures are the touchstone whereby Christians examine all real or supposed revelation. In all cases, they appeal to the law and to the testimony, and try every spirit thereby." Letters, Vol. II (February 10, 1748), p. 117.

34. Wesley, Works, Vol. VIII, p. 271. Mildred Wynkoop argued against any kind of prescriptive legalistic inter-

pretation of Wesley. For Wynkoop, both sin and righteousness were solely dependent on our relationship with God. She stated that "the most fruitful way to interpret Wesleyan, or holiness theology, is by way of offering the 'interface' concerning which it speaks as a personal relationship between man and God." Wynkoop, p. 168.

35. Charles Jones, p. 85.
36. Upham, Divine Union, p. 288.
37. Ibid.
38. Ibid., p. 286.
39. Upham, Interior Life, p. 259. The language at this point bears similarity to William Sangster's argument against the term "eradication." Sangster quotes from Sugden: "But sin is not a thing; it is a condition of balance amongst our natures." Sangster, p. 113.
40. Upham, Interior Life, p. 260. H. Orton Wiley included the whole chapter (in abbreviated form) of Upham's on "The Idea of Spiritual Liberty" in his chapter "Christian Ethics or the Life of Holiness" for his systematic theology. Over the past forty years, this work has been the most widely used theological text among holiness seminaries, colleges, and Bible schools.
41. Ibid., p. 261.
42. Ibid., p. 262.
43. Ibid., p. 265.
44. Haroutunian, p. 172.
45. Upham, Mental Philosophy, Vol. II, p. 199.
46. Ibid.
47. Faust and Johnson, pp. xxxviii-xc.
48. Ibid., p. 252.
49. Ibid., pp. 362-364.
50. Ibid., p. lxxxvi.
51. Ibid.
52. Ibid., p. xcv.
53. Upham, Mental Philosophy, Vol. II, p. 281.
54. Ibid., p. 282.
55. Ibid.
56. Ibid., p. 283.
57. Ibid., p. 285.
58. Ibid., p. 286.
59. Upham, Divine Union, p. 96. Upham also penned in reference to transcendentalism: "There is a system of philosophy supported by a great and memorable name, and none the less memorable because he who bore it pursued his sublime and difficult studies in the woods of America, which

maintains that virtue consists in the love of being in general." Letters, p. 390.

60. Ibid., p. 113.
61. Ibid., p. 123.
62. Upham, Letters, p. 392.
63. Ibid.
64. Upham, Divine Union, p. 107.
65. Conforti, p. 115.
66. Upham, Catherine Adorna, p. 19.
67. Upham, Interior Life, p. 17.
68. Ibid., p. 149.
69. Henry B. Smith, p. 643.
70. Upham, Divine Union, p. 319. Upham was quite Aristotelian in stating as he did that love and justice, as well as other attributes of character, need to balance out each other. He would have agreed with Thomas Oden, who wrote: "Although agape may be present and experienced in certain peak moments of interpersonal meeting, we cannot reasonably expect such love to be the sustained basis of interaction, since sacrificial love involves the disavowal of power. Justice at the interpersonal level seeks an equitable ordering of power in the light of mutual self-interest. Justice is not capable of bestowing upon personal transactions the conditions of ideality and perfection. It may give more concreteness to love under the conditions of human estrangement, however, than could a purer idealism." Thomas C. Oden, Game Free (New York: Harper and Row, 1974), p. 128.
71. Upham, Interior Life, p. 210. Upham saw no polarization between love and justice. Upham would not have agreed with the following from Edward Long, which explicates the dualism of Emil Brunner: "Love is regarded as the practical principle for dealing with the conflicting claim found in situations of power. Emil Brunner throws these two norms into sharp antithesis. For him love is confined to personal situations; justice is the only norm for the order of society." E. L. Long, Jr., Conflict and Compromise (Philadelphia: The Westminster Press, 1954), p. 77.
72. "Review of Archibald Alexander's Outlines of Moral Science," Princeton Review, p. 24.
73. Adam Clarke, Christian Theology (Salem, Ohio: Convention Book Store, 1967), pp. 78-79.
74. Upham, Catherine Adorna, p. 125.
75. The Kantian categorical imperative is to "So act as to treat humanity whether in thine own person or in that of any other in every case as an end withal, never as a

means only." Edward Leroy Long, Jr., A Survey of Christian Ethics (New York: Oxford University Press, 1967), p. 5.

At several points within the book, I have used terms which define particular ethical modes or methodologies for forming ethical norms. Among them are such words as "descriptive," "deliberative," "relational," "institutional," and "operational." For further definition of these terms, see the text above by Edward Long, Jr.

76. Upham, Manual of Peace (New York: Leavitt, Lord, and Company, 1836), p. 28.

77. Upham was most influenced in his ideas of peace, by William Ladd, who was active in the American Peace Society, and formulated principles for a congress of nations. Upham met with him on several occasions and was impressed by his work. Upham highlighted his life to illustrate what God could do through "a limited agency, a single individual to effect the destiny of nations and good in the whole of society." Upham, Divine Union, pp. 323-325.

78. William Allen, "Congress of Nations," Quarterly Observer, Vol. II (January 1834), p. 14.

79. Ibid., p. 24.

80. Ibid., p. 23.

81. Upham, Manual of Peace, p. 133. Upham was influenced by Rev. George Bush, who was active in the American Peace Society, and wrote on the subject of "pacifism." In a letter written on May 2, 1836, Upham wrote to George Bush: "I believe myself, (and I would propose the matter for your consideration), that the Society never can prosper and never will do much good, until it takes the high ground, that all wars, both offensive and defensive, are opposed to the spirit of the Gospel, and are sinful. When we take this ground, we shall have a character; people will know where to find us, and we shall act vigorously. As far as my information goes the thorough and active peace men are generally dissatisfied with the position, which the society now occupies." From the Simon Gratz Collection, The Historical Society of Pennsylvania.

82. Upham, Manual of Peace, p. 134.

83. Ibid., p. 157.

84. Ibid., p. 158.

85. Upham, Absolute Religion, p. 278.

86. Upham, Catherine Adorna, p. 131.

87. H. Richard Niebuhr, Christ and Culture (New York: Harper and Bros., 1951), p. 185.

88. Upham, Manual of Peace, p. 386.
89. Ibid., p. 148.
90. Ibid., p. 335.
91. Ibid., p. 388.
92. Niebuhr, p. 143.
93. Upham, Manual of Peace, p. 406.
94. Ibid., p. 42.
95. Ibid., p. 43.
96. Ibid., p. 45.
97. Ibid., p. 174.
98. Ibid., p. 26.
99. Timothy Smith, Revivalism and Social Reform, p. 215.
100. Ibid., p. 199. At this point, Smith is speaking of the Phoebe Palmer enclave and certainly not the Oberlin perfectionists who were so ideological that they could give at least partial sanction to John Brown's raid. But not even at Oberlin was there common consensus as to appropriate action for the Christian.
101. Upham, Manual of Peace, p. 267.
102. David Davis, in his article, "The Emergence of Immediatism in Antislavery Thought," relates moral action to the religious experience of individual and corporate guilt. He suggests that a person who experiences "a romantic frame of mind, a hostility--to all dualism of thought and feeling, an allegiance to both emotional sympathy, and abstract principle, an assumption that mind can rise above self-interest and a belief that ideas, when held with sufficient intensity can be transformed into irresistible moral action," would be an immediatist. Upham evidenced all of these characteristics but yet was forced into a gradualist position. Davis's thesis was true of Oberlin, and the romanticist, Harriet B. Stowe, but not for Upham and many other evangelicals.

A somewhat opposite thesis is taken by Edward Madden when he states, "there is little or no connection between concepts of moral law and commitments on specific moral issues." Edward Madden, Civil Disobedience and Moral Law in Nineteenth Century American Philosophy, p. 69.

Davis's article would also lead someone to believe that gradualism and immediatism were simple concepts, when actually both were very difficult to define as there were many degrees of each. David Brion Davis, "The Emergence of Immediatism in British and American Antislavery Thought," John M. Mulder and John F. Wilson (ed.), Religion in American History (Englewood Cliffs, N.J.: Prentice-Hall, Inc., 1978), pp. 236-253.

103. Leonard Woods, Jr., "On Political and Ecclesiastical Reform," Literary and Theological Review, Vol. II (June 1835), pp. 344-364, p. 357.

104. Upham, Divine Union, p. 190.

105. Upham stated to Alpheus S. Packard during the Civil War, "I have been in the habit, Brother P. (he declared) of referring everything to the providence of God, and I can and do trust Him and commit all into his hands." Packard, p. 21.

106. Upham, Religious Maxims, p. 69. In a letter to Rev. John Orcutt, D.D., April 20, 1870, Upham had not given up hope for a migration of blacks from America to Africa for redemption of the continent. "I have been unable to separate in my thoughts and in my deepest convictions the connection of the disenthralled and regenerated slave with the liberation of the land from which he came.... In this great work, which constitutes a part of God's remedial system for the restoration of the world, colonization can now nobly lead. The way is now open for more energetic and widely-extended action, without the fears and doubts, and the liabilities to error which have perplexed the past." The letter was published by the American Colonization Society, and is available at the Yale University Library. This letter is also insightful as to Upham's cultural and sociological views of the "negro."

The little mention of colonization in the main evangelical antislavery periodical of the 1830's and 1840's, The New York Evangelist, evidences that for the revivalistic abolitionists of the Northeast, colonization was not a viable action. The publication pointed out the inconsistency and shallowness of the American Colonization Society for electing four times straight, a slaveholder for its president. The following statement issued by its president, Henry Clay, from Kentucky in 1837, reveals its contrasting goals regarding abolitionism. "Regarding the American Colonization Society as the only practical scheme ever presented to public consideration for separating advantageously to all parties, the European descendents upon this continent from the free people of color, the descendents of Africans, with their own consent, and of ultimately effecting a more extensive separation of the two races with the consent of the states, and individuals interested, and I shall continue to cherish the highest interest in the success of the Society, and will contribute whatever is in my power to promote its prosperity." The New York Evangelist (January 14, 1837), p. 10.

The fact that there is no mention of Upham in this periodical (save for the article of Harriet Beecher Stowe on Upham's Interior Life) is evidence of Upham's nonactive role in revivalism and abolitionism.

107. Upham, Letters, p. 34.

108. Concerning Lyman Beecher's proposed plan for the assimilation of abolitionism and colonizationism, Gilbert Barnes commented, "Like Beecher's 'famous technique' of 'Evangelical Assimilation of Calvinism and New Theology,' this plan for assimilating the conflicting programs of colonization and abolition was unworkable." Gilbert Barnes, The Antislavery Impulse, 1830-1844 (New York: D. Appleton-Century Companies, 1933).

109. Ibid., p. 96.

110. Upham, The Manual of Peace, p. 138.

111. Ibid., p. 145.

112. Ibid., p. 150. But as to how the slave trade at home is to be suppressed, Upham is unspecific. "If when we do right ourselves, by breaking the yoke of bondage and treating the millions of Africans in Christian countries as our fellowmen, the great evil of the slave trade does not cease and die of itself, then we shall be called upon with some show of propriety to answer the inquiry concerning the application of force." Upham never got around to answering the inquiry.

113. Ibid., p. 373.

114. Francis McConnell, John Wesley (New York: Abingdon Press, 1939), p. 242.

115. Leonard Woods, Jr., "On Political and Ecclesiastical Reform," p. 361.

116. Upham, Manual of Peace, p. 29.

117. Ibid., p. 26.

118. Ibid., p. 228.

119. At this point, Upham's ethic seems to be quite teleological, in that, punishment is for the good of society. Contrast this with Madden's assessment of Mahan's deontology: "Moreover, this justification of punishment can be only that someone deserved it and not that the administrator of punishment will promote the well-being of society or the ultimate well-being of the individual punished. For Mahan, these are beneficial consequences of punishment, to be sure, but they cannot be the justification of punishment. Punishment, like reward, can be justified only in terms of fairness, justice, and desert." Madden, Civil Disobedience, p. 64.

120. Upham, Manual of Peace, p. 229.

121. Ibid., p. 235.

122. Forty-three years after his death, 1915, a letter was addressed to Thomas Upham from a California legislator "for assistance in securing authoritative evidence concerning capital punishment in the state of Maine." Newspaper article: "Receive Letter for Professor 50 Years Dead." On file at Bowdoin College.

123. Upham, Manual of Peace, p. 250.

124. Upham, Divine Union, p. 168.

125. Ibid., p. 343.

126. Ibid., p. 342.

127. Ibid., p. 322.

128. It should not be inferred that ecumenism did not characterize the early holiness movement. Actually, as we already argued, the opposite is true of both Phoebe Palmer's meetings and the National Association for the Promotion of Holiness.

128. Upham, Ratio Discipline, p. 65.

129. Upham, Absolute Religion, p. 197.

130. Upham, Interior Life, p. 22.

131. See the letter written by Phebe Upham to Phoebe Palmer on p. viii, Phoebe Palmer, Promise of the Father (Salem, Ohio: Schmul Reprint, 1981), original 1859. The letter concerns women's rights: "It gives me pleasure to add that my husband, who has given no small degree of attention to this subject, coincides with these views." Palmer quoted Upham: "One of the results of God's great work which is now going on in the world will be to raise and perfect woman's position and character. The darkest page in human history is that of the treatment of woman. But when, in the progress of divine truth, it is understood that man cannot fulfil his own destiny, and is not the completion of himself,--he will also be restored to that which is a part of himself, and will thus perfect, in completed unity, that would otherwise remain in the imperfection of an undeveloped and partial nature" (p. 53).

132. Donald Dayton, "The Social and Political Conservatism of Modern American Evangelicals: A Preliminary Search for the Reasons," Union Seminary Quarterly Review Volume XXXII, Number 2 (Winter 1977), p. 75.

133. Timothy Smith, Revivalism and Social Reform, p. 154.

134. Wilson Smith, p. 197.

135. Upham, Absolute Religion, pp. 199-200.

136. Ibid., pp. 202-203.

137. Ibid., p. 202.
138. Ibid., p. 206.
139. Ibid., p. 207.
140. Ibid., p. 266.
141. McConnell, p. 216. McConnell points out that in Wesley's *Standard Sermons*, there is no sermon on heaven or hell.
142. Phebe Upham's account of the death of her husband. Original on file in Bowdoin College Library.

Chapter VII

A NINETEENTH-CENTURY PSYCHOLOGY OF HOLINESS THEOLOGY

Thomas Upham's theological works, especially Principles of the Interior Life, may be one of the best attempts of the first half of the nineteenth century to place pietism within a psychological context. Upham's common-sense mental philosophy bears little resemblance to the later depth psychology of Freud, the case histories of James, and much less to the clinical research of the twentieth century. But even Freud could have profited from Upham's demonstration that there is a healthy common ground between religion and psychological investigation.

Upham was not so much a pioneer as he was a systematizer, or a builder, upon the foundations of Locke, Edwards, Burton, Rush, and others, who had gone before him. His exploration of basic drives, feelings, and instincts, through the commonsense method of introspection, observations of the behavior of others, and illustrations found in his omnivorous reading, all served to weave a psychological thread throughout his explications of spiritual experience.

The Laws of the Mind

The premise behind Upham's theology is the same as the premise behind his psychology, i.e., that there are fundamental laws operative within the universe. To the extent that man is in harmony with these laws, such is the degree to which he possesses mental and spiritual health. The dichotomy between mental wholeness and spiritual wholeness becomes somewhat obliterated.[1] There is a single drive in man toward a noncompartmental psychosomatic harmony. Both insanity and spiritual sickness result from lack of alignment with the fixed principles that have their foundation in nature.[2] Man is created to be both mentally healthy and holy. Lack of perfection in each, or disordered action, is more a philosophical, psychological--and even a physical--discord, than it is a positive taint of evil or a demonic affliction. For Upham, the witchcraft "delusion" in seventeenth-century New England could have been explained by natural causes, had man the medical and psychological insight he has today.[3]

Mental Laws of Belief

The content of belief is both a psychological and religious phenomenon. Believing the wrong thing may not only be due to lack of knowledge or to spiritual blindness but to some defect in the norm of belief that is inherent to proper mental function. Belief in God is both a proper mental function and a spiritual drive quickened by prevenient grace. Upham wrote:

> The mind has its nature and its laws; and, although it cannot be diseased or disordered in the same way that a material existence may be, yet sound philosophy does not forbid the supposition that it may possibly be susceptible of derangement in such way and degree as may be consistent with its own nature. Take, for instance, the susceptibility of belief. The state of mind which we call belief has its laws, and may be regarded as a universal attribute of the mental nature. In other words, all men have this susceptibility. Furthermore, in the great mass of mankind, it exists nearly the same degrees, and exhibits the same manifestations.[4]

For Upham, the natural mental laws of belief were foundational to a supernatural gift of faith. In fact, faith unto salvation was more of a quickening or an illumination of natural laws than it was a power imported from another world. As reason is an original mental law, man will not believe what he cannot reasonably accept.

Unlike Kierkegaard, Upham believed that the command to believe could only be carried out to the extent that it was fortified by reason.[5] Equally important are: reliance on memory, the witness of others, and the consciousness that one's perception of the relationship between objects is congruent and in keeping with known comparative facts, equality, differentiation, etc. Upham was not saying that religious belief is a purely natural process. What he did contend is that God does not require a faith that is a denial of natural mental laws.

> What ever may be said on the subject there must be, and there are, certain original grounds, certain fundamental laws of belief, which in every analysis of our knowledge are fixed, and permanent boundaries, beyond which we cannot proceed.[6]

Does the above suggest that Upham might have disbelieved miraculous intervention that defies natural law? He made no overt negation of this, but the tautology suggests that miracles do not play a significant part in God's economy. For instance, in regards to visions, voices, etc., that may appear to be of supernatural origin, Upham was inclined to look for natural causes or disordered mental action, especially of the senses.[7] Such phenomena as trances and physical agitations he explained by purely natural principles.[8]

Apparent miracles find their cause in the inspiration of God, the suggestions of Satan, or the "movements of a strangely disordered physical system operating upon, or in connection with a highly-excited state of the intellect and the feelings."[9] Upham was inclined to discount the first and go with the latter causes.

> If a man has a trance, a vision, and especially if he has a revelation, and can sustain it by such miracles as sustained the divine messages of Christ and the apostles, we readily admit that he is entitled to a hearing. But, in the first place, we know of no such cases. And in the second place, if we did, it would furnish no decisive grounds of inference in favor of the piety of such persons.[10]

But Upham was not interested in demonstrating conclusively whether a particular observable manifestation could, or could not be related to natural causes. His particular contention was that sensationalism is detrimental to a healthy psychology of belief. Thus, a clear call is present in Upham's writing for a faith that is beyond seeing or knowing either as perception or as demonstrable fact.[11]

Weak faith desires a demonstrable manifestation from God. But strong faith, even though it has an inclination to rely on the visible and tangible, is gradually weaned from depending on empirical certitude.[12] No matter how extensively God manifests himself, the finite must always exercise faith when grasping the infinite.[13] The will must exist to accept what God decides to keep beyond the grasp of human knowledge.

> The love of manifestations, of that which is visible and tangible, in distinction from that, which is addressed to faith, is one of the evils of the present age. Men love visions, more than they love holiness. They would have God in their hands, rather than in their hearts. They would set him up as a thing to be looked at, and with decorated cars would transport him, if they could realize what their hearts desire, from place to place, on the precise principles of heathenism; because, being weak in faith, they find it difficult to recognize the existence, and to love and to do the will of an "unknown God."[14]

Emotions

Likewise, helpful to a full assurance of faith, a faith that operates on a steady, psychological keel, is a trust in the eternal immutability of God. This kind of faith excludes all reliance in fluctuating emotions. Upham would not exclude rational belief or emotional commitment, but true faith has to be one step beyond each.[15] There will be emotional urgency behind true religion that recognizes ultimate value, but healthy religion will not rest on belief which fluctuates with emotional moods. We are to leave the regulation of our feelings to the wisdom of God, who in his providence will suitably regulate the emotions to the occasion or circumstance. The secret to controlling the emotions is acquiescing to whatever circumstances God chooses to send. Even though divested self-interest will prevent an individual from being spiritually crippled by the emotions, one must recognize that feelings, because of the laws of the mind, will accompany particular circumstances and, for the healthy mind, will be in keeping with the occasion.[16] Thus, Upham did not advocate a stoical religion or principles of mind control. These are not necessary, he said, to achieve a proper worship or

prayerful attitude.[17] One should not attempt to regulate suitable religious feelings; instead

> the mind should be religiously quiet, that is to say, it should on religious considerations, cease from itself, from its selfish interests, its fears in relation to God's veracity, its prejudices, all inordinate passions, everything, in short, which is inconsistent with leaving itself, in submissive and deeply confiding repose, in the hands of God.[18]

The above statement is integral to Upham's premise that entire sanctification should be defined as perfect love. The assurance that one is sanctified wholly is the consciousness of a will to love rather than to experience a highly joyful and rapturous excitement.[19] Joy, as emotion, terminates in itself; true love desires the glory of God and the good of others.[20] Upham is wary of spiritual sensuality, which leads the Christian to focus on his or her self while losing sight of the highest good, i.e., the glory of God and welfare of others.[21] Emotions should be abiding love, which constantly seeks the will of God. Never should they be an end in themselves.

> If he is the highest object of our love, we shall desire no higher happiness than that of constant communion with him, and of being always united to him by oneness of will. Thus, all may be said to be in him, and he in us; and that eternal rest of the soul, which constitutes the true heaven, will be commenced here. Then we shall have the true joy--calm, deep, unchangeable. Love goes before, joy comes after. Love is the principle of action; joy is the reward.[22]

Sanctification as Psychological Restoration

The historical revivalistic matrix of the first Great Awakening occasioned Edwards' and Wesley's defense, to the best of their ability, of the observable phenomena. Removed from revivalistic measures and confined to the classroom, Upham was much more interested in what happens internally regarding the conversion-sanctification process.

An overview of Upham's understanding of the mind would be helpful to any reader of this book. (See Appendix A.) The crucial point of spiritual recovery for man concerns the benevolent affections. Man was created with a supreme love to the creator. It was natural for primitive man (Adam), before the fall, to place God first in his affections to the extent that the natural affection to God has been obliterated.

Though Upham is not dogmatic concerning the extent of man's fall, the fall has so damaged the image of God that instincts and propensities have gained inordinate dominance over the benevolent affection, i.e., over supreme love to God. Complete restoration means that man's affection will be restored to its proper object; entire sanctification is the full exercise of the original principle of love to God that keeps the subordinate principles in their place.

> The appetites, the propensities, and the domestic affections still exist; but such is the ascendancy of love to the Supreme Being, that every inordinate tendency is rebuked, and they all resolve in the circle which God in the beginning assigned to them.[23]

The above was crucial to Upham's understanding of the holy life that he wrote about over and over again and an area commonly left ambiguous by Wesleyan contemporaries. The propensities and instincts are in themselves wholesome; their inordinancy arises not because they are corrupted, tainted or diseased but because they have been deprived of their check, their safety valve. The positive psychological approach emphasized increased restoration; the theological one emphasized death, annihilation, and extermination. Upham wrote: "Holiness does not annul, or even alter, the laws of nature, but only restores and perfects their action."[24] He observed from history that:

> Many pious persons, at different periods in the history of the church, have maintained that the various propensities and affections should not merely be crucified in the true scripture sense, viz, by being reduced from an irregular to a subordinate and holy action, but should be exterminated. In accordance with this opinion, obviously erroneous as it is, many persons of both sexes, some of them distinguished for

> their learning and their rank in life, have avoided, by a permanent principle of action, everything that could please the appetites or gratify the demands of our social nature.[25]

Inward Congruity and Harmony

An individual reaching sanctifying grace has achieved total internal, psychological, and spiritual harmony. The moral perfection of the universe is extended to the individual; God's divine harmonious rule governing the macrocosm is applied to the microcosm. Both the individual and his world will become a well-ordered machinery, each gear properly meshed, ratioed, and oiled. A unity and integration of personality exists whereby the supreme love of God, "reduces all principles of action and all motives into one. God in everything, and God through Christ in himself, thus, harmonizing himself not only with God, but with everything which God does and is."[26]

Holiness was not so much a miracle as it was God applying his already established laws. Upham could investigate the principles of holiness, therefore, just as he investigated the laws of the mind and of the world.[27] "God works *gradatim*, step by step; by the gradualism of continually developed law, and not by the impromptus and ejaculations of blind effort, without any wise and permanent principles as the foundation of that effort."[28]

The desire of God to put man at harmony with himself and the world around him is the theological corollary to Upham's psychological premise that the mental operations are intricately linked together and that change of one operation affects subsequent operations.[29] If one part of the mind inhibits the maximum efficiency of some other function or act, then a person is not really free. The sanctified person is free to function according to the natural laws of creation and God's original intention. Liberty is the ability of each faculty to fulfill its nature properly.[30]

> We hold it to be self-evident that no being, attribute, or faculty can be considered as free in the highest sense of that term, whenever there is a violation of

> the elements of its nature or what is the same thing when there is an interruption or hindrance from another source of the tendencies of the elements.[31]

Spiritual tranquility is present if God has harmonized the mind by way of religious influences. Appetites are subdued, conflicts are resolved within the propensities, and appetites and "all [are] in their place operating where they aught to operate and not operating where they aught not to operate."[32] The supreme love to God subordinates all other mental activities and mitigates "that inward jarring, which had formerly existed, thought in conflict with thought, passion, and conscience asserting rights which it could not maintain.[33]

Throughout his spiritual writings, Upham consistently explicated the moral need for man to have an undivided self reconciled to a unified God. Love regulated by rectitude is the controlling principle by which God acts, and the same single-eyed motive must belong to man. "It is self-evident, that a man, who is variant with himself, acting partly from good and partly from bad motives, can never be in perfect union with a being who is one with himself and acts only from a holy nature."[34] Just as God's mind is able to make perfect adaptation and adjustment to all the vicissitudes of his Creator, man, because he is in harmony with God makes perfect adjustment to the circumstances of life.[35] The tranquility that the Holy Spirit brings is "not the rest of inaction," or "of impassive stagnation, but of emotional and moral harmony."[36] In the words of William James: "The saintly person becomes exceedingly sensitive to inner inconsistency or discord, and mixture and confusion grow intolerable."[37]

Upham's psychology of holiness exemplifies the bridge between transcendental idealism and Wesleyan perfectionism. Note the similarity of language present in both the previous statement and the following one by Orestes A. Brownson, written in 1836:

> We are beginning to perceive that Providence, in the peculiar circumstances in which it has placed us, in the free institutions it has given us, has made it our duty to bring out the ideal man, to prove, by a practical demonstration, what the human

> race may be, when and where it has free scope for the full and harmonious development of all its faculties. In proportion as we perceive and comprehend this duty, we cannot fail to inquire for a sound philosophy, one which will enumerate and characterize all the faculties of the human soul, and determine the proper order and most efficient means of their development....[38]

A Psychology of Duty and Obligation

The point at which man is most conscious of mental freedom and interior harmony is in obedience to God. Upham wrote that "the occasion, on which we are conscious of mental freedom, in the highest degree, is to be found in a condition of the mental acts, conformed to the requirements of the Supreme Being."[39] Here, one of Upham's most unique contributions to a psychology of religion came into focus. Upham divided moral sensibilities into two different planes of operation--moral emotions (desires) and moral obligations. The word "plane" seems most apropos because obligations are a higher mode of moral operation than are emotions.

In a sense, the man who has had a change of heart acts out of spontaneity to holy emotions and affections that have been transformed by the grace of God. This psychological description of man's moral choices affirmed the Edwardian argument that man acts according to his strongest desire or motive and, hence, is not truly internally free. But since Upham divided affections into emotions and obligations, every moral issue was open-ended. In Upham's thought, not even the Christian has automatic responses to do the right thing; each individual must make difficult moral decisions.

The person who is psychologically and spiritually free is one who does what he ought to do and not necessarily what he wants to do. Moral obligations are the key area in which the Holy Spirit can empower an individual; this is because obligatory feelings are the arbitrator between the individual desires and moral emotions. A stalemate may exist--or perhaps perfect agreement between individual desires and moral emotions--according to the particular moral issue being confronted. Emotions make pronouncements and moral judgments on the character of something that has taken place or is presently taking place but, "the states of mind involving obligation and duty have reference to the future: to something that is either to be performed, or the performance of which is to be avoided."[40] Thus the will always has two classes of mental states to take into consideration: "Desires and feelings of obligation."[41] If man operated only according to his desires, where would moral worth, courage, or moral accountability lie?[42] Desires fluctuate with the emotions. Again, Upham accented Wesley's emphasis on the sanctification of the will: "A will steadily and uniformly devoted to God is essential to a state of sanctification, but not an uniformity of joy or peace of happy communion with God."[43]

Habit Formation

Maturing of the sanctified person and strengthening of moral fortitude entails more than a single act of hallowing grace and even more than the ongoing acts of the Holy Spirit. Holy disposition needs to be strengthened through continual use and exercise. A truly holy heart may have to wrestle against antecedent habits that were ingrained within the personality before the experience of living fully for God.[44] Even after redemption from self-love and selfish attitudes and in consequence of previous "habits of inordinate exercise, there may be a strong tendency, which requires constant resistance, to resume its former position of irregularity and sin."[45] Upham seems to have been saying that an instantaneous act of grace can free man from conscious sinful acts, but only undergoing a process of hallowing grace over a period of time can purge the unconscious from acquired dispositions. As faith is strengthened by habit,[46] so the conscience is strengthened by perpetual right use.

The will of man to obey God in all circumstances can become invigorated, perfected, and well-established only through habit.[47] This process will require the concurrence of our own efforts with the operations of divine grace.[48] Upham suggested that the practice of humbling ourselves before others and placing their desires before ours, even in matters of moral insignificance, will help in strengthening and preparing the will for those moral matters that really count.[49]

Denying ourselves in small things will enable us to deny ourselves in matters of major importance. "Such are the laws of the human mind, that indulgence in the latter will take away our strength, and deprive us of victory in the former."[50]

Upham was not without practical suggestions. For instance, when our actions are misrepresented and we are falsely accused and we are tempted to retort back or come to our own defense--those times we must practice silence. "To be silent, therefore, in ordinary cases is best in every respect; not only because it is the course indicated by true religion but because it aids in breaking down the irregular and sinful action of the will."[51] Sanctification in its highest sense can only take place as the laws of habit are reinforced. The Christian may be victorious but powerful, accumulated laws of nature will call for watchfulness, prayerfulness, vigilance, and even struggling.[52] The above is quite similar to what Sydney G. Dimond called Wesley's "continual inhibition of instincts by habits."[53] In the same context, he wrote:

> This piece of self-analysis illustrates the difference between inhibition and repression of instincts. The evil of repression arises from the fact that it is a refusal of direct attention, which forces the impulse into disguise and concealment, where it enacts its own uneasy private life subject to no inspection and no control. There is a wholesome directness and an open confrontation of instinctive tendencies with all their implications, evident in Wesley's behavior, that differs entirely from the damming up and ignoring of impulses which is the cause of pathological conditions.[54]

The above demonstrates a truth that was not always made clear in holiness teaching, i.e., that the experience of entire sanctification does not necessarily guarantee holy living. The intellect must receive, during its early development, a vigorous course of moral education in which precepts of righteous living are understandable.[55] Christ's promise that "the truth shall make you free" indicates the integral part the intellect plays in religious and moral development.[56]

In Upham's estimation, a well-balanced knowledge "is

naturally effective in a very high degree, in the renovation of the character and the support of just morals."[57] Upham unequivocally states in a secular textbook (if there was such a thing in 1840): all moral education that does not include foundational, religious training and the knowledge of God, is defective.[58] Education and correct habit formation are psychologically indispensable to the development of religious life. The pivotal truth for the development of strong character and integrity is that activity of a tendency strengthens it, and repression weakens it.[59] "Whatever is good and commendable in that part of our nature may be strengthened by repetition and encouragement; on the other hand, whatever is evil may be weakened and gradually done away by an opposite system of repression."[60]

Mental Health

Upham, more than any other holiness writer of the nineteenth century, wrote of the relationship of religion to mental health. A relationship with God keeps the mind from getting overly agitated and provides psychological fortification against disturbances that may come from persecution or criticism.[61] Contentment within is the hallmark of the sanctified, who fully accept the will of God in their lives. "He who frets at events, frets at God; he, who is not acquiescent in events, is at war with God."[62] The sanctified are psychologically equipped to minimize those events which worry others, because they do not attach to them undue importance.[63] A proper value system, which views events and things through God's priority scale, does not allow the mind's eye to exaggerate and distort beyond true limits. Everything is kept in proper perspective, i.e., within the light of eternity and brought to its proper size. "Events, therefore, which leave the man of faith in quietness of spirit, disturb and agitate the natural man, unloose the tongue of suspicion and complaint, and fill the world with his outcries."[64] Psychological detachment and distance prevent the man of faith from overpersonalizing the events that surround him and from internalizing the occurrences of life. The ideal state for Upham is the mental stability that prevails amidst afflictions and diversities, this being "the true preventive of the alternating system in religious experience, the system of elevations, and depressions, of inordinate heat and inordinate cold."[65]

Upham's Weltanshauung, which viewed everything as ordered by God, brought coherence and meaning to life. There is an intellectual defense against all events that would rob man of inner tranquility. Concerning death, Upham wrote: "The feeling appropriate to it is sorrow, but even when we consider that being an event in Providence, it is an event ordered in divine wisdom, the appropriate feeling is not only sorrow but sorrow mingled with acquiescence and patience."[66]

Upham would have clearly understood Reinhold Niebuhr's exhortation to accept those things beyond our control. No matter how desirable a thing may appear to be to us, if the law of providence stands in our way it cannot be done.[67] Complete submission to the Holy Spirit as well as surrender of "self-interested plans" will bring release from "uneasy, agitated, and excited feelings."[68]

The mind of the sanctified person "has acquired, as it were, a divine flexibility in virtue of which it accommodates itself with surprising ease and readiness, to all the developments of Providence, whether prosperous or adverse."[69] Mental and spiritual union with the perfect mind--the absolute mind of the universe--bring perfect peace.[70]

Upham, clearly, perceived Madame Guyon as the epitome of mental victory over suffering and adversity. He viewed her as a prototype of those who maintain psychological freedom in the midst of temporal threat.[71]

Wholeness

So far personality integration, mental harmony, and inner reconciliation have been discussed. Upham's explication of man's psychological impulse to wholeness rivals twentieth-century theories. More aware than any other holiness writer, he made it apparent that the call to spiritual perfection, maturity, fullness, wholeness, and the teliosis of the New Testament carries with it psychological connotations. Both Wesleyans and modern psychoanalysts have called for human beings to face their carnal mind, or shadow side, in order for the duality in personality to be fused or healed. What Upham sought was the individual's willingness to admit to a basic human selfishness that dictates a constant desire to protect self-interest. For Jungian Edward Whitmont, it is "only when we realize that part of ourselves which we have not hitherto seen or preferred to see, can we proceed to question and find the sources from which it feeds, and the basis on which it rests," can wholeness and integration within, take place.[72]

Upham's work constitutes the longest chapter within holiness theology which foreshadowed Jung's conviction that freedom, autonomy, and wholeness cannot be brought about by creeds, or social mores but by the "incontrovertible experience of an intensely personal reciprocal relationship between man and an extramundane authority."[73] Upham, unlike Jung, saw God as more than a projected archetype created by the universal needs of trust, consolation, or the desire for a benevolent father figure. Wholeness can be psychologically imparted only as we form a day-by-day relationship with a whole and personal God.

Wholeness for theological perfectionism means full conformity to the life and person of Christ. Holiness is the fullness of Christ within, a law written on the heart rather than on a tablet of stone. Regeneration means that a person is born of the Spirit, but sanctification means that the Christian is wholly filled with God. Jung confirmed the metaphysical archetype of wholeness as found in Christ and quoted St. Augustine: "Therefore, our end must be our perfection, but our perfection is Christ."[74] Oneness with the God image, writes Jung

> is in exact agreement with the empirical findings of psychology, that there is an ever present archetype of wholeness which may easily disappear from the purview of consciousness illuminated by conversion recognizing it in the figure of Christ.[75]

Though Jung was not offering the historical God-man, only a dogma which speaks of a metaphysical fact, he was very close to a Wesleyan or Uphamian perspective when he spoke of consciousness illuminated and enabled by conversion to see the possibility of wholeness in Christ.

Sanctification of Physical and Psychological Drives

Not articulated as clearly as twentieth-century theories of self-identity, self-congruence, and self-actualization, Upham's writings alerted Christians to be in touch with their real selves and not work under the illusion of super-spirituality. "Holy persons like others, retain the attributes appropriate to man's nature, differing from the same attributes in others in respect only, that they are deprived of irregularities of action, and are entirely subordinate to the divine will."[76] Not that contemporary holiness writers denied those sanctified their humanity--George Peck stated:

> The entirely sanctified minister will still have about him his natural or constitutional infirmities. He will probably be no more accurate or fluent than before, and may not be so much so as many others of far less religious attainments.[77]

But in comparing Peck's statement and those of other holiness authors with Upham, two apparent differences emerge. Peck uses the word "infirmities," which in holiness terminology implies that humanity is an impediment to authentic spirituality. The human constitution is not a composite of characteristics and traits to be utilized by the Holy Spirit to the glory of God. Instead, the characteristics and traits ameliorate what God would and could do in a person's life if they were absent.[78] Nineteenth-century holiness theology cannot be accused of Gnosticism. At the same time, however, the relationship of humanity to God is most often set in the context of the flesh warring against the Spirit. The teaching virtually never is that the created attributes of man are gifts of the Creator to the created to be "sanctified and meet for the master's use." Also, these traits were never named or enumerated, much less related in an instructive way to the operations of God's grace.

Upham attempted to do the above in Interior Life, making his work a unique chapter in antebellum holiness literature. In keeping with his mental philosophy, Upham first affirmed that natural principles--such as the desire of life, the desire of food, the desire of knowledge, the desire of society--have their place, their laws, their use.[79] To be sure, if the desire gains ascendancy over the will of God, guilt is incurred. But even here the emphasis is not just on guilt but on the potential for man's being relieved from inner "misery," and experiencing happiness by allowing the Holy Spirit to control human drives. The psychological principle for man's unfulfillment is this:

> If they meet with a present gratification, they always lay the foundation for their own re-existence. In the shape of subsequent and still stronger desires, which will fail of being gratified. A mind which is under the dominion of such urgent but ungratified desires, can never be at rest--can never be happy.[80]

The rule for eating and drinking is that it should be done according to the laws of nature and that its pleasure should not be an end in itself.[81] "The Saviour ate and drank without prejudice to his holiness, because he did so in fulfillment of the laws of nature."[82] Sex is given to us by the benevolent hand of God and is designed by Him for nothing but good.[83] The secret to the right use of these appetites is to use them according to God's design. Enslavement to any desire will mar the image of Christ within the soul and prevent God from revealing the face of his affectionate love. Upham urges:

> Upon all persons who wish to live a life of true holiness, the great importance of being in such a manner, in the exercise and indulgence of the appetites, as fulfill, and nothing more than fulfill, the intention of nature, or rather the intention of the wise and benevolent author of nature.[84]

Malevolent Affections

In no other area did Upham's understanding of the human psyche help him to clarify a misconception in sanctification theology more than his explication of the malevolent affections or emotions. Anger, resentment, and displeasure are as natural and God-given as positive feelings. Their moral character is to be determined by their teleological assessment. Are the feelings expressed to gratify selfish ends or for the betterment of others and for the glory of God? Instinctive resentment that is spontaneous does not have a religious or moral character at all, because it does not allow for a process of reasoning.[85] But Upham warned that anger, more than other emotions, is particularly liable to perversion and excess.[86] The awareness that all have sinned, and that Christ was unjustly offended and yet forgave, should be primary in preventing the indulgence of passion and in allaying passion's effects.[87]

Interpersonal Psychology

The most satisfying chapter on the importance of interpersonal relationships in psychological and spiritual development is Upham's "Union with God in the Redemption and Sanctification of the Family." Upham foreshadowed modern theories of imaging and the importance of modeling relationships in references to the analogy of faith. Within the nature of things, God has established the eternal pattern that men need each other, and that the sexes complement each other. We can only be happy in one another. Each person has the right to love and to be loved. What Upham called the "duality of existence," Buber called the "I-thou" relationship.

> But this duality of existence, which is constituted into unity by the unchangeable hand of the affections, cannot be perfectly happy except in some object, possessing a like infinity of character, which may be regarded, speaking after the manner of men, as "a procession or emanation" from the two. And this reproduction of itself, infinite in its nature, perfect in its love, and by an everlasting generation, "constitutes and completes the adorable family of the Trinity."[88]

This particular essay reveals Upham at the peak of his psychological astuteness, especially as his perceptiveness related to the holiness of God. Life, love, wholeness, and happiness are neither byproducts of holiness nor entire sanctification, as others would seem to imply. But all of the attributes are inherent to the perfection of God's nature, and they are experienced by man to the extent that he accepts the laws inherent to the very being of God, laws which God desires to extend to His entire creation. God is the center of the universe, and all things must be aligned with

Him.[89] The microcosm of the home or family must have its center in God, just as the universal sphere of all existence needs to be perfectly oriented to the absolute frame of reference. Without this absolute frame of reference, which is the essence of holiness, life and love will be amiss.

The family unit is the prime paradigm of what God wants to accomplish in all of His creations. God's design for the family is a relationship of holy love, but man and woman can realize the maximum that this love offers only if they experience divine union.

> A love being, that is to say, a being whose central principle of movement is holy love, cannot see its own love, because it is the nature of holy love, to turn its eyes from itself, and to see the wants, and to seek the good of another. But being unable to see itself in itself, when it sees and recognizes itself imaged forth in the bright heart and countenance of another, it seeks the company of such a being by a natural impulse, and rejoices in it "with joy unspeakable." In other words, the issues of perfect happiness are from the meetings and unions of true or pure love. It is not merely soul meeting soul, but the divine rushing into the arms of the divine. Stated in still other terms, the happiness of love consists, more than anything else, in seeing the face of love. This is the philosophy, not more of the true joy of earth, than it is the true joy of heaven.[90]

The God-head, which is the prototype of the nature of things, required an object to love throughout eternity; thus, the relationship of the father to the son, the eternal word.[91]

To be psychologically and spiritually complete, a human being must have an infinite object to love.[92] The holy love between a man and a woman is an extension of the love of God and has existed for all eternity. This holy love, which is the essence of spiritual sanctification, is in no way limited to union between the opposite sexes. "To love and to be loved, and in such a manner as to secure the highest happiness is the sacred right of all moral beings...."[93]

Upham obviously believed that the optimum matrix for

such a completion in one another is the family unit. It is within the family unit that the nurture of holy love begins. Upham was not unaware of the psychological formation of the God-concept, as exemplified by the earthly father in his relationship to the family.[94] Thus, the author stressed father's importance as family priest and his authority as a true representation of his heavenly Father. In a sense, Upham was saying, "show me what is happening in the family in terms of psychological commitment and spiritual fidelity, and I will show you what is happening in the world."

> He, who is not true to his father and mother, his wife and children, his brother and sister, being false at the centre, is not, and cannot be true to his neighborhood, his nation, and mankind. How is it possible for him to be true in his affections, when the truth of affection is not in him?[95]

A Psychology of Attainability

One of the standard arguments used by Christian perfectionists was that men would not seek after spiritual ideals if they did not believe these ideals were attainable. If properly understood in its context, the exhortation of Jesus was a command to be realized, "Be ye therefore perfect even as your Father in heaven is perfect." George Peck wrote that "defection is always the result of resting in low attainments."[96] The philosophical mind of Mahan made much of this argument: "Whatever a man regards as impracticable or thinks it absolutely certain that he never will perform, the changeless laws of mind render it impossible for him to aim at or intend to perform."[97] In answer to those who pointed to the saints who did not believe they had attained sanctification, the essence of Mahan's response was this: if all saints believed they would not or could not attain, no wonder they did not.[98]

For Finney, the whole debate pivoted on this one issue: "The real question is, has grace brought this attainment so within our reach, that we may reasonably expect to experience it in this life?"[99]

The above issue was a psychological corollary to Upham's three-fold division of the mind. That which a person weakly accepted, or believed intellectually, resulted in ambivalent feelings. The power of the will to act is proportionate to the depth of emotion attached to the object, which calls for some degree of commitment. Doubt brings despair and discouragement, which in time weakens the hope that a goal can be reached. Strong volitions never exist in respect to those things that we believe to be wholly beyond our reach. Upham went on to write: "Accordingly, we find it to be generally the fact that, whenever the possibility of securing any object in view is decidedly doubtful, the voluntary act, imbibing a sort of contagious hesitancy, becomes wanting and weak."[100]

Here was a psychological explanation for faith and the commitment of the will; these were the two foundational pillars for Phoebe Palmer's optimism, which was grounded in the belief that in the things of the kingdom entire sanctification can be an immediate reality for the serious minded. This view was not unlike the increasingly popular optimism in the kingdom of nineteenth-century America, that said "where there is a will, there is a way."

If the path could not be found, the responsibility for lighting the way of holiness rested on the shoulders of the individual traveler; it did not depend on the eternal lamp that was ever faithful. Nathan Bangs affirmed:

> ... the promise is made to those that seek. Do I seek? Yes, Then I have a right to expect that I shall find. But many shall seek and shall not be able to find. Have I sought without finding? Then have I not sought aright. The fault is in me and not in God. I must, therefore, search and find out the hindering cause.[101]

As long as a person disputes either the existence or the possibility of sanctification, attainment is an impossibility. The psychological principle is a corollary to Upham's synergism that God does not arbitrarily sanctify an individual within the dictates of his sovereignty. "Who can reasonably expect to be holy that does not put forth volition, a fixed, unalterable determination with divine assistance to be so?"[102]

The Holy Spirit did the work but he could not act without the human ingredients of positive mental attitude and exercise of freedom to overcome spiritual inertia. The first step to becoming holy was a resolve to be holy. Timothy Merritt, in the very first full-length treatise on Christian perfection written in America, stated:

> When the resolution is fully formed, that you will seek holiness, immediately set your face against all sin, even all the corruptions of your heart, confessing and bewailing them, and begging God for Christ's sake to take them all away, and fill you with righteousness.[103]

True to a conditional theology, there was the psychological confidence that if man takes the first step, God will take the second; "...if in the fixed purpose of our minds, we consecrate ourselves to him, to do, as far as in us lies, his whole will then, and not otherwise, we can believe that he will be to us, and do for us, all that he has promised in his holy word."[104]

Upham devoted the last half of his life to encouraging Christians toward a spiritual ideal that to a certain extent required perseverance and a "fixed tenacity of purpose"[105] but on the other hand was received through a simple act of faith. Upham's psychology of attainment was not unlike the reasoning of David Roberts, who implied that it is psychologically unhealthy to condemn men for failing to embody agape, especially if they are told that Christ's example is beyond the reach of the race.[106] "This doctrine scolds them for not being replicas of Christ and then scolds them if they believe that they could be."[107] After all, if a man seeks for holiness, what does he have to lose? It was the pragmatism and idealism articulated by William James at the turn of the century:

> The difference between willing and merely wishing, between having ideals that are creative and ideals that are but pinings and regrets, thus, depends solely either on the amount of steam pressure chronically driving the character in the ideal direction, or on the amount of ideal excitement transciently acquired.[108]

Conclusion

The laws of psychological health bear a strong

resemblance to the principles of spiritual maturity, which are discussed throughout Upham's writings. Upham's division of the mind enforced Wesley's teachings that sanctification takes place primarily in the will rather than in the emotions. The restoration of the will brings control to the propensities and instincts, but not without discipline and training. Human appetites are not evil in themselves, but they need, daily, to be submitted to sanctifying grace.

The secret to mental tranquility is a right value system, i.e., attaching to events and objects their due importance; this means a person must estimate everything in the light of a supreme love to God. Sanctification parallels a psychological thrust within the human personality toward wholeness, integration, congruence, inner reconciliation and mental harmony. Upham placed humanity in a much more positive light than his contemporaries did, especially concerning innate drives and malevolent affections.

Though Upham fell somewhat short of twentieth-century teaching in his explication of interpersonal development, he made a significant contribution to the relationship of spiritual maturity to sociality, family nurture, imitation, etc. Not the least important of his contributions was the psychological theory supporting the belief that holiness of heart and life could be attained in this world.

Notes

1. This is unclear in Wesley and is a moot question in the nineteenth-century holiness movement. But holiness writers generally agreed that a person could be holy in intention while sick in mind. Bear in mind Wesley's teaching that holiness was consistent with a "thousand nameless defects." Contemporary holiness writers have concluded that one can be morally sanctified while remaining mentally and physically depraved. Richard Taylor writes: "The result of Adam's sin and separation from the presence of God was a depraved or degenerated moral nature. Losing his health and perfeciton, his nature became diseased and warped and out of line. Inevitably, man's mind and body were greatly impaired because of this depravity and his continued sinning so that he has become subject to countless mistakes of judgment, deficiency of knowledge, lapse of memory, faulty

reasoning and perceptive faculties, physical deformities, abnormalities and peculiarities of temperament, disease, pain, and decay. But since none of these infirmities have a moral quality in them, they must not be considered part of the Adamic depraved moral nature, or original sin...." Richard S. Taylor, *A Right Conception of Sin* (Kansas City, Mo.: Nazarene Publishing House, 1939), pp. 96-97.

2. Thomas C. Upham, *Outlines of Disordered Mental Action* (New York: Arno Press, reprint of 1868 edition), p. 63.

3. Ibid., p. 99.

4. Ibid., p. 119.

5. Upham, *Mental Philosophy*, Vol. I, p. 46. At this point Upham crosses the threshold of the thoughts of Edwin Starbuck and William James. Starbuck's empirical investigation took as its premise that "there is no event in the spiritual life which does not occur in accordance with immutable laws." Paul E. Johnson, *Psychology of Religion* (New York, Nashville: Abingdon Press, 1945), p. 22. Where Upham differed from the empiricists at the turn of the century, was in his lack of systematic research methodology such as surveys, questionnaires, and case studies. Of course, there is the continuing question as to what part the supernatural plays in religious experience for Starbuck and James. James left open-ended the question as to the predominance of a *sui generis* experience beyond psychological and cultural causation.

6. Ibid., p. 43.

7. Upham, *Outlines of Disordered Mental Action*, pp. 91-93.

8. Upham, *Life of Faith*, p. 85.

9. Ibid., p. 87.

10. Ibid., p. 88.

11. Ibid., p. 143. That faith must be beyond absolute undoubtable demonstration is inherent to the meaning of faith and is a superfluous statement. William James wrote: "Faith means belief in something concerning which doubt is still theoretically possible: and as the test of belief is willingness to act, one may say that faith is the readiness to act in a cause, the prosperous issue of which is not certified to us in advance." Orlo Strunk, Jr. (ed.), *Readings in the Psychology of Religion*, "A Definition of Faith" by William James (Nashville: Abingdon Press, 1959), pp. 196-197.

12. Upham, *Life of Faith*, pp. 147-148.

13. Ibid., p. 150.

14. Ibid., p. 153.

15. David Roberts argues that secure faith "rests upon an integration between rational belief and emotional commitment." David Roberts, Psychotherapy and a Christian View of Man (New York: Charles Scribner's Sons, 1950), p. 72.

16. Ibid., p. 374.

17. Ibid., p. 375.

18. Ibid., p. 376.

19. Upham, Interior Life, p. 125.

20. Ibid., p. 126.

21. Ibid., p. 127.

22. Ibid., p. 129. Upham was leery of high emotional experience, believing that often it was a counterfeit for true sanctification of character. He wrote: "Many persons seem to be more solicitous for strong emotions than for right emotions. It would perhaps be a fair representation of their state to say the burden of their prayer is, that their soul might be like 'the chariots of Arminadib,' or that like Paul, they may be caught up into the third heavens. They seem desirous perhaps almost unconsciously to themselves, to experience or to do some great as well as some good thing." Upham, Religious Maxims, p. 37.

23. Upham, Mental Philosophy, Vol. II, p. 225.

24. Upham, Divine Union, p. 290.

25. Upham, Interior Life, p. 184.

26. Upham, Madame Guyon, Vol. II, p. 340.

27. Upham, Divine Union, p. 6.

28. Ibid., p. 4.

29. I use the word "operation" because Upham did not believe the mind could be separated into physical (material) departments or faculties. His divisions of the mind were for the purpose of describing the functional processes and psychological characteristics.

30. Upham, Will, p. 17.

31. Ibid., p. 242.

32. Upham, Life of Faith, p. 256.

33. Ibid. Inward tranquility because of supreme love to God or "relating absolutely to the absolute," was a core teaching of Kierkegaard's: "One who distinguishes absolutely has a relationship to the absolute telos and ipso facto, also a relationship to God.... It keeps the mob of relative ends at a distance, in order, that the absolutely, distinguishing individual may effect a relationship to the absolute.... In the midst of the finite and its manifold

limitations in order to forget the absolute distinciton, it proposes to be for the individual his absolute inwardness, and as for other things, he may be an alderman, and so forth. But the maximum of attainment is simultaneously to sustain an absolute relationship to the absolute end and a relative relationship to relative ends" (pp. 369-371). Soren Kierkegaard, Concluding Unscientific Postscript (Princeton, N.J.: Princeton University Press, 1941). Translated by David F. Swenson and Walter Lowrie.

34. Upham, Life of Faith, p. 467.
35. Upham, Divine Union, p. 364.
36. Ibid.
37. William James, Varieties of Religious Experience (New York: Longman, Green, and Company, 1923), p. 290. To illustrate minds free from anxiety and experiencing mental security, harmonious disposition and psychic serenity, James utilizes Upham's biographies of Madame Guyon and Catherine Adorna (pp. 287-289).
38. Perry Miller (ed.), The Transcendentalists (Cambridge: Harvard University Press, 1960), p. 108.
39. Upham, Will, p. 235.
40. Ibid., p. 305.
41. Ibid., p. 307.
42. Ibid., p. 308.
43. Wesley, Letters, Vol. VI, p. 68.
44. Upham, Interior Life, p. 364.
45. Ibid., p. 365.
46. Upham, Life of Faith, p. 33.
47. Upham, Divine Union, p. 162.
48. Ibid., p. 163.
49. Ibid., p. 164.
50. Ibid.
51. Ibid., p. 165.
52. Upham, Madame Guyon, Vol. I, p. 133.
53. Sydney G. Dimond, The Psychology of the Methodist Revival (London: Oxford University Press, 1926), p. 64.
54. Ibid., p. 65.
55. Upham, Mental Philosophy, Vol. II, pp. 356-357.
56. Certainly Wesley believed this as he was perhaps a greater disseminator of religious literature than anybody in the history of the church before his time.
57. Upham, Mental Philosophy, Vol. II, p. 360.
58. Ibid., p. 361. The full quote from Merle Curti, which I refer to in the introduction, is as follows: "As late

as 1848, Webster's Elementary Speller, of which a million copies were being sold annually, was outspoken in its religious character. Children who studied this famous 'blueback' learned that 'God governs the world with infinite wisdom,' makes the ground to bring forth fruit for man and beast, and is to be worshipped with prayer on beginning the day and before retiring at night. They were also told that the laws of nature are sustained 'by the immediate presence and agency of God,' and that hence they were never to complain of unavoidable calamities. Further, they were taught that the immortality of the soul had been rarely disputed; that the Scriptures were to be examined 'daily and carefully'; that pastors did not like to see vacant seats in church, and that the devil is the great adversary of man. 'We are apt to live forgetful of our continual dependence on God,' and it should never be forgotten that it is a solemn thing to die and appear before Him for judgment." Merle Curti, The Social Ideas of American Educators (Totowa, N.J.: Littlefield, Adams and Company, 1959), p. 17.

59. Ibid., p. 264.

60. Ibid., p. 363. Upham is not using repression in the Freudian sense, which forces desires and instincts from the view of consciousness to survive in the unconscious. From a healthful psychological point of view, Upham should have used the word "suppression." See pp. 277-280. Philip Reiff, Freud: The Mind of the Moralist (Chicago: The University of Chicago Press, 1959).

61. Upham, Life of Faith, p. 214.

62. Ibid., p. 261.

63. Ibid., p. 270.

64. Ibid.

65. Ibid., p. 380.

66. Upham, Divine Union, p. 197.

67. Ibid.

68. Upham, Interior Life, p. 299.

69. Ibid., p. 262.

70. Upham, American Cottage Life, p. 138.

71. Ibid., p. 135

Mental Freedom

By Madame Guyon

A little bird I am, Shut from the fields of air;
And in my cage I sit and sing to Him, who placed me there;
Well pleased a prisoner to be Because, My God it pleases thee

O, it is good to soar These bolts and bars above,
To Him, whose purposes I adore; Whose providence I love;
And in the mighty will to find The joy, the freedom of the mind

72. Edward Whitmont, The Symbolic Quest (Princeton, N.J.: Princeton University Press, 1969), p. 165.

73. C. G. Jung, The Undiscovered Self (Boston: Little, Brown, and Company, 1957), p. 31.

74. C. G. Jung, Collected Works, Vol. XX, Part I (London: Routledge and Kegan Paul, Ltd., 1958), p. 275.

75. Ibid., p. 40.

76. Upham, Interior Life, p. 161.

77. George Peck, p. 438.

78. This does not mean that holiness writers believed that infirmities could not bring glory to God, but the emphasis was that God would turn bad into good not that traits were positive in themselves. J. A. Wood wrote: "Freedom from these [infirmities] can not be expected in this world. We must wait for deliverance from their imperfections until this mortal puts on immortality. These infirmities, so numerous and various, are the common inheritance of humanity. They are not signs; they are innocent; and although they are our misfortune, they are included in the 'all things' which, by the grace and blessing of God, shall work together for our good." Perfect Love, p. 41.

79. Ibid., p. 177.

80. Ibid., p. 181.

81. Ibid., p. 180.

82. Ibid., p. 181.

83. Ibid., p. 182.

84. Ibid., p. 183.

85. Upham, Mental Philosophy, Vol. II, p. 141.

86. Ibid., p. 179.

87. Ibid., p. 81.

88. Upham, Divine Union, p. 296. Thomas Oden argued that man can learn about interpersonal relationships through studying God's self-disclosure as a trinity of being. Oden stated: "My thesis is that the history of language of the person has emerged under the tutelage of trinitarian theology and classical patristic Christology." Thomas C. Oden, Game Free, p. 117.

89. Upham, Divine Union, p. 291.

90. Ibid., p. 294. Upham speaks here of the "I-thou" relationship, the divine human encounter that is the prototype of all other relationships. Rob Staples, in an

unpublished Ph.D. dissertation on Christian perfection argues against an understanding of static attainment but rather for an ongoing "I-Thou" relationship. "But faith is no mere single response; it is a continuous succession of responses to the Divine Giver. Holiness is not a static possession. It is given moment by moment, dependent upon the receptivity and responsiveness of faith." p. 214. Rob Staples, "John Wesley's Doctrine of Christian Perfection: A Reinterpretation." Unpublished Ph.D. dissertation, Berkeley, California: Pacific School of Religion, 1963.

91. Ibid., p. 296.

92. Ibid., p. 298.

93. Ibid., p. 304.

94. Ibid., p. 307.

95. Ibid., p. 310. Upham does not fully explicate the term "imaging," but his belief that human love as exemplified in the family, reflects that which is eternal and divine, makes Dennis Kinlaw's references to the writing of Charles Williams apropos: "It is an human experience that images something eternal. It is part of what scripture means by the _imago Dei_. When this is realized, we see that it is a divine category with a human counterpart (image), which helps us understand ourselves. He who is love made us like Himself.... He has built into us a human need and a human experience that in counterpart symbolizes in a human relationship this ultimate personal experience with God. Thus, a sanctity derives to human love from the sacredness of the reality which it images." Dennis F. Kinlaw, "Charles Williams' Concept of Imaging Applied to the 'Song of Songs,'" _Wesleyan Theological Journal_, Vol. 15, No. 1 (Spring 1981), p. 91. Kinlaw goes on to point out that the person who looks at life as an expression of the divine, sees life as good in itself as a gift of God and not simply an allegory of something better. This is exactly the philosophical approach of Upham to the world around him and its possibilities. Theological perfection was not a negating and waiting for something better. Expressed in the words of Kinlaw, Upham firmly believed that "The gifts of God must not be slighted for a pseudospirituality" (p. 91).

96. George Peck, p. 16. For the difference between the psychological drive for perfection and the spiritual desire for Christian perfection, see W. S. Taylor, "Perfectionism in Psychology and in Theology," _Canadian Journal of Theology_, Vol. V, No. 1 (July 1959), p. 177. "Whatever one may think of these distinctions in the meaning of the term

sinlessness, it seems quite clear that Christian perfection is conceived in terms of religious attitude rather than in terms of ethical observance. It is a life dominated by faith in and love to God, rather than by a struggle to act in strict conformity to ideal maxims. It is basically a personal response rather than a personal achievement. The perfect man is one who has moved into a new dimension of living, whose system of motives has been transformed by his inclusion within the new order of grace and faith. The effect is to remove the obsessional compulsiveness which so often characterizes the striving for what Ritschl would call quantitative conformity, without lessening an effort to realize his ideal."

97. Asa Mahan, Scripture Doctrine of Christian Perfection (Boston: D. S. King, 1839), p. 46. Attainability in this life was the key issue that separated the Wesleyan-Oberlin perfectionists from the opponents of the doctrine. The simple issue created a schism between the two opposing parties within evangelical Protestantism, a great schism that could not be crossed by a bridge made of synthetic semantics. For Mahan, one was on one side of the gulf or another; there was no in between. He wrote in his "Reply to Dr. Woods": "You will permit me hereto notice what appears to me as manifest inconsistency in admitting what you have respecting the provisions and promises of grace, and the maintaining that the question whether complete sanctification in this life is an object of rational expectation, is not the great question of practical interest with us as Christians." Asa Mahan, "President Mahan's Reply to Dr. Woods," Guide to Christian Perfection, Vol. III, No. 7 (1842), p. 183.

98. Asa Mahan, Ibid., p. 193.

99. Upham, Will, p. 75.

100. Ibid., p. 80. See "Upham on Spiritual Life" from the Biblical Repertory and Princeton Review (Philadelphia: 1846), Volume XVIII. The article stated and attempted to refute: "The author propounds a certain doctrine respecting the necessary and universal connexion of a sense of obligation, in the human mind with a given intellectual perception of the possibility of something the relation of a certain feeling to an exercise of the understanding on a given object" (p. 293).

101. Nathan Bangs, "Christian Perfection: How to Attain It," Guide, Vol. XXXVII, p. 168.

102. Upham, Interior Life, p. 27.

103. T. Merritt (ed.), The Christian's Manual: A Treatise on Christian Perfection (New York: 1840), p. 140.

104. Upham, Interior Life, p. 29.
105. Ibid., p. 33.
106. David Roberts, p. 123.
107. Ibid.
108. William James, Varieties of Religious Experience, p. 266.

Chapter VIII

THE WARFIELD CRITIQUE

A comparison of Benjamin B. Warfield[1] and Thomas C. Upham reveals a paradox of nineteenth-century American theology. Both men were steeped in Scottish common-sense realism, and both gave reason primacy in Christian experience. The affinity stopped there, however.

According to Warfield's theological perspective, Upham had three strikes against him: mysticism threatened the transcendence of God, Arminianism depreciated God's sovereignty, and perfectionism mitigated against the Westminter Confession's teaching on total depravity and, in Warfield's mind, could never be disassociated from John Humphrey Noyes' antinomianism.[2] Whatever Calvinism there remained in Upham made him, in Warfield's eyes, all the more inconsistent. George Marsden summed up Warfield's assessment of Keswick exponent, Lewis Sperry Chafer; the summary applies to Upham as well:

> The essence of Warfield's criticism was, as he put it in a review of a work by young Lewis Sperry Chafer, that the Keswick teacher was plagued by "two inconsistent systems of religion struggling together in his mind." One was Calvinist, so that he and his "coterie" (one of Warfield's favorite words) of evangelists and Bible teachers often spoke of God's grace doing all; but behind this Calvinist exterior lurked the spectres of Pelagius, Arminius, and Wesley, all of whom made God's gracious working subject to human determination. The resulting synthesis, Warfield said, was "at once curiously pretentious and curiously shallow."[3]

Mysticism

But Pelagius, Arminius, and Wesley were not those friends of Upham who rankled Warfield most. That dubious distinction belonged to religious enemy number one: mysticism. Mysticism struck at the root of Warfield's apologetic, i.e., all truth must be primarily proved by, founded on, and reasoned from the external authority of the scriptures. In other words, Upham internalized Scottish common-sense philosophy while Warfield externalized it. Upham reasoned from within while Warfield reasoned from without. It was intuitive rationalism against scholastic rationalism, and intuitive rationalism was too suggestive of Kant and Ritschl to suit Warfield. In comparing a mystic with a true evangelical, Warfield wrote:

> The mystic, on the other hand, tends to substitute his religious experience for the objective revelation of God recorded in the written Word, as the source from which he derives his knowledge of God, or at least, to subordinate the expressly revealed Word as the less direct and convincing source of knowledge of God to his own religious experience. The result is that the external revelation is relatively depressed in value, if not totally set aside.[4]

Lack of External Authority

Mysticism, transcendentalism, and liberalism all smelled of, at best, excessive immanentism--and, at worst, pantheism--to Warfield. Upham had fused the inner light of mysticism, Scottish reliance on inner consciousness, and natural theology. And, as an internal buttress to doubt, he'd added skepticism, and philosophical speculation.

From Warfield's point of view, not enough external data existed to form a basis for the synthesis. Religious historical facts and biblical authority for Warfield could not be replaced by Wesleyanism's and mysticism's subjective reliance on spiritual experience. In Warfield's estimation, immanentism ("which confounds the natural and the supernatural") and subjectivism ("which makes subjective experience the standard of authority") could not withstand the inroads of higher criticism and evolution.[5] "Christianity rests on external authority and for the very good reason that it is not the product of men's religious sentiment but it is the gift of God."[6]

Warfield made little allowance for receiving the gift of God in any other way. God could be directly understood through the scriptures and, using them, infallibly interpreted. In William Livingston's words: "Such a method in theology does not and cannot allow for the richness and variety of religious experience."[7] Warfield had little esteem for man's using psychology as an investigative tool to understand his relationship with God. Hermaneutically speaking, therefore, Upham started off on the wrong foot. Warfield was confident that no fields of study other than exegesis were necessary to knowing God. Using scripture, as an objective statement of fact, an individual was able to eliminate the subjective element, i.e., the point of view of the observer that stands between the facts and the observer's report of the facts.[8] In Warfield's estimation, Upham's psychology was not about to do that. The difference in methodology was clearly articulated by Livingston:

> If theology is the "science of faith," then it is as a branch of psychology. If theology is the "science of the Christian religion," then it is a branch of history. In the former case, the subject matter of theology will consist of the subjective experiences of the heart, and the task of apologetics will be to discover what is the objective basis for such experiences.... If however, theology is the science of God, then it deals not with subjective experiences nor with the history of thought, but with a body of objective facts.[9]

Warfield's Overall Assessment of Upham

Warfield's 122-page essay on Upham, "The Mystical Perfectionism of Thomas Cogswell Upham," is the lengthiest critique of Upham's writings. Much of Warfield's negation represented the stock arguments that late nineteenth-century fundamentalistic Calvinism posed against Wesleyan-Arminianism.[10]

But Warfield was not without some complimentary things to say about his subject. He made note of Upham's excellent family background, his conspicuous ability, and his intellectual acuity.[11] Referring to the time Upham gave spiritual counsel to Henry Boynton Smith, Warfield did not hesitate to call the Bowdoin professor a "devoted man of God."[12] For Warfield, the bottom line regarding Upham's worth is that the good of Upham's life outlived the poison of his doctrine.

> Loved by all who knew him; admired by all who came into contact with him, whether in person or in his printed works; he lived his quiet life out in a somewhat remote academic center, and has left behind him little more than the sweet savor of an honored name. Perhaps in his case, we can reverse Mark Antony's maxim and say that the good he did lives after him and the evil has been largely interred with his bones.[13]

Methodology of Critique

Warfield attacked by using innuendos and by accusing Upham of guilt by association. He proceeded in this way: first, he pointed out a theological error that Upham made, perhaps; next, because the accusation could not be substantiated in Upham's writings, Warfield partially amended his charge or demonstrated why his insinuation, in fact, was probably not true. By that time, however, doubts regarding Upham's unorthodoxy had been planted in the mind of the reader.

A prime example of this modus operandi occurred when Warfield implied that Upham had begun to seek holiness (or his "second conversion") when he became anxious that the blood of Christ was no longer sufficient for him and "that he [Upham] was uneasy--increasingly so--so long as he had nothing but Christ's righteousness to rest upon."[14] Since Warfield knew that nothing in Upham's testimony even remotely hinted at a lack of reliance on the blood of Christ, he went on to write: "It is probable, however, that he intends no more than to convey a strong impression of the distress, the consciousness of his shortcomings gave him, and his consequent increasing anxiety to be completely delivered from them."[15]

The only thing wrong with the latter statement is the "probable"; what Upham wanted was to move from Romans chapter seven to Romans chapter eight, a transition that necessitated an even greater reliance on the merits of Christ. Upham doubted the efficacy of relying fully on the merits of Christ's blood no more than the apostle did who had been converted on the Damascus road. The essence of the Wesley-Oberlinian and Uphamian argument is that the blood of Christ was to be relied on not only for justification, but also to be fully and individually appropriated for sanctification.

> We must be enabled to say, if we would realize the astonishing cleansing and healing efficacy there is in the Gospel of God, that he is My God, of the Savior, that he is My Savior. We must be enabled to lay hold on the blessed promises, and exclaim, These are the gifts of my Father, these are the purchase of My Savior, these are meant for Me.[16]

Guilt by association abounds through Warfield's commentary. Upham's teaching on the dispensation of the Holy Spirit is compared with John Humphrey Noyes' chialistic perfectionism by way of Bousuet's commentary that compared Fenelon and Madame Guyon to Montanus; a commentary on Montanus, therefore, was indirectly related to Upham, enabling Warfield to use a catch-all historical label, Montanism, to obscure and camouflage a personality that in many ways is on the opposite end of the theological continuum, not to mention being of dissimilar psychological temperament.

Again Warfield set the record straight: "Neither Madame Guyon nor Upham were Montanists."[17] So why even bring up the name of Montanism, which was synonymous with fanaticism and, for the early church, was the case in point for extreme expressions of spirituality? According to Warfield, both Madame Guyon, and Upham shared with Montanus the fanatical assertion that the culminating dispensation of the kingdom of God--the dispensation of the Spirit--had been introduced by them.[18] But Warfield failed to produce a single statement in the writings of either Madame Guyon or Upham to support this accusation.

His pattern was to clear his prey from an accusation while, at the same time, making another accusation. Somehow a linking of Montanus to Upham by way of Bousuet deserved a commentary on Rufus Jones' treatment of John the Scot (the latter taught the progressive dispensations of the coming Kingdom). Warfield concluded a commentary on John the Scot, Joachim of Fiori, Gerard of San Donnino, and Amaury of Bene, with a reference to their antinomianism.[19] Thus, Upham received the same accusation as Wesleyan perfectionism, antinomianism, a tendency which was absent in Upham, and which Wesley vehemently fought against. Warfield stated:

> It is this form of the conception rife among the Baptists and Ranters of seventeenth century England which reappears in the mystical perfectionists of Western and Central New York at the end of the first quarter of the nineteenth century, and is proclaimed with the confidence of strong conviction by Upham.[20]

Relating Upham to the Ranters and to John Humphrey Noyes' Oneidan community--via many personalities in between--required a strong sense of historical and theological imagination.

Quietism

It would be easier to critique Warfield's treatment of Upham, if Warfield had contented himself with unraveling what Upham actually thought and wrote regarding specific issues--especially the historical premises of Quietism. But Warfield assumed that a good deal of what was true concerning Quietism was also true about Upham. For Warfield, there were only three kinds of mystics: bad, worse, and worst. In the final analysis, Warfield believed, all mysticism "makes its appeal to the feelings as the sole, or at least as the normative, source of knowledge of divine things."[21] Rather than give a systematic review of the way in which Upham identified with the seventeenth-century Quietists or how he differed with them, Warfield's effort was, ostensibly, to critique a Quietism that was superimposed upon Upham. Thus Upham was introduced to a late nineteenth-century and early twentieth-century American fundamentalist camp, wearing a costume that the Bowdoin professor would neither fully have claimed nor possibly have even recognized.

As Warfield and Knox pointed out, it is true that Upham

was anachronistic in his evangelical treatment of Madame Guyon, but his treatment of her is not an adequate excuse for Warfield having reversed the procedure of dressing Upham in seventeenth-century Quietist language. The following, though true perhaps of Madame Guyon, was in no sense true of Upham.

> Faith we must bear in mind, however, was in Madame Guyon's view, a "work," that is to say, a virtue, a virtuous disposition, that particular virtuous disposition which above all others prepared and opened the soul for the reception of divine things.[22]

The extreme example of the above may be found between pages 381 and 390. Warfield wrote there an explication of Quietism as seen mostly through the eyes of Rufus Jones, but Warfield never once mentioned Upham. Instead he made a blanket statement that, on the surface, concerned all that had gone before in that chapter. "This is the doctrine in the terms of which Upham undertook to express what, after all is said, remained in substance, the Wesleyan doctrine of Christian perfection."[23]

Warfield referred specifically to two issues. The first concerns the central idea of Quietism and centers on such issues as passivity, indifference, abandonment, and annihilation.[24] Little doubt exists that Upham attempted to explain these characteristics in acceptable terms; he himself admitted that they were adapted to his own theological scheme and that they reflected traits of his own personality.[25]

Nature

Meriting further inspection is the other characteristic of Quietism, about which Warfield comments. He differentiated seventeenth-century Quietism from Reformation theology in the following manner:

> The Quietists' preoccupation, in other words, was not with sin, but with nature. The Protestant, whose preoccupation was with sin, did not look for the annihilation of nature, but for the eradication of its sin. But what the Quietist sought to be delivered from, was

> self. It was not a purified nature he sought but a superior nature.[26]

Warfield interpreted the Quietists as teaching that sin can only be negated as the natural life is destroyed or absorbed by the divine. In Madame Guyon's opinion, "there is no solution short of the complete annihilation of the individual self in which sin inheres the absolute spoiling of every particular thing to which the soul clings in its sundered selfhood."[27] Warfield claimed that the Quietists sought for a divinization of nature, or at least a deliverance from it because they believed man's problem was not original depravity in the Reformation sense but the "utter miserables of the creature."[28] What Warfield described is a Gnostic concept of evil that makes sin inherent to nature or matter as an essential element of created existence. Closely related is Catholicism's contempt of nature as well as a superficial dualism of the natural and supernatural, which gives rise to the doctrine of the need of superadditum grace.

Defining Upham in terms of all this was the coarsest mistake that Warfield made, an error apparently inspired by only a partial reading of the Bowdoin professor.

Perhaps Upham's view of original sin is suspect, but in no way, after reading all of Upham, could anyone have inferred a pessimism regarding the natural man. That natural man can be realigned and restored--as opposed to displaced--was inherent to Upham's perspective as a moral philosopher and to his belief in uniformity of law, the immutability of God's law, as well as the inherent good in God and His creation, both animate and inanimate. To be truly natural is to live by the laws that God originally intended for man; nothing contradictory is needed or desired. (This is not to say that nothing antecedent or additional is needed, i.e., the grace of God).

Upham was one who, along with Scottish philosophers, believed that "the purpose of philosophy was to analyze the nature of the human mind in order to discover the laws of human nature so that man would be able to know them and follow them to comply with God's design."[30] For Upham it was simply grace added to, not displacing, a scientific methodology that not only investigated maximum performance levels but hoped for optimum achievement. Instantaneous sanctification would not bring the perfection of the original natural man, but progressive sanctification would increasingly realize Edenic standards. Anthropological confidence is a foundational premise for both Upham's theology and philosophy.

Warfield himself wrote how the Spirit of God, according to Upham, does not negate the appetites, propensities, and affections but works in and through them to accomplish his directions and desires. "It is by purifying them that He guides us in pure paths; by elevating them that He brings us to exalted actions."[31] Yet, Warfield went on to say that what had deflected Upham's exposition from the truth was his "undertone" of sympathy accompanied by "false antagonism of the natural and the supernatural which dominates the thoughts of his Romanist teachers."[32] What Warfield actually did was attack one of Upham's most important contributions--the non-depreciation of God-given gifts. But Warfield quoted Upham, "We are not required to eradicate our natural propensities and affections but to purify them. We are not required to cease to be men but merely to become holy men."[33]

Determinism

Warfield's scattered treatment of "Upham's Doctrinal Teaching," makes it very difficult to give an extensive treatment of any one criticism. The author jumped from topic to topic and did not fully develop his accusations. He began his critique by attacking Upham's explanation of the will and by concluding that Upham was caught in the dilemma that he himself had created while trying to demonstrate that man is master of both his and God's action. But, Warfield wrote, "at the bottom of [Upham's] heart, he knows that man is determined in all his action."[34] (This unresolvable philosophical problem has already been commented on.) Warfield demonstrated his own rigidity when he came up with another standard Calvinistic syllogism: "Free consent means moral merit and moral merit means a salvation according to works."[35]

The dilemma, "damned if you do and damned if you don't" belonged to Warfield. He was critical of human initiative that made God "the instrument of our disposal."[36]

At the same time, he negated passivity that mitigated against striving, agonizing, and working out our own salvation.[37]

Degrees of Reception

Of more substantial worth was Warfield's attempt to demonstrate how Upham had mechanically compartmentalized the mind in order to give a psychological explanation to the parable of the sower. Warfield denied that a person may receive religious truth, feel emotive about it, yet not experience religion. Quoting directly from Upham will reveal the professor's true meaning:

> But if the experience stops here, in such a manner as to constitute a merely emotional experience, and without reaching and affecting a still more inward and important part of the mind, as seems sometimes to be the case, we cannot with good reasons, regard it as a truly religious experience.[38]

Note that Upham said a "truly religious experience"; by this he meant true religion. In answer to the suggestion that religious truth did not always evolve into a commitment of the will, Upham did not argue and said it was the normal course that, as Warfield implied, intellectual perception would have no effect whatsoever on the affections and will.[39] Warfield retorted that the

> human soul is a unit and cannot be aroused except through a prior movement of the intellect, so every movement of the intellect must be felt in the emotional nature--and through it, in those affections which Upham calls desires and in the will.[40]

I would not argue for the correctness of Upham's psychological explanation of the mysteries of godliness, or as to why grace takes greater effect in some lives than in others. I will make only two comments. First, the premise that true religion needs to extend to the will was foundational to both Wesley's and Upham's concept of entire sanctification, to their identification of sin with known willful transgression of the law of God, and to the developed theory of nineteenth-century holiness proponents that entire sanctification could not take place--because of theological and psychological reasons--without a willful consecration of the self to God.

Secondly, Warfield did not have any options either in evaluating Upham's explanation of various depths of spiritual reception or in describing the difference between nominal belief in God and Christian commitment to God. His theological presupposition that only the saved or elect could receive or be excited by truth, ruled out a psychological progression that may stop short of the will. Degrees of reception are, in every respect, according to God's sovereign preparation of the human heart. Note the lack of psychological explanation in the following from Warfield:

> The reason why some who hear the word go on to fruit bearing and others do not, is that the natural process of growth is arrested in mid course in the one case and not in the other. The reason why it does it, is that it does it.[41]

Charge of Hedonism

Warfield agreed with Upham's assertion that love was the motive for creation, but when Upham suggested that God's desire for man's happiness entered into his purpose for creation, Warfield saw red. It is proof "that Upham adopts the hedonistic theory of ethics prevalent in the New England of his day, according to which happiness is the *summum bonum* over general benevolence, or the love of being in general, the principle of all virtue."[42]

Once again we have an innuendo, a statement taken out of context and not fully developed. Upham designated love to God--not happiness--as the highest good. Warfield's insinuation did not agree with the totality of Upham's ethics, which was deontological, nonutilitarian, and highly influenced by a mystical disinterested benevolence. How could Warfield charge Upham with the mistaken idea that God and holiness can be sought apart from a desire for gifts and graces[43] and, at the same time, accuse him of hedonism? Upham did not advocate a teleology of happiness any more than Samuel Hopkins did. Upham was constantly arguing for a nonutilitarian understanding of God's love.

> It is a great practical principle in the religious life, that a state of suffering furnishes the test of love. When God is pleased to bestow his favors upon us, when his blessings are repeated every hour, how can we tell whether we love him for what he is or for what he gives? But when, in seasons of deep and varied afflictions, our heart still clings to him as our only hope and only joys, we may say, "Thou knowest all things. Thou knowest that I love thee."[44]

Use of Providence

Warfield's criticism of Upham in regards to Madame Guyon's use of providence is well taken. The criticism is three-fold.

First, this use of providence provides an intellectual defense for the adverse events of life because it sees all things from the wisdom of God. In fact, Warfield himself may have been as guilty of this view as Upham was, because, in keeping with his Calvinistic presuppositions, Warfield saw the hand of God as a primary cause of events. He wrote:

> Despite this display of timidity in giving expression to the whole truth, the statement shows clearly as its main matter that Upham believed in the universal providence of God and had the courage to say so. Calvin says it better; but it is good to have it said at all, and that directly in the interest of holy living.[45]

Warfield was rightly critical of Upham's optimism that God's providence could be understood and, hence, man could order his life by it. But there is a truth; if man accepted God's providence, i.e., his place in life, there would be more individual and civic harmony in the world. On the other hand, one wonders if Upham wrestled sufficiently with acquiescence to the rule of God and the psychological dimension of personal initiative.

Secondly, Warfield was further justified in his pointing out that acquiescence leads to an unrealistic divorce of human emotions from events and a callousness to not only the feelings of self but to the feelings of others as well.

Thirdly, Warfield's most astute observation--in the entire treatise possibly--was that the mystical use of providence tends to be anthropocentric.

> It may, often does, end in erecting our individual self into something very like the focus of the universe and conceiving of everything and everybody in the circumference of the circle thrown out from ourselves, as a center, as existing for us alone.[46]

In regards to Madame Guyon's suggestion that the death of her father and daughter would strip her of those props and dependences that were preventing her further sanctification, Warfield humorously commented that "such purposes of God made it quite dangerous to live within the reach of the as yet only partially sanctified affections of a saint."[47] Contact with the partially sanctified is "almost as perilous as contact with a live wire."[48] The psychological tendency to interpret events as they relate to self is an infantile urge for coherence and meaning, which Upham was not advanced enough to censure.

Definition of Perfection

Warfield was extremely delighted (actually demonstrating his ignorance of Wesleyan subtleties) that Upham taught only a relative perfection or a mitigated perfection. He seemed to think he'd discovered Upham's Achilles heel, a vulnerability that defined perfect love as "a love which is free from selfishness, and which is conformed to its object, so far as a knowledge of its object is within our reach in our present fallen state."[49]

Warfield was right, but not novel or acutely insightful, that "perfection is not conceived as perfection," i.e., absolute perfection.

The fact that he sometimes used the word perfection as Upham meant it to be used and at other times used the word in the sense of absoluteness (he doesn't want anyone to use it, unless they mean it in the latter sense) without distinguishing between the two, produces the following superfluous and speculative issue: "Of course, we may raise the question whether this argument proves that perfection expands with growing knowledge, or that there can be no such thing as perfection until knowledge is perfect."[50] The simple answer is that even though Upham teaches that knowledge can be a means of holiness growing by degree (it is already perfect in nature), perfection will not be absolute in this life; neither will knowledge be perfect. So why ask, when at this stage of existence, do we see only through a glass darkly?

Throughout his treatise, Warfield demonstrated his irritation at the very word "perfectionism." Apparently, he was unwilling to consistently use the word as Upham, Oberlinians, and Wesleyans define it. The word, in an unqualified sense, made his victim look ridiculous. Even though he admitted to the difference existing between the radical, utopian, antinomian perfectionists and the Wesleyan-Oberlin emphasis,[51] Warfield stated that, for the former, Wesleyanism was in the background and "supplied everywhere a starting point and everywhere gave a certain dignity and stability to the movement."[52]

The following demonstrates that Warfield could never make up his mind whether the "perfectionists" claimed too much or too little, or whether they were legalists or antinomians. In other words, one never is quite sure whether Warfield was arguing against under-spirituality or against super-spirituality.

> That is to say, Christian perfection differs from all kinds of perfection precisely in this, that it is not real perfection. That is a pity, if true, and provokes the jibe that one may be then a perfect Christian it seems without being a perfect man. We are face to face here, in other words, with that antinomian tendency which is the nemesis that follows on the heels of all forms of perfectionism.[53]

It is astonishing to read a very clear seven-page (pp. 445-452) summary of Upham's doctrine of perfection and find not one serious accusation. "Whatever may be the difficulties to a perfectionist of the idea of a developing holiness, however, Upham frankly teaches that idea, and gives it very rich expression."[54]

Warfield was far kinder to Upham than he was to Mahan

and Finney. He stated that Finney gave us less a theology than a system of morals; God could be eliminated from it entirely without essentially changing its character. Everything related to Finney was simply an expression or extension of Pelagius[55] and Nathaniel Taylor.[56]

Finney opted for sanctification as the keeping of the whole law; Upham and the Methodists spoke of evangelical perfection. So to present Finney and Upham in the same volume created the critic's dilemma. Must he attack Finney for opting for more or attack Upham for opting for less? Upham's evangelical perfection sat much better with Warfield than did Finney's assertion that Christian perfection is total obedience to the law of God, and that man, therefore, can be as morally perfect as God.[57] Warfield was quick to key in on the confusions in Finney, pointing to the discrepancies present between objectivity and subjectivity, and relativity and absoluteness as it relates to "natural ability." Warfield wrote:

> Obligation here is interpreted in terms of ability with the result that each man becomes a law to himself, creating his own law; while the objective law of God, the standard of holiness in all is annulled, and there are as many laws and many standards of holiness as there are moral beings.[58]

Defect in the Doctrine of Depravity

The most serious defect to be found in Upham's theory of perfection is his identifying with Nathaniel Taylor. Thus, an accusation of neglecting the innate corruption of the heart is made against him and is not made against the Wesleyans or Quietists. Madame Guyon had a clearer concept of "that secret power within us which continually draws as to evil."[59] On the same topic, Warfield approved of Samuel Harris' conclusion in his review of Upham's biography of Madame Guyon.

> We are never perfect till the effects of corrupt nature and of sinful habit are eradicated, till self-denial ceases in the extinction of all tendency to selfishness and not the mere restraining of it, till we are restored to a state of spontaneous delightful universal coincidence with God's will....[60]

In other words, because Upham's theory of original sin was defective, his theory of perfection was likewise defective.

If Warfield wanted an "eradication theory" holiness, he should have turned to some of his contemporaries--W. B. Godbey and Beverly Carradine, for example. But Samuel Harris did not think Upham defective in this matter; neither did that Calvinistic author think it a mistake to hope for attainment of such perfection in this life, even if the possibility of that attainment was somewhat of an illusion. Harris' stance was this: if one is going to teach actual attainment in this life, let him strive for a high standard rather than for a low one. He wrote:

> The grand error of perfectionism lies not in maintaining that some actually attain perfection in this life. That is a minor and comparatively harmless error, pertaining merely to a question of fact. But the dangerous error is, in teaching that to be perfection which is not--it is the element of antinomianism perpetually appearing--the lowering of the standard of moral obligation, not merely to the capacity, but to the present habits and attainments of men.[61]

Motherhood and Fatherhood of God

The most damaging blow inflicted by Warfield relates to a development in Upham which had nothing to do with his perfectionism. Nevertheless, since the development had to do with the doctrine of the Trinity, it behooved Warfield to place this bit of heresy at the beginning of his treatise. The embryo of the heresy was Upham's teaching on the duality of existence, "and on his belief that for every soul there is a complimentary [sic] soul especially between the sexes."[62] According to Warfield, the idea was fully developed in W. Hepworth Dixon's Spiritual Wives (1868), but Upham did not mention Dixon by name.[63] The teaching presumed that if all of life is directed by providence, why should not marriages be made in heaven? It also served as an argument for God's design of the two becoming one flesh and for the absolute law of monogamy. Upham writes:

> There seems, then, to be a just and adequate foundation for the doctrine, for which we find some inclination

> and glimpses from time to time in experimental writers, that all holy beings have their correspondences. That is to say, they have other beings in the same rank of existence, who, in their physical though purified and perfected nature, in intellect and affections, and also in providential position, correspond to their own necessities, and which constitute, therefore, the completion or complement of their physical part, and of their perceptions and loves.[64]

While Upham believes that this principle was applicable to all Christians and their relationships, he thought that its ideal application fit most comfortably within the context of marriage. If Upham had stopped here, he would have escaped applying the duality of existence to the Father and to the Holy Spirit, who in turn become the Father and Mother of the Trinity, who produced the Son. This unfortunate development appears in Upham's last book, Absolute Religion, a work so highly metaphysical, freethinking, and verbose that it would leave any systematic theologian with a nightmare of loose ends as well as with the obsession that the book needed to be "tidied up." (The work would have appealed much more to Margaret Fuller and Ralph Emerson than to Princeton fundamentalists.) But Warfield was kind enough to admit "that these grotesque speculations are not a fair sample of the substance of Upham's teaching."[65]

Upham himself made no apology. In order for a human Motherhood and Fatherhood to become one, there had to be an eternal Mother and Father cooperating throughout eternity.[66] The very first man was made in the image of God and he was a combination of both masculine and femine elements.[67] Upham cited Jewish writings to support his description of "Sophia," a maternal principle within the Godhead.[68] According to Upham, the logos in John's Gospel is identified with this maternal principle. Upham quoted at least a dozen obscure sources for his doctrine and also some sources not so obscure--Philo, Clement of Alexandra, and the mystic, Jacob Boehme. Concerning the writing of the latter he wrote:

> If we understand him rightly, it was the Sophia, the Wisdom or Maternal Essentio or Personality of the Godhead, which incarnated itself in Christ, and which caused him in a mother's spirit, though in male form,

> to endure his great sufferings in behalf of a world which was to be born into a saved and regenerated life of him and through him.69

Of course, it does not help Upham's credibility that he quoted from such sects as the Familists, Shakers, and Bible Communists. It seems, as Warfield had already noticed, that the Bible Communist publication "The Berean," was a major source for Upham. The periodical stated "that woman as well as man should have her archetype in the primary sphere of existence; that the Receptive as well as the Active principle, subordination as well as power; should have its representative in the Godhead."70

Upham quoting Theodore Parker on the subject confirmed his solidarity with transcendentalism. Although Scripture does not clearly declare the doctrine, Upham believed it had been and would be taught by the Holy Spirit. This kind of progressive revelation did not sit well with the closed canon biblicism of Warfield. In a sense, Upham's chapter is an unfortunate one. But in another sense, it represents the kind of eclectic investigative search for truth, wherever it might be found, that typified Upham's mind-set. As a scholar, Upham prized that mind-set even more than he prized a particular label, even if it meant forfeiting the label that was most important of all, at least to a Warfield--orthodoxy.

Conclusion

Mysticism and mental philosophy internalized Upham's Scottish commonsense philosophy. It served to polarize him from Warfield's biblical rationalism, at least, in Warfield's estimation. Much of what Warfield had to say was inherent to the nineteenth-century Calvinistic-Arminian debate. He superimposed mysticism on Upham to such an extent that he presented an inaccurate concept of Upham's teachings, especially in regards to the "natural" life. Admitting that Upham's psychological explanations of spiritual experience were difficult to understand (such as the relationship of the affections and will), Warfield offered little evidence that he had sorted through what Upham was explicating.

Warfield was correct in describing the unhealthy use of

providence by Upham. He could have been more accurate in his criticism, however, if he had defined the word "perfection" and consistently used it as Upham had. But Upham's weak concept of depravity left him open to the accusation that his idea of perfection was limited because it did not adequately deal with the "effects of corrupt nature." Warfield reminded us, as would even many Wesleyans, that Upham's concepts of disinterested benevolence were unrealistic. His most damaging blow struck at Upham's unorthodox remarks on the Trinity, a highly metaphysical concept developed in the last days of Upham's life.

Notes

1. Benjamin Breckinridge Warfield (November 5, 1851-February 16, 1921) succeeded Archibald Hodge as professor of didactic and polemic theology at Princeton Theological Seminary in 1887. The D.A.B. reports that "He published some twenty books on Biblical and theological subjects besides pamphlets and addresses. This production he maintained by indefatigable intense study in New Testament criticism and interpretation, patristic theology, especially that of the Reformed churches, and considerable fields of church history. By command of modern language he kept constantly abreast of theological scholarship" (p. 453). The focus of this chapter will be Warfield's 1,100-page diatribe against perfectionistic theology, entitled Perfectionism (New York: Oxford University Press, 1931).

2. See Benjamin B. Warfield, "John Humphrey Noyes and his 'Bible Communists,'" Bibliotheca Sacra, Volume LXXVIII (1921), pp. 37-72. Warfield wrote, "In this perfectionist sect, we have therefore the opportunity to observe a perfectionism working itself out in life under leadership strong enough to enable it to go its own way, along the line of a development distinctly logical although narrow and inconsiderate, untrammeled by considerations derived from tradition, whether religious, ethical or social, and unaffected by the universal judgement of the community in which it lived" (p. 39). (I have emphasized a phrase which is representative of the fact that whenever Warfield discussed perfectionism, he had antinomianism lurking in the back of his mind. Antinomianism was perfectionism worked out to its logical conclusion.)

3. Marsden, p. 98.

4. Benjamin B. Warfield, Studies in Theology (New York: Oxford University Press, 1932), p. 655.

5. William Livingston, The Princeton Apologetic As Exemplified by the Work of Benjamin B. Warfield and J. Greshan Machen, 1880-1930 (Yale, 1948), pp. 334-335. Unpublished Ph.D. dissertation.

6. Ibid. Quoted from Warfield by Livingston, p. 186.

7. Ibid., p. 343.

8. Marsden states: "Increasingly, modern thought suggested that the points of view of the observer stood between the facts and his report of the facts. This would suggest that even the most honest and authoritative accounts of the past would be altered in detail by the observer's point of view. At Princeton, however, the ideal for truth was an objective statement of fact in which the subjective element was eliminated almost completely. In their view, scripture did just that. Although they did not deny the human element, divine guidance was thought to produce accounts where the warp from point of view had been virtually eliminated." Marsden, p. 114.

9. Livingston, p. 174. An article in the Biblical Repertory and Princeton Review, "Upham on Spiritual Life," was critical of Upham's formulation of spiritual truth by a subjective, psychological, introspective method, "... the texture of his book throughout is wrought on the presumption that these instructions are applicable to all Christians as guides of their exertions for spiritual advancement and tests of their success.... The grand difficulty lies in applying abstract tests of religious feeling.... What satisfaction can we obtain by asking a candidate for admission to the church whether his affections are such as indicate a change of nature or whether he has only experienced such a change in his feelings as mere natural affections may undergo?" Biblical Repertory and Princeton Review, Vol. XVIII (1846), pp. 314-317.

10. In fact at the root of all Warfield's criticism are the tensions that marked the Calvinistic-Arminian debate. For instance, Warfield states "Clearly, we shall need the 'new heart,' before we can conceive the faith that is to make us this new heart. Faith, this faith, cannot come into existence except as the product of the new heart: the heart it enters is already the new heart." p. 436. The above represents the consistent Calvinistic argument that since the heart is totally depraved, faith and repentance can only take place after sovereign regeneration. Such an attempt to

place the eternal God within a time sequence salvation scheme is beyond (not worth) the scope of this paper. Wesley solved the problem with prevenient grace which is not so carefully worked out in Upham. Also notice the argument in the Biblical Repertory and Princeton Review, which is essentially Calvinistic and makes no allowance for prevenient grace. "It is a desire which can have no place in a mind not already holy, and the degree of holiness in the heart is the only degree in which this desire what ever they may be which attend it, are the fruit of holiness already in the heart. They are the effect of which holiness is the cause; and the Christian, when he makes the entire consecration of himself to the service of God, does it rather from an impulse of holy feeling within him than from a regard to holy feeling which he does not possess, and which he may thereby acquire." "Upham on Spiritual Life," Biblical Repertory and Princeton Review, p. 300.

11. Warfield, Perfectionism, p. 343.
12. Ibid., p. 351.
13. Ibid., p. 459.
14. Ibid., p. 352.
15. Ibid.
16. Upham, Interior Life, p. 45.
17. Warfield, Perfectionism, p. 368.
18. Ibid.
19. Ibid., p. 369.
20. Ibid.
21. Warfield, Studies in Theology, p. 651.
22. Warfield, Perfectionism, p. 379.
23. Ibid., p. 391.
24. Ibid., p. 385.
25. Upham was astute enough to recognize that traits which are normally credited to piety may be the result of psychological temperament. "There are some persons, who, in addition to the rectification of the outward nature, have had a degree and kind of inward experience, which is truly remarkable. It is not an experience which, properly speaking, can be described as sanctification; but it is sometimes taken for it. These persons have been much exercised on the subject of a holy life; they have experienced much anxiety in regard to it; and in consequence of the new views which they have had, and the inward victories they have obtained, have been the subjects of a high degree of joy. Sometimes the joy, owing in part, I suppose, to some peculiarities of mental character, is sudden, intense, overwhelming.

They suppose themselves wholly and forever conquerors." "Thomas Upham's Life of Madame Guyon," The New Englander, Vol. VI (April, 1848), p. 174.

26. Warfield, Perfectionism, p. 389.
27. Ibid., p. 390.
28. Ibid., p. 388.
29. Ibid., p. 383.
30. French, p. 85.
31. Warfield, Perfectionism, p. 404.
32. Ibid., p. 405.
33. Ibid., p. 410.
34. Ibid., p. 417.
35. Ibid.
36. Ibid., p. 493.
37. Ibid., p. 497.
38. Upham, Interior Life, p. 140.
39. Warfield, Perfectionism, p. 420.
40. Ibid.
41. Ibid., p. 421.
42. Ibid., p. 424.
43. Ibid., p. 398.
44. Upham, Religious Maxims, p. 46.
45. Warfield, Perfectionism, p. 427.
46. Ibid., p. 430.
47. Ibid., p. 431.
48. Ibid.
49. Warfield, Perfectionism, p. 447.
50. Ibid., p. 452.
51. In fact, in footnote #52, p. 70, of "Noyes and His Bible Communists," Warfield quotes Asa Mahan's eight characteristics of radical perfectionism, which differentiate them from the Wesleyan-Oberlin doctrine.
52. Ibid., p. 55. This is in spite of the following footnote from Warfield: "Charles G. Finney, in his Views of Sanctification, (1840), p. 136, says: 'So far as I can learn, the Methodists have been in great measure if not entirely exempt from the errors held by modern Perfectionists.' He is not in this, however, speaking of the sources upon which the Perfectionists drew for their membership, but of the teaching current in the Methodist Church in contrast with theirs. He does, however, add that 'Perfectionists, as a body, and I believe with very few exceptions, have arisen out of those denominations that deny the doctrine of entire sanctification,'--and this doubtless was true of the perfectionists he had in mind, if taken as a general fact. It was not, however, the whole truth" (p. 69).

53. A comment on Robert Pearsall Smith. Warfield, Perfectionism, p. 528.

54. Ibid., p. 452.

55. Ibid., p. 193.

56. Ibid., p. 33. In Warfield's estimation, Nathaniel Taylor was possibly the most guilty party of the nineteenth century for producing theological error. Concerning radical antinomian, communitarian perfectionism, Warfield wrote: "But the most effective forces in the production of the prevalent perfectionism were derived from quite different quarters particularly from the Pelagianizing theories of the will emanating from New Haven." "Noyes and His Bible Communists," p. 55.

57. Warfield, Perfectionism, p. 58.

58. Ibid., p. 70.

59. Ibid., p. 455.

60. Ibid.

61. Samuel Harris, "Upham's Life of Madame Guyon," The New Englander, Vol. VI (1848), p. 173. It was at this very point that a previous article in The New Englander attacked Upham, i.e., for setting the standard of perfection too low. "To speak of sanctification as completed in those who still exhibit such imperfections as flow from our fallen condition, and our connection with Adam, and require the application of Christ's blood, those who are not able to assert absolutely and unconditionally that they have been free from sin, at least for any great length of time, appears to us to be a very singular and unauthorized use of terms." "Theories of the Christian Life," The New Englander, Vol. III, (1845), p. 390.

62. See the chapter on "Union with God in the Redemption and Sanctification of the Family." Upham, Divine Union, pp. 290-314.

63. Warfield, Perfectionism, p. 364.

64. Ibid., p. 295.

65. Warfield, Perfectionism, p. 370.

66. Upham, Absolute Religion, p. 49.

67. Ibid., p. 50.

68. Ibid., p. 53.

69. Ibid., p. 61.

70. Ibid., p. 65. What the theologian calls "imaging," the psychologist calls "projection." This particular doctrine of Upham's, which describes a kind of God that possesses both masculine and feminine traits, would provide a strong case for Carl Jung's teaching on "archetypes." Thus, this

God would fulfill the unconscious and repressed anima (female) side of man and the animus (masculine) side of woman. Upham, by noting that the Madonna represents the Motherhood concept in Roman Catholicism provides the perfect example of a psychological projection of either the anima or maternal matrix, which creates a religious or universal symbol. See also Carl G. Jung, Man and His Symbols (New York: Dell Publishing Company, 1964), pp. 186-198.

EPILOGUE

Suppose we could reincarnate Thomas Upham. Where would he go? What would he do? He would be too religious for the secular setting. His presumed absolutes would be termed narrow-minded by the "scientific mind." Open confession of Jesus Christ would possibly preclude his being hired at Bowdoin.

Even in a pseudo or nominal religious setting, his piety would appear to be irregular and his moral stances would seem queer. For the intelligensia, a conservative label is tantamount to academic anemia. Upham would be queried, "What was that you said about values? A person who doesn't believe in moral relativism and value-free education just doesn't function well in the contemporary classroom. We begin from ground-zero here at State University, and, of course, that means no religious assumptions."

No problem. Dr. Upham could find a job at a fundamentalist school, right? Even though he would be a part of a cognitive minority and nothing he wrote would ever see the outside world, still he could openly flaunt his spirituality and utter his moral platitudes in the classroom.

But Upham's theology was not systematic. He quoted little scripture; he wasn't quite clear on his articulation of total depravity--and his mind was so curious. Even though he was convinced of the existence of absolute truth, he was always looking for truth in the most unlikely places (i.e., beyond the denominational discipline)--in psychology and philosophy, mainline churches and sects, established institutions and communes. His catholic spirit prevailed in all situations.

Thomas Upham was convinced that ultimate truth <u>can</u> be discovered, but that fresh nuances appear that ought to be savored and expounded. His personal library was filled with the latest books. Who could tell what he might read today, maybe even items censored from the school library. Listening in, we would probably hear the following reply: "Dr. Upham, you are not dogmatic enough, your hermaneutic is a bit wishy-washy, and you are too accommodating to sociology and psychology. In fact, you are just too liberal. Our only source is the Bible, and if it isn't stated in the Bible, you had better leave it alone! Besides, your pacifism wouldn't fit in here, and where did you get those queer ideas about capital punishment? Don't you know that in the Bible...?"

To help our friend through his disappointment, we explain: "Tom, it's different now from when you were around the first time. When your contemporary Horace Mann commented on public education in the United States, he said, '...our system earnestly inculcates all Christian morals; it founds its morals on the basis of religion.' But our secular system today takes the opposite religious belief, that morals and religion should be completely separated. Perhaps you could get a job with the Peace Corps or the American Friends Service Committee. Your transcendentalism would fit in well with their visionary idealism, and they're not really concerned about what you believe. Writing, you say? Possibly for 'Sojourners Magazine' or some other similar radical periodical. But you are not quite dogmatic enough for them.

"You see, Tom, our society is dominated by a 'new class,' technocrats, who believe that all knowledge is teleological, an end for building more economical transportation, a more luxurious life-style, a more adequate defense system, and a more efficient information-gathering process--you know, corporate up-and-comers pursuing excellence by way of nutrients, vitamins, exercise, and of course, more money. But in spite of our glitter, there are a few problems: five-thousand teenagers committed suicide last year; a million and a half babies were aborted. Experts predict that by 1990, half the homes in America will have a single parent living in them. Of course, there is the constant threat of our world being totally obliterated by nuclear war. Oh well, everything can't be perfect.

"What was that you said about true virtue and the inviolability of human life? Is there really such a thing as spiritual and natural law that can bring order to our society and stability to my own life? I've heard a lot about love, but I've never heard anything about holy love. You mean you wrote all of those books and you can't find a job? Why don't you start a new university and call it, Spirit and Intellect? Of course, Madelyn O'Hare, Timothy Leary, Lawrence Kohlberg, and other autonomous types would not fit in. And you wouldn't obtain the endorsement of Jerry Falwell, Bob Jones, Jay Adams or other B. B. Warfield protégés. But I'll bet thousands of people searching for hope and wholeness would show interest--those who suspect that a holy and just God may exist, a God whose eyes run to and fro throughout the whole earth beholding the evil and the good."

It almost seems ironic that Americans today can be so confoundingly optimistic, yet dwell on the brink of destruction. They are such experts at love, but at the same time the urban masses are increasingly estranged. Dr. Upham reminded us that Americn idealism zenithed just before the time during which our country almost committed suicide. Yet, one vast difference separated his day and ours. Upham's writings beckoned America to a transcendent God while today's church and a host of self-help gurus have proclaimed a new gospel. This latest gospel calls for self-esteem, self-actualization, and self-accentuation. It proclaims that inferiority complexes and self-doubt are greater threats than "rulers of darkness" and "spiritual wickedness in high places."

Upham understood that the human battle was both psychological and spiritual. The educational world has retained the former and dropped the latter and has almost persuaded the American church to follow suit. This particular divorce has spawned a multitude of illegitimate children, small coups d'etat by a myriad of cults. People <u>are</u> looking for answers.

For Upham, the secret of recovery and stability lay in a correct frame of reference--faith in an immutable, holy God. The only real hope for personal maturity rested with a perfect God. Only then would peace and harmony exist within God's creation. To look within the human breast for the complete answer was futile. If there were no God, there could be no solution to the human dilemma.

In summary, Upham's writings added credibility to the theology of the holiness movement. His psychological and theological investigations lent an unprecedented intellectual breadth to Wesleyan perfectionism; a theology discovered through spiritual thirst and intellectual pursuit is more impressive than a dogma inherited from ancestors. Upham's "spiritual discovery" resulted in a creativity and freedom of expression that was not as concerned with augmenting someone else's ideas as it was with ascertaining truth. The same openness and inquisitiveness that led him to Phoebe Palmer's parlor prevented Upham from leaving a neat theological package to his posterity. The picture we have is of a free-flowing mind, a mind housing the magnanimous thoughts that characterized transcendentalism.

Was Upham a "Wesleyan perfectionist"? If key points of holiness doctrine such as "crisis experience" identifies one as such, the answer is "yes." But to simply answer "yes" would identify Upham as an institutionalist, and an institutionalist he was not. To accept every jot and tittle of a single person, group, or denomination, was not his style.

One of the delights of spiritual pursuit is being open to that part of God's message which the Holy Spirit in His wisdom deems fit to apply. Upham was confident that the Holy Spirit had satisfied his spiritual hunger. He attempted through his writings to actualize in others that which had actualized him. Being an instrument of love and life was far more important for Thomas Upham than maintaining theological shibboleths and correct semantics. I suppose Wesley would have said, "Amen!"

Appendix A:

UPHAM'S UNDERSTANDING OF TOTAL MENTAL FUNCTIONING

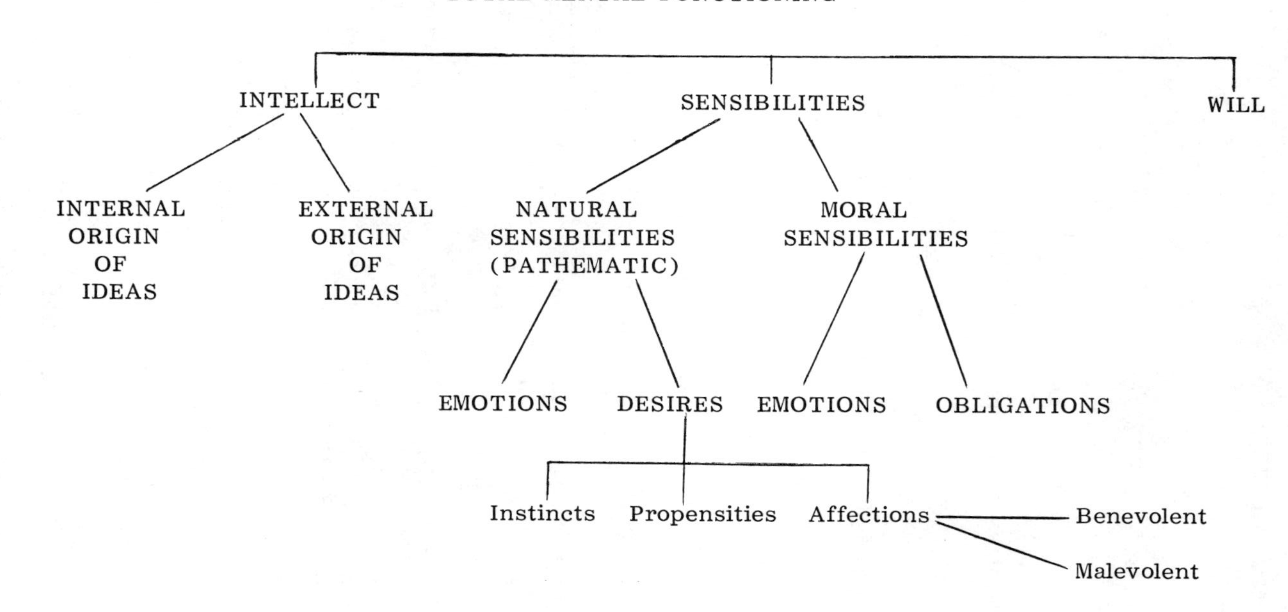

BIBLIOGRAPHY

PRIMARY SOURCES

Books by Thomas Cogswell Upham

Absolute Religion. New York: G. P. Putnam's Sons, 1873.

American Cottage Life. Boston: American Tract Society, 1850.

Christ in the Soul. New York: Warren, Broughton and Wyman, 1872.

Divine Union. Boston: George C. Rand and Avery, 1856.

Elements of Mental Philosophy. Two volumes. New York: Harper and Brothers, 1855.

Inward Divine Guidance. Philadelphia: G. W. McCalla, 1887.

Letters: Aesthetic, Social and Moral. Philadelphia: H. Longstreth, 1857.

The Life of Faith in Three Parts. Boston: Waite, Peirce and Company, 1845.

Life, Religious Opinion and Experiences of Madame Guyon. London: H. R. Allenson, Ltd., 1908.

Madame Catherine Adorna. Boston: Waite and Peirce, 1845.

The Manual of Peace. New York: Leavitt, Lord, and Company; Brunswick: J. Griffin, 1836.

Outlines of Imperfect and Disordered Mental Action. New York: Harper and Brothers, 1865.

A Philosophical and Practical Treatise on the Will. New York: Harper and Brothers, 1851.

Principles of the Interior or Hidden Life. Boston: Waite and Peirce, 1845.

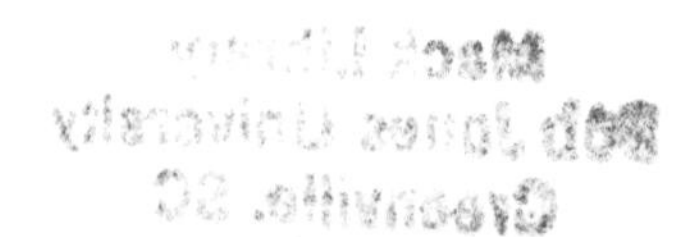

Ratio Discipline or the Constitution of the Congregational Churches. Portland, Me.: William Hyde, 1844.

Religious Maxims. Boston: Waite, Peirce, and Company, 1846.

Religious Offerings. New York: Leavitt, Lord and Company, 1835.

Periodical Articles by Upham

"Illustrations from Personal Experience." Guide to Holiness, Vol. IV (September 1842), pp. 49-54.

"The Immutability of Moral Distinctions." Biblical Repository and Quarterly Observer, Vol. VI (July 1835), pp. 117-136.

"Marks or Characteristics of Perfect Love." Guide to Christian Perfection, Vol. II (August 1840), pp. 25-28.

"On the Three Forms of Love: Namely, of Benevolence, of Complacency, and of Union." Guide to Christian Perfection, Vol. XV, No. 19 (1849), pp. 97-100.

"Peculiar Dangers Attending a State of Holiness." Advocate of Christian Holiness (July 1872), pp. 13-15.

"Professor Upham's Experience." The Advocate of Christian Holiness, Vol. XII, No. 1 (January 1880), pp. 76-78.

"Religious Maxims Having a Connection with Holiness." Guide to Christian Perfection, Vol. VII, No. 6 (June 1845), pp. 121-123.

"Religious Maxims Having a Connection with the Practice of Holiness." Guide to Christian Perfection, Vol. II, No. 8 (February 1840), pp. 169-172.

"Thoughts on Holiness: The Naturalness of a Truly, Holy Life." Guide to Holiness, Vol. XIV, No. 11 (1848), pp. 25-28.

Books by John Wesley

Explanatory Notes upon the New Testament. London: The Epworth Press, 1954.

Journal of the Rev. John Wesley. Edited by Nehemiah Curnock. London: Epworth Press, 1938.

Letters of the Rev. John Wesley. Edited by John Telford. London: Epworth Press, 1931.

A Plain Account of Christian Perfection. London: Epworth Press, reprinted 1952.

Wesley's Doctrinal Standards, The Sermons. Edited by N. Burwash. Salem, Ohio: Convention Bookstore, 1967.

Wesley's Standard Sermons. Edited by Edward H. Sugden. London: The Epworth Press, 1921.

Works. London: Wesleyan Conference Office, 1872. Reprinted Grand Rapids, Michigan: Zondervan Publishing House, no date given.

Miscellaneous Primary Sources

Edwards, Jonathan. A History of the Work of Redemption. New York: American Tract Society, no date.

_______. The Works of President Edwards. New York: Jonathan Leavitt and John F. Trow, 1843.

Erikson, Erik H. Insight and Responsibility. New York: W. W. Norton and Company, 1964.

Fenelon, François. Christian Perfection. New York: Harper and Brothers, 1947.

_______. Fenelon's Letters to Men and Women. Edited by Derek Stanford. London: Peter Owen Ltd., 1957.

Fichte, Johann G. The Vocation of Man. Indianapolis: The Bobbs-Merrill Company, Inc., 1956.

Freud, Sigmund. Civilization and Its Discontents. New York: W. W. Norton, 1961.

Guyon, Madame. The Exemplary Life of the Pious Lady Guion. Translated from her own account by Thomas Digby Brooke. Philadelphia: Joseph Crukshank, 1804.

_______. A Short and Easy Method of Prayer. Translated from the French by Thomas D. Brooke. Included in autobiography above.

_______. Spiritual Torrents. Translated from the Paris edition of 1790 by A. W. Marston. London: H. R. Allenson, Ltd.

James, William. Varieties of Religious Experience. New York: Longman, Green, and Company, 1923.

Jung, Carl G. Collected Works. London: Routledge, and Kegan Paul Ltd., 1958. Vol. XX, Part I.

_______. Man and His Symbols. New York: Dell Publishing Company, 1964.

_______. The Undiscovered Self. Boston: Little, Brown, and Company, 1957.

Kierkegaard, Soren. Concept of Dread. Translated by Walter Lowrie. Princeton, N.J.: Princeton University Press, 1944.

_______. Concluding Unscientific Postscript. Translated by David F. Swenson and Walter Lowrie. Princeton, N.J.: Princeton University Press, 1941.

The New Chain Reference Bible. Edited by Frank Charles Thompson. Indianapolis: B. B. Kirkbride Bible Company.

OTHER NINETEENTH-CENTURY SOURCES

Books

Blakey, Robert, Esq. History of the Philosophy of Mind, Vol. IV. London: Trelawney William Saunders, 1848.

Caldwell, Merritt. The Philosophy of Christian Perfection. Philadelphia: Sorin and Ball, 1848.

Clarke, Adam. Christian Theology. Salem, Ohio: Convention Bookstore, 1967. Original edition, 1835.

Cleaveland, Nehemiah. History of Bowdoin College from 1806 to 1870. Boston: James R. Osgood and Company, 1882.

Curtis, Olin. Forty Witnesses. New York: Phillips and Hunt, 1888.

Finney, Charles G. Lectures on Systematic Theology. Oberlin, Ohio: Oberlin Press, 1847.

_______. Memoirs of the Rev. Charles G. Finney. London: Hodder and Stoughton, 1876.

_______. Views of Sanctification. Oberlin: James Steele, 1840.

Fish, Henry C. Primitive Piety Revived. Boston: Congregational Board of Publication, 1855.

Foster, Randolph. Nature and Blessedness of Christian Purity. New York: Harper and Brothers, 1851.

Hughes, George. Days of Power in the Forest Temple. Boston: John Bent and Company, 1873.

_______. Fragrant Memories of the Tuesday Meeting. New York: Palmer and Hughes, 1886.

Inge, William Ralph. Christian Mysticism. London: Methuen and Company, 1899.

Lawrence, Robert F. The New Hampshire Churches. Claremont, N.H.: The Claremont Manufacturing Company, 1856.

Lee, Luther. Elements of Theology. New York: Miller, Orton, and Mulligan of Syracuse, 1856.

McDuffee, Franklin. History of the Town of Rochester, New Hampshire: From 1722 to 1890. Manchester, N.H.: The John B. Clarke Company, 1892. Vol. I.

Mahan, Asa. Out of Darkness into Light. London: Wesleyan Conference Office, 1875.

_______. Scripture Doctrine of Christian Perfection. Boston: D. S. King, 1839.

Merritt, T. (ed.). The Christian's Manual: A Treatise on Christian Perfection. New York: T. Mason and G. Lane, 1840.

Palmer, Phoebe. Entire Devotion to God. Salem, Ohio: Schmul Publishers, no date given. Original in 1855.

_______. Faith and Its Effects. London: no publisher or date given.

_______. The Way of Holiness with Notes by the Way. New York: Lane and Scott, 1850.

_______. Pioneer Experiences. New York: W. C. Palmer, Jr., 1872.

_______. Promise of the Father. Salem, Ohio: Schmul Reprint, 1981. Original, 1859.

Palmer, Walter. Life and Letters of Bishop Hamline. New York: Carlton and Porter, 1866.

Peck, George. The Scripture Doctrine of Christian Perfection. New York: Carlton and Phillips, 1854.

Peck, Jesse D. The Central Idea of Christianity. Louisville: Ky.: Pentecostal Publishing Company, first edition, 1902. Original edition, 1858.

Ralston, Thomas Neeley. Elements of Divinity. Nashville: Cokesbury Press, 1924.

Récéjac, E. Essay on the Bases of the Mystic Knowledge. New York: Charles Scribner's Sons, 1899.

Smith, Elizabeth L. Henry Boynton Smith: His Life and Work. New York: A. C. Armstrong and Sons, 1881.

Smith, Hannah Whitall. The Christian's Secret of a Happy Life. Westwood, N.J.: Fleming H. Revell Company, 1952.

Sprague, William B. Lectures on Revivals of Religion. Albany, N.Y.: Packard and Van Benthuysen, 1832.

Steele, Daniel. Love Enthroned. Salem, Ohio: Schmul Publishers, 1961.

_______. Milestone Papers. New York: Eaton and Mains, 1878.

Stevens, Abel. Life and Times of Nathan Bangs, D.D. New York: Carlton and Porter, 1863.

Stowe, Charles Edward. Life of Harriet Beecher Stowe. Boston: Houghton Mifflin and Company; New York: The Riverside Press, 1889.

Stowe, Harriet Beecher. Old-Town Folks. Cambridge, Mass.: The Belknap Press of Harvard University, 1966.

Upham, Frank Kidder. Descendants of John Upham of Massachusetts. Albany, N.Y.: Joel Munsell's Sons, 1892.

_______. Genealogy and Family History of the Uphams of Castine, Maine, and Dixon, Illinois. Newark, N.J.: Advertiser Printing House, 1887.

Upham, Phebe Lord. The Crystal Fountain. Philadelphia: J. B. Lippincott and Company, 1877.

Walker, Williston. A History of the Congregational Churches in the United States. New York: The Christian Literature Company, 1894.

Watson, Richard. Life and Letters of Mrs. Phoebe Palmer. New York: W. C. Palmer, Jr., 1876.

Wheatley, Richard. Life and Letters of Mrs. Phoebe Palmer. New York: W. C. Palmer, Jr., 1876.

Wood, J. A. Perfect Love. Boston: Degen, Estes, and Company, 1866.

_______. Purity and Maturity. Abridged by John Paul. Kansas City, Mo.: Beacon Hill Press, 1950.

Woods, Leonard. History of the Andover Theological Seminary. Boston: James R. Osgood and Company, 1885.

Periodicals

Allen, William. "Congress of Nations." Quarterly Observer, Vol. II, No. 3 (January 1834), pp. 5-24.

"Archibald Alexander's Outlines of Moral Science." The Princeton Review (January 1853), pp. 1-43.

Bangs, Nathan. "Christian Perfection: How to Attain It." Guide to Christian Perfection, Vol. XXVII (1855), pp. 168-173.

Bangs, W. M. K. "Strictures on Professor Upham's Philosophical Works." Methodist Magazine and Quarterly Review, Vol. XVII (1836), pp. 299-318.

Beecher, Edward. "The Nature, Importance, and Means of Eminent Holiness Throughout the Church." American National Preacher, Vol. X, No. 110 (July 1835), pp. 193-224.

Beecher, Lyman. "Lyman Beecher's Personal Testimony to 'The Blessing of Sanctification by Simple Faith in Christ.'" Guide to Christian Perfection, Vol. VII (1845), p. 23.

"Believe Ye Receive and Ye Shall Have." Guide to Christian Perfection, Vol. XXV (1854), pp. 166-171.

Clay, Henry. "Regarding the American Colonization Society." New York Evangelist (January 14, 1837), p. 10.

"Criticism of a Visitor." Oneida Circular (January 7, 1874), pp. 18-19.

"Dr. T. C. Upham." Guide to Holiness, Vol. XVI (1872), p. 152.

Dutton, S. W. "The Relation of the Atonement to Holiness." Monthly Religious Magazine, Vol. XV (January 1856), pp. 19-35.

"Early Rochester Sketches." Rochester, New Hampshire Courier (December 14 & 21, 1888).

"Entire Sanctification: Its Nature." Guide to Christian Perfection, Vol. IV (1842), pp. 224-225.

Hall, G. Stanley. "The History of American College Textbooks and

Teaching in Logic, Ethics, Psychology, and Allied Subjects." *American Antiquarian Society* (April 1894), pp. 137-161.

Harris, Samuel. "Thomas Upham's Life of Madame Guyon." *New Englander*, Vol. VI (April 1848), pp. 165-176.

"Importance of a Knowledge of Mental Philosophy to the Christian Minister." *Christian Review*, Vol. III (September 1838), pp. 428-442.

Lawrence, E. A. "Leonard Woods." *Congregational Quarterly*, Vol. I, No. 2 (April 1859), pp. 105-124.

Loveland, D. H. "Believe You Have It and You Have It." *Guide to Christian Perfection*, Vol. XXIX (1856), pp. 150-151.

"Madame Guyon." *Christian Examiner*, Vol. LXLIII (November 1847), pp. 317-324.

Mahan, Asa. "President Mahan's Reply to Dr. Woods." *Guide to Christian Perfection*, Vol. III, No. 7 (January 1842), pp. 153-186.

_______. "The Spiritual Writings of Prof. Thomas C. Upham." *Oberlin Quarterly Review*, Vol. IV (January 1849), pp. 100-127.

"Man's Dependence on the Grace of God, for Holiness of Heart and Life." *The Christian Spectator*, Vol. VII (1835), pp. 28-33.

Palmer, Phoebe. "An Act of Faith." *Guide to Christian Perfection*, Vol. XXVII (1855), pp. 136-137.

_______. "The Methodist Ministry." *Guide to Christian Perfection*, Vol. XXVI (July 1854), pp. 1-6.

Peck, George. "Dr. Upham's Works." *Methodist Quarterly Review*, Vol. XXVIII (April 1846), pp. 248-265.

Peck, Jesse. "Entire Sanctification and Its Condition." *Guide to Christian Perfection*, Vol. XXVII (1855), pp. 78-84.

"Perfectionism: Upham's Life of Faith." *Christian Examiner*, Vol. XL (1846), pp. 397-398.

"Permanent Sanctification." *Guide to Christian Perfection*, Vol. II (1841), pp. 42-45.

Pond, Enoch. "Review of Upham on the Will." *Literary and Theological Review*, Vol. II (March 1835), pp. 148-168.

Smith, Henry Boynton. "Review of Upham's Mental Philosophy."

Literary and Theological Review, Vol. IV (December 1837), pp. 621-659.

Stowe, Harriet Beecher. "The Interior Life or Primitive Christian Experience." Guide to Christian Perfection, Vol. VIII (1845), pp. 13-18.

"Theories of the Christian Life." New Englander, Vol. III (1845), pp. 373-392.

"Theory of Temptation." Methodist Quarterly Review, Vol. XXIV (January 1842), pp. 142-161.

"Thoughts on the Relation of Mental Philosophy to Theology." Christian Spectator, Vol. VII (1835), pp. 76-89.

Turner, J. H. "The Witness of the Spirit." Guide to Christian Perfection, Vol. XXVII (1855), pp. 178-179.

"The Two Witnesses." Guide to Christian Perfection, Vol. XVI (1849), pp. 101-105.

"Upham on Spiritual Life." Biblical Repertory and Princeton Review, Vol. XVIII (1846), pp. 275-319.

Vaughn, Robert. "American Philosophy." British Quarterly Review, Vol. XII (February-March 1847), pp. 88-119.

"Wesleyanism and Taylorism." Methodist Quarterly Review, Vol. XLII (1860), pp. 656-669.

"Witness of the Holy Spirit." Guide to Christian Perfection, Vol. I (May 1840), pp. 241-244.

"Witness of the Spirit: Does the Holy Spirit Witness to the Fact of a Man's Entire Consecration to God?" Guide to Christian Perfection, Vol. XVII (1855), pp. 40-43.

Woods, Leonard, Jr. "Christianity and Philosophy." Literary and Theological Review, Vol. I (September 1834), pp. 483-509.

_______. "On Political and Ecclesiastical Reform." Literary and Theological Review, Vol. II (June 1835), pp. 344-364.

Woods, Leonard, Sr. "Examination of the Doctrine of Perfection as Held by Rev. Asa Mahan, President of Oberlin Collegiate Institute: Rev. Charles Fitch, and Others Agreeing with Them." Literary and Theological Review, Vol. VIII (January 1841), pp. 166-189.

TWENTIETH-CENTURY SECONDARY AND INTERPRETATIVE SOURCES

Books

Ahlstrom, Sydney E. A Religious History of the American People. Garden City, N.Y.: Image Books, 1975.

Barbour, Brian M. American Transcendentalism. Notre Dame, Ind.: University of Notre Dame Press, 1973.

Barnes, Gilbert. The Antislavery Impulse, 1830-1844. New York: D. Appleton-Century Companies, 1933.

Berkower, C. K. Faith and Sanctification. Grand Rapids, Mich.: W. B. Eerdmans Publishing Company, 1952.

Brett, George. A History of Psychology. London: George Allen and Unwin Ltd., 1921. Three Volumes.

Cannon, William. The Theology of John Wesley. Nashville: Abingdon Press, 1946.

Cell, George Croft. The Rediscovery of John Wesley. New York: Henry Holt, 1935.

Cheney, Mary Bushnell. Life and Letters of Horace Bushnell. New York: Charles Scribner's Sons, 1903.

Clark, Elmer. The Small Sects in America. Nashville: Abingdon Press, 1949.

Conforti, Joseph A. Samuel Hopkins and the New Divinity Movement. Grand Rapids, Mich.: Christian University Press, 1981.

Cox, Leo G. "The Imperfections of the Perfect." In Further Insights into Holiness. Edited by Kenneth Geiger. Kansas City, Mo.: Beacon Hill Press, 1963, pp. 179-195.

Cox, Leo G. John Wesley's Concept of Perfection. Kansas City, Mo.: Beacon Hill Press, 1964.

Curti, Merle. The Social Ideas of American Educators. Totowa, N.J.: Littlefield, Adams and Company, 1966.

Davis, David Brion. "The Emergence of Immediatism in British and American Antislavery Thought." In Religion in American History. Edited by John Mulder and John Wilson. Englewood Cliffs, N.J.: Prentice-Hall, Inc., 1978, pp. 236-253.

Dictionary of American Biography. Article on Thomas Upham by Kenneth C. M. Sills. New York: Charles Scribner's Sons, 1936. Vol. XIX.

________. Article on Benjamin B. Warfield by Robert Hastings Nichols, 1936. Vol. XIX.

Dieter, Melvin E. The Holiness Revival of the Nineteenth Century. Metuchen, N.J.: The Scarecrow Press, Inc., 1980.

Dimond, Sydney G. The Psychology of the Methodist Revival. London: Oxford University Press, 1926.

Edwards, Jonathan. "Dissertation Concerning the End for Which God Created the World (1765)." In New World Metaphysics. Edited by Giles Gunn. New York: Oxford University Press, 1981, pp. 112-114.

Faust, Clarence H., and Thomas H. Johnson. Jonathan Edwards: Representative Selections, with Introduction, Bibliography, and Notes. New York: Hill and Wang, 1962.

Fay, Jay Wharton. American Psychology Before William James. New York: Octagon Books, 1966.

Figgis, J. B. (ed.). Keswick from Within. London: Marshall Brothers, 1914.

Flew, R. Newton. The Idea of Perfection in Christian Theology. Oxford: Clarendon Press, 1934.

Foster, Frank Hugh. A Genetic History of the New England Theology. Chicago: The University of Chicago Press, 1907.

Gilbertson, Catharine. Harriet Beecher Stowe. Port Washington, N.Y.: Kennekat Press, Inc., 1937.

Grider, J. Kenneth. Entire Sanctification: The Distinctive Doctrine of Wesleyanism. Kansas City, Mo.: Beacon Hill Press, 1980.

Handy, Robert T. A Christian America: Protestant Hopes and Historical Realities. New York: Oxford University Press, 1971.

Harford, Charles F. (ed.). The Keswick Convention. London: Marshall Brothers, 1907.

Harkness, Georgia. Mysticism: Its Meaning and Message. Nashville: Abingdon Press, 1973.

Haroutunian, Joseph. Piety Versus Moralism. New York: Henry Holt and Company, 1932.

Harris, Merne, and Richard S. Taylor. "The Dual Nature of Sin." In The Word and the Doctrine. Edited by Kenneth Geiger. Kansas City, Mo.: Beacon Hill Press, 1965, pp. 89-117.

Hatch, Louis C. The History of Bowdoin College. Portland, Me.: Loring, Short, and Harmon, 1927.

Helmreich, Ernst Christian. Religion at Bowdoin College: A History. Brunswick, Me.: J. S. McCarthy Company, Inc., 1981.

Hertzler, Joyce O. The History of Utopian Thought. New York: The Macmillan Company, 1923.

Johnson, Paul E. A Shopkeeper's Millennium. New York: Hill and Wang, 1978.

________. Psychology of Religion. New York and Nashville: Abingdon Press, 1959.

Jones, Charles. Perfectionist Persuasion: The Holiness Movement and American Methodism, 1867-1936. Metuchen, N.J.: The Scarecrow Press, Inc., 1974.

Jones, Rufus. New Studies in Mystical Religion. New York: The Macmillan Company, 1927.

Knox, Ronald. Enthusiasm: A Chapter in the History of Religion. New York: Oxford University Press, 1950.

Koberle, Adolf. The Quest for Holiness. Minneapolis: Augsburg Publishing House, 1936.

Kuhn, Harold B. "Ethics and the Holiness Movement." In Insights into Holiness. Edited by Kenneth Geiger. Kansas City, Mo.: Beacon Hill Press, 1962, pp. 241-261.

Lindstrom, Harold. Wesley and Sanctification. London: The Epworth Press, 1956.

Long, Edward Leroy, Jr. A Survey of Christian Ethics. New York: Oxford University Press, 1967.

________. Conscience and Compromise. Philadelphia: The Westminster Press, 1954.

McConnell, Francis. John Wesley. New York: Abingdon Press, 1939.

Maclear, James F. "The Republic and the Millennium." In Religion in American History. Edited by John Mulder and John Wilson. Englewood Cliffs, N.J.: Prentice-Hall Inc., 1978, pp. 181-198.

Madden, Edward H. Civil Disobedience and Moral Law in Nineteenth Century American Philosophy. Seattle: University of Washington Press, 1968.

_______, and James E. Hamilton. Freedom and Grace: The Life of Asa Mahan. Metuchen, N.J.: Scarecrow Press, Inc., 1982.

Marsden, George. Fundamentalism and American Culture. New York: Oxford University Press, 1980.

Mead, Sidney E. "Denominationalism: The Shape of Protestantism in America." In Denominationalism. Edited by Russell E. Richey. Nashville: Abingdon Press, 1977, pp. 70-105.

_______. Nathaniel William Taylor. Chicago: The University of Chicago Press, 1952.

Miller, Perry (ed.). The Transcendentalists. Cambridge: Harvard University Press, 1960.

Monk, Robert C. John Wesley: His Puritan Heritage. Nashville: Abingdon Press, 1966.

Moore, Robert L. John Wesley and Authority: A Psychological Perspective. Missoula, Mont.: Scholars Press, 1979.

Moorhead, James H. American Apocalypse: Yankee Protestants and the Civil War: 1860-1869. New Haven, Conn.: Yale University Press, 1978.

Niebuhr, H. Richard. Christ and Culture. New York: Harper and Brothers Publishers, 1951.

_______. The Kingdom of God in America. New York: Harper and Row, 1937.

_______. Social Sources of Denominationalism. New York: Henry Holt and Company, 1929.

Oden, Thomas C. Game Free. New York: Harper and Row, 1974.

_______. Structures of Awareness. Nashville: Abingdon Press, 1969.

Outler, Albert (ed.). John Wesley. New York: Oxford University Press, 1964.

Peters, John L. Christian Perfection and American Methodism. New York: Abingdon Press, 1956.

Piette, Maximin. John Wesley in the Evolution of Protestantism. New York: Sheed and Ward, 1937.

Rieff, Philip. Freud: The Mind of the Moralist. Chicago: The University of Chicago Press, 1959.

Riley, Woodbridge. American Thought. Glouchester, Mass.: Henry Holt and Company, 1915.

Roback, A. A. History of American Psychology. New York: Library Publishers, 1952.

Roberts, David. Psychotherapy and a Christian View of Man. New York: Charles Scribner's Sons, 1950.

Rose, Delbert R. "Christian Perfection, Not Sinless Perfection." In Insights into Holiness. Edited by Kenneth Geiger. Kansas City, Mo.: Beacon Hill Press, 1962, pp. 107-128.

Sanford, Charles. The Quest for Paradise. Urbana: University of Illinois, 1961.

Sangster, William. The Path to Perfection. New York: Abingdon Press, 1943.

Schneider, Herbert W. A History of American Philosophy. New York: Columbia University Press, 1963.

Shipman, William D. The Early Architecture of Bowdoin College. Brunswick, Me.: Brunswick Publishing Co., 1973.

Simpson, Alan. "The Covenanted Community." In Religion in American History. Edited by John Mulder and John Wilson. Englewood Cliffs, N.J.: Prentice-Hall Inc., 1978, pp. 17-27.

Smith, H. Shelton; Robert T. Handy; and Lefferts A. Loetscher. American Christianity: Interpretation and Documents. New York: Charles Scribner's Sons, 1963.

Smith, Timothy L. Revivalism and Social Reform. New York and Nashville: Abingdon Press, 1957.

Smith, Wilson. Professors and Public Ethics: Studies of Northern Moral Philosophers Before the Civil War. Ithaca, N.Y.: Cornell University Press, 1956.

Starkey, Lycurgus M., Jr. The Work of the Holy Spirit: A Study in Wesleyan Theology. Nashville: Abingdon Press, 1962.

Strunk, Orlo, Jr. (ed.). Readings in the Psychology of Religion. "A Definition of Faith" by William James. Nashville: Abingdon Press, 1959.

Taylor, Mendell. Exploring Evangelism: History, Methods, Theology. Kansas City, Mo.: Nazarene Publishing House, 1964.

Taylor, Richard S. A Right Conception of Sin. Kansas City, Mo.: Nazarene Publishing House, 1939.

Tocqueville, Alexis de. "Democracy in America." In Ideology and Power in the Age of Jackson. Edited by Edwin C. Rozwenc. New York: University Press, 1964, pp. 17-22.

Trethowan, Illtyd. Mysticism and Theology. London: Geoffrey Chapman Publishers, 1974.

Trueblood, D. Elton. A People Called Quakers. New York: Harper and Row Publishers, 1966.

Turner, George Allen. The More Excellent Way. Winona Lake, Ind.: Light and Life Press, 1952.

_______. The Vision Which Transforms. Kansas City, Mo.: Beacon Hill Press, 1964.

Tuttle, Robert G. John Wesley: His Life and Theology. Grand Rapids, Mich.: Zondervan Publishing House, 1978.

Underhill, Evelyn. The Mystic Way. New York: E. P. Dutton and Company; London: J. M. Dent and Sons, Ltd., 1914.

_______. Mysticism. New York: E. P. Dutton and Company, 1961.

Walker, Williston. Ten New England Leaders. New York: Silver, Burdett and Company, 1901.

Warfield, Benjamin B. Perfectionism. New York: Oxford University Press, 1931.

_______. Studies in Theology. New York: Oxford University Press, 1932.

Warren, Austin. New England Saints. Ann Arbor: The University of Michigan Press, 1956.

Whitmont, Edward C. The Symbolic Quest. Princeton, N.J.: Princeton University Press, 1969.

Wiley, H. Orton. Christian Theology. Kansas City, Mo.: Beacon Hill Press, 1943. Volume III.

Williams, Colin W. John Wesley's Theology Today. Nashville: Abingdon Press, 1960.

Wood, A. Skevington. The Burning Heart. Minneapolis: Bethany Fellowship, Inc., 1978.

Wynkoop, Mildred B. A Theology of Love. Kansas City, Mo.: Beacon Hill Press, 1972.

Periodicals

Ahlstrom, Sydney E. "The Scottish Philosophy and American Theology." Church History, Vol. XXIV (1915), pp. 257-272.

Arnett, William. "Entire Sanctification." The Asbury Seminarian (October 1975), pp. 24-45.

"Bowdoin College's Gentle Apostle of Peace." Lewiston Journal (February 27, 1915).

Cardno, J. A. "The Aetiology of Insanity: Some Early American Views." Journal of the History of the Behavioral Sciences, Vol. IV, No. 2 (1968), pp. 99-108.

________. "The Birds Are Rather Big for Ducks: Criterion and Material in History." Journal of the History of the Behavioral Sciences, Vol. V, No. 1 (1969), pp. 68-72.

________. "Idiocy, Imbecility: An Early American Contrast." The Psychological Record, Vol. XVIII, No. 2 (1968), pp. 241-245.

Curti, Merle. "The Great Mr. Locke: America's Philosopher, 1783-1861." Huntington Library Bulletin, No. 11 (April 1937), pp. 107-151.

Davis, Merrill R. "Emerson's Reason and the Scottish Philosophy." New England Quarterly, Vol. XVIII (June 1944), pp. 209-228.

Dayton, Donald. "The Social and Political Conservatism of Modern American Evangelicals: A Preliminary Search for the Reasons." Union Seminary Quarterly Review, Vol. XXXII, No. 2 (Winter 1977), pp. 71-80.

Gabriel, Ralph H. "Evangelical Religion and Popular Romanticism in Early Nineteenth Century America." Church History, Vol. XIX (1950), pp. 34-47.

Hamilton, James E. "Nineteenth Century Philosophy and Holiness Theology: A Study in the Thought of Asa Mahan." Wesleyan Theological Journal, Vol. XIII (Spring 1978), pp. 2-15.

Howard, Ivan. "Wesley Versus Phoebe Palmer: An Extended Controversy." Wesleyan Theological Journal, Vol. VI, No. 1 (Spring 1971), pp. 31-39.

Kinlaw, Dennis F. "Charles Williams' Concept of Imaging Applied to the 'Song of Songs.'" Wesleyan Theological Journal, Vol. XV, No. 1 (Spring 1981), pp. 85-92.

Kohlberg, Lawrence. "Developmental Approach to Moral Education." Humanist (November and December 1972), pp. 14-16.

Mullen, Lawrence K. "Holy Living: The Adequate Ethic." Wesleyan Theological Journal, Vol. XIV, No. 2 (Spring 1981), pp. 85-92.

Smylie, James. "Uncle Tom's Cabin Revisited." Interpretation: A Journal of Bible and Theology (1973), pp. 67-85.

Staples, Rob. "Sanctification: A Phenomenological Analysis of the Wesleyan Message." Wesleyan Theological Journal, Vol. VII (March 16, 1972), pp. 3-16.

Taylor, W. S. "Perfectionism in Psychology and in Theology." Canadian Journal of Theology, Vol. V, No. 1 (1959), pp. 170-177.

Warfield, Benjamin B. "John Humphrey Noyes and His 'Bible Communists.'" Bibliotheca Sacra, Vol. LXXVII (1921), pp. 37-72.

ARCHIVES, PAMPHLETS, AND UNPUBLISHED SOURCES

Arnett, William. "John Wesley: Man of One Book." Unpublished Ph.D. dissertation, Madison, N.J.: Drew University, 1954.

Bowdoin College Archives. Extensive clippings on Thomas C. Upham. Bowdoin, Maine.

French, Stanley G., Jr. "Some Theological and Ethical Uses of Mental Philosophy in Early Nineteenth Century America." Unpublished Ph.D. dissertation, University of Wisconsin, 1967.

Hale Family Papers, from the New Hampshire Historical Society. Concord, New Hampshire.

Howard, Vernon. "The Academic Compromise of Free Will in Nineteenth Century American Philosophy." Unpublished Ph.D. dissertation, University of Wisconsin, 1965.

Jeremiah Mason Papers, from the New Hampshire Historical Society. Concord, New Hampshire.

John Kelly Papers, from the New Hampshire Historical Society. Concord, New Hampshire.

Kimball, Gayle Hallie. "The Religious Ideas of Harriet Beecher Stowe: Her Gospel of Womanhood." Unpublished Ph.D. dissertation, University of California at Santa Barbara, 1976.

Lee, James. "The Development of Theology at Oberlin." Unpublished Ph.D. dissertation, Madison, New Jersey, Drew University, 1952.

Livingston, William. "The Princeton Apologetic As Exemplified by the Work of Benjamin B. Warfield and J. Greshan Machen, 1880-1930." Unpublished Ph.D. dissertation, New Haven, Connecticut, Yale, 1948.

McNulty, Frank John. "The Moral Teachings of John Wesley." Unpublished S.T.D. thesis, Washington, D.C., Catholic University of America, 1963.

Packard, Alpheus. "The Life and Character of Thomas C. Upham." Brunswick, Maine: Joseph Griffin, 1873.

Pierce, H. M. Presidential Address at the Commencement of Rutgers Female College. New York: Cushing, Barbua and Company, 1870.

Simon Gratz Autograph Collection. The Pennsylvania Historical Society, Philadelphia, Pennsylvania.

Smith, Timothy L. "Biblical Themes in the New England Renaissance." An unpublished essay sent to this writer by the author.

Staples, Rob. "John Wesley's Doctrine of Christian Perfection: A Reinterpretation." Unpublished Ph.D. dissertation, Berkeley, California, Pacific School of Religion, 1963.

Thompson, Claude H. "The Witness of American Methodism to the Historical Doctrine of Christian Perfection." Unpublished Ph.D. dissertation, Madison, New Jersey, Drew University, 1949.

Upham, Nathaniel G. "Rebellion, Slavery, Peace." Concord, N.H.: E. C. Eastman, 1864. Address delivered at Concord, New Hampshire, March 2, 1864.

"Upham on Colonization." A letter to John D. Orcutt. Published by the American Colonization Society. Available at Yale University Library.

White, Charles. "Phoebe Palmer: Her Life and Thought." An unpublished manuscript reviewed by this author.

BIBLIOGRAPHIES

Jones, Charles Edwin. A Guide to the Study of the Holiness Movement. Metuchen, N.J.: The Scarecrow Press and the American Theological Library Association, 1974.

National Union Catalogue. Pre-1956 imprints.

Williams, Joseph. A Bibliography of the State of Maine, from the Earliest Period to 1891. Portland, Me.: The Thurston Print, 1896. Volume II.

INDEX